school success for kids with

Emotional and
Behavioral
Disorders

school success for kids with

Emotional and
Behavioral
Disorders

Michelle R. Davis,
Vincent P. Culotta, Ph.D.,
Eric A. Levine, Ed.D.,
& Elisabeth Hess Rice, Ed.D.

PRUFROCK PRESS INC.
WACO, TEXAS

Library of Congress Cataloging-in-Publication Data

School success for kids with emotional and behavioral disorders / by Michelle R. Davis ... [et al.].
    p. cm.
Includes bibliographical references.
ISBN 978-1-59363-431-5 (pbk.)
1. Problem children--Education. 2. Emotional problems of children. 3. Behavior disorders in children. 4. Special education.
5. Teaching. I. Davis, Michelle R. (Michelle Renee), 1972-
LC4801.S338 2011
372.94--dc22
                        2010035137

Copyright © 2011, Prufrock Press Inc.
Edited by Lacy Compton
Cover and Layout Design by Marjorie Parker

ISBN-13: 978-1-59363-431-5

Printed in the United States of America.

At the time of this book's publication, all facts and figures cited are the most current available. All telephone numbers, addresses, and website URLs are accurate and active. All publications, organizations, websites, and other resources exist as described in the book, and all have been verified. The authors and Prufrock Press Inc. make no warranty or guarantee concerning the information and materials given out by organizations or content found at websites, and we are not responsible for any changes that occur after this book's publication. If you find an error, please contact Prufrock Press Inc.

Prufrock Press Inc.
P.O. Box 8813
Waco, TX 76714-8813
Phone: (800) 998-2208
Fax: (800) 240-0333
http://www.prufrock.com

Contents

Part I

Background and Perspective

chapter 1

chapter 2

chapter 3

Part II

Schools and Classrooms

chapter 4

Acknowledgments

THIS book represents the cumulative experiences of scores of children, adolescents, and families struggling for more than just a good education; many children are challenged to find a sense of identity and value. It is because of these families' perseverance that we are able to share their stories and better understand their needs.

Michelle and the authors share appreciation for Maria Hammill's excellent contributions in her medical issues chapter. Her empathetic, understanding manner and ability to support families with school demands is unique. Michelle's deep gratitude for the support and love from her husband, family, and friends is unending. Michelle is especially grateful for the opportunities she has had to serve her community and the many extraordinary educators who do so every day.

Vince would like to thank his mentors, colleagues, and coauthors who have taught him more from their actions than could be acquired from books. He also wishes to thank Trisha Sanderson for her endless energy, and the staff of NeuroBiological Associates for truly caring about the children we serve. To his wife Cheryl, and daughters Stephanie and Anna—their patience, encouragement, and love remind him why we strive to make a contribution and leave things just a little better than we found them.

Eric acknowledges his wife Gretchen for her wisdom, experience, patience, love, and tolerance over the years. Eric feels fortunate to have had the opportunity to wear many professional hats. Without Gretchen's quiet yet thoughtful guidance, it would not have been possible for him to do the things he has been able to do. Eric would like to acknowledge his children Erika and Alex for simply being who they are, his many friends and colleagues, and of course, the children and families with whom he has had the opportunity to serve.

Lisa would like to thank her colleagues at The George Washington University for their support and dedication to preparing teachers for students with the most challenging behaviors. In addition, she would like to acknowledge her husband Lacy for his patience, humor, and unflappable support. Sara, Lacy, and Austin, Lisa's children, also deserve recognition because they fuel her passion to advocate for good teachers for all children.

To our editor, Lacy Compton, thank you for your guidance and leadership, keeping us focused on how we best communicate to serve children.

Introduction

D O you know a child or adolescent who is battling depression, anxiety issues, or anger issues? Are you the parent or teacher of a student who is misunderstood and who ends up isolated in the community or in school? This book is about the countless numbers of students and their families who are living with the invisible but very real emotional and behavioral disabilities. These students can shut down and refuse to interact, cut themselves, starve themselves, refuse to follow directions, or incite other students or adults. These students are not helpless or beyond help, they are simply misunderstood and often mistreated. This book tells their stories and offers some basic solutions that are so often ignored in schools.

Challenging behaviors can mask a child's potential, strengths, and talents; interfere with academic success; and impair the fulfillment of a productive and happy life. Parents and teachers who work with students with emotional and behavioral challenges often are desperately searching for information about successful interventions. They are seeking professionals who understand their students and who can tell them how to help. Children and adolescents with challenging behaviors can be successful in school and in life, but they need strength-based, caring interventions. This cannot occur, however, with the current philosophies and practices in place in our schools. Nationally and worldwide, failure to attend to the needs of children with social, emotional, and behavioral challenges could result in a crisis so profound that all of us are likely to be affected. Now is the time to transform our education system and the way we serve and educate students with social, emotional, and behavioral difficulties. There *are* interventions that work. This book is designed to provide parents and educators with tools for school success, including schoolwide and classroom interventions and evidence-based interventions for individual students.

School success for students with challenging behaviors is one of the most important issues in education, mostly because the societal implications for underserving or misunderstanding this group of children are so great. Students with challenging behaviors whose needs are not met will be adults with poor social skills either unnoticed or noticed for the wrong reasons. Children who suffer with the symptoms of oppositional defiance, mood, conduct, or other disorders often are talented, but their gifts have not been uncovered. They often are situated with one foot in the world of possible unemployment and discord and one foot in the world of possibility. Children with challenging behaviors have the lowest grade point averages, lowest high school graduation rates, and the largest unemployment rates compared to any other group. Educators and parents have a ripe opportunity to now take advantage of the educational research and understanding of biological and brain-based factors for challenging behavior and transform education for this important and growing group of students.

When the outcomes of students with identified emotional or behavioral disabilities are studied, the results are dismal. More students with emotional differences drop out than graduate with diplomas (National Center for Education Statistics, 2008; Wagner, Kutash, Duchnowksi, & Epstein, 2005). In general, people with mental health and behavioral problems tax our communities when they are unemployed, incarcerated, or upsetting themselves and others. Despite the shift from establishment of the rights of children with disabilities to international implementation of rights, our efforts to provide proper and sufficient supports for children with EBD have failed. There is still a wide gap between federal legislation and policy requiring the use of evidence-based methods for children who are at risk for developing, or have been identified with, an emotional or behavioral disability and actual school-based services provided (Kutash, Duchnowski, & Lynn, 2006).

To powerfully counter these outcomes and problems, parents and professionals must intervene early and swiftly with scientifically proven methods that build upon each individual's strengths. Escalating public awareness, proliferating neuroscience research, and an explosion of data regarding negative outcomes show us that this is now the time to transform the way we provide needed academic, behavioral, and mental health services in education.

It's generally well known that, from infancy to adulthood, a child's behavior, control, expression of emotions, and social skills improve and typically reach a point where the child independently uses social, behavioral, or emotional skills. But for up to 20% of children, these milestones do not occur, and school support is necessary. Research shows us that skills in these areas can be developed when the right amount and type of proven methods are provided under the right conditions (Kauffman & Landrum, 2009). Research has shown the brain is malleable and open to intervention. Students with challenging behaviors *can* learn social, emotional, and behavioral skills.

Whether a child is experiencing mild social, emotional, or behavioral difficulties, or whether the child is already known to have a disability, these issues can be treated and changed through schoolwide, classwide, and individual interventions. In this book, children with challenging behaviors are described with many faces on a continuum— from transient behaviors related to a trauma, to serious behaviors requiring hospitalization or residential placement.

Unlike other school problems, behavior challenges are especially complex because dealing with behaviors involves opinion, perspective, and consideration for the interaction between and among the child's support systems. Indeed, assessing and addressing behaviors often is more art than science, although progress is being made in the study of methods that work to improve school success.

Historically, how we teach children with interfering behaviors has related to our collective perception about how people with differences should be educated, and this includes how we perceive the cause of behaviors. Educators have developed more of an ecological perspective about behavior, which includes better understanding about the biological, environmental, family, and school factors that need to be addressed for school success. Some of the common misperceptions about behaviors are discussed in the Myths and Truths tables found at the beginning of each chapter.

Children with challenging behaviors often are smart, talented, and creative. But their behaviors can be described as oppositional, defiant, disrespectful, depressed, or anxious. These behaviors can overshadow or overcome a child's strengths. Kids who struggle with behavior are not a small group. At least 6% to 10% of school-aged students have some degree of emotional or behavioral disorder. Yet, only 1% of school-aged students receive formal services (Kauffman & Landrum, 2009). This gap means that there may be up to 9.5 million students who struggle with challenging behaviors in our neighborhood schools who are not likely receiving the services they need to be safe, productive, and independent citizens (Wagner et al., 2005).

If you have picked up this book, perhaps you are trying to better understand your child or searching for new tools and strategies for helping talented but troubled students. Perhaps you know someone like the children we introduce in Chapter 1. Perhaps you are considering a career in working with students with emotional or behavioral disabilities. Because there are about 60 million students and staff members in America's schools, there is a widespread opportunity to make a difference in the education of youths with social, emotional, and behavioral difficulties. If you are a concerned educator or parent of a student with challenging behaviors, this book is for you.

Part I

Background and Perspective

chapter 1

The Many Faces of Students With Challenging Behavior

TO be successful in school and in life, individuals must have strong emotional and behavioral skills. After all, academic and other skills are useless unless individuals can get along, follow routines and structures, and generally behave well in a group. All of us likely know someone affected by a child with challenging behavior. Students who have the invisible disability of an emotional or behavioral challenge often are marginalized or avoided because they do not fit with "the norm." Families struggle with finding the right learning and social opportunities for their children. With up to 10 million children at risk for developing an emotional or behavioral disorder, and more than 60 million children and staff in America's schools, there is a great concern to make visible the needs of those struggling with challenging behaviors.

Myth	Truth
Mental illness is a personal problem, not a societal concern.	Depression affects about 121 million people around the world and causes about 850,000 deaths by suicide each year (World Health Organization, 2010).
Kids with challenging behaviors are making poor choices. Kids are in control of behavior choices.	There is interplay between a child's brain, biology, family, community, and school. All of these should be considered for school success.
Behaviors are the parents' fault.	There is no research to demonstrate fault of behaviors. Research does show, however, that effective parent-school partnerships are critical for school success. Partnerships are most effective when blame for behaviors is not assigned. Legal requirements don't take into account the cause of behavior, but effective evaluation of behavior will evaluate the cause.

When behavioral issues interfere with learning or relationships with others, families and professionals must work together to create strength-based interventions. Interventions at the school level, the classroom level, and at the individual level should be used to support individual growth and family functioning. Interventions from the vantage point of multiple professions should inform the intervention plan.

This chapter will answer the following questions:

- What is the prevalence of children with challenging behavior in the U.S.?
- How is the book structured, and how can the reader use the book?
- Who are the children discussed in this book?
- What is a continuum of behaviors and why is that important?

Prevalence

The answer to the question, "Who has an emotional or behavioral challenge?" is a complex one. The problem with identifying challenging behaviors is that there is always a subjective element to assessing behavior. What is "disrespectful" in one class, in one geographical area, or to one culture may not be to another. What is "oppositional," "abnormal," or "atypical" may not translate from classroom to classroom or state to state. This ambiguity to define "normality" has prevented many professionals over time from defining challenging behaviors and from progressing on the science of studying effective interventions for students with these issues. Never in the history of American education has more than 1% of the school-aged population received services for special education under the disability category of emotional disturbance or emotional behavioral disorder. However, some researchers estimate that as much as 20% of all children should be identified to receive such services (Kauffman & Landrum, 2009).

Of the approximately 53 million children in the more than 100,000 schools in the United States, at least 3 million children are identified with serious social, emotional, and behavioral difficulties. As seen by the very low number of children who are eligible to receive formal services—only about a half million children—it is widely understood that there is a vast underserving of kids with challenging behaviors in our schools (Kutash et al., 2006). Researchers estimate that more than 10 million children are affected by a mental health problem (Kauffman & Landrum, 2009).

This large number of students with emotional and behavioral challenges face difficulty in their everyday functioning at home, in school, and in the community. The outcomes for this important group of students are currently the poorest when compared with other disability groups (Kutash et al., 2006). Emotional and behavioral challenges often are surrounded with denial, shame, or embarrassment.

However, there *are* promising interventions that can remove some of the obstacles students face. We welcome you to our conversation about how we believe this is the right time to transform the education of children and adolescents. We write this book from our perspectives as parent, neuropsychologist, psychiatrist, teacher, advocate, administrator, and researcher and hope it will bring professionals and families hope and strategies for school success.

How to Use This Book

This book is for parents and educators, and it focuses on school success. You can read it straight through or just read the sections that apply directly to you. There are questions that guide each chapter, a section on relevant myths and facts in each chapter, and reproducible Tools at the end of several of the chapters. There are special sections that show examples and highlight legal information for families. We hope this structure will provide parents and educators with practical, ready-to-use resources that work for children with challenging behavior.

The first part of the book, Chapters 1, 2, and 3, discusses global topics, such as how history, attitude, and perspective-taking skills are important for adults as we teach and parent kids with challenging behavior, and how perception and culture affects the education of kids with challenging behavior. The topics then become focused on schools and classrooms in Chapters 4 and 5, which explore how important the whole school community and classwide interventions can be and delve into the use of discipline in schools. Chapters 6, 7, 8, and 9 look into how best to evaluate the child's needs and develop and deliver individual student plans. Chapters 10, 11, and 12 provide a detailed exploration of Conduct, Oppositional Defiant, personality, and other disorders, and neurological, medical, and biological factors that affect the education of kids with challenging behavior. Finally, the last chapter is about what parents and educators need to know to create a successful future for a child.

Who Are These Kids?

We, the authors of this book, believe that students with emotional and behavioral challenges are talented, smart, and valuable members of our society who often go unnoticed, underserved, or wrongly served. When we talk about children and adolescents with social, emotional, and behavioral challenges, we are including a whole continuum of students. Some students are at risk of developing behavior problems, while others have been diagnosed with specific disorders or have educational disabilities.

There are many faces of kids with emotional and behavioral challenges. Some students with challenging behaviors have difficulty with authority and with slight efforts can be educated in general education classrooms. Others have extreme aggression, opposition, anxiety, or depression but are unidentified in the special education system. Still other students have been identified in the special education system and have an identifiable emotional or behavioral disorder (EBD) for which they require special education. There is one thing that all of the children who struggle with behavior share: All children and adolescents with emotional and behavioral challenges live with *invisible* disabilities. These invisible disabilities are as real as diabetes, high blood pressure, or epilepsy and affect how children and adolescents function. We believe that the very real and often painful disabilities these students live with are not caused by "bad parenting" or "just bad personalities." We believe students with behavior, social, and emotional difficulties deserve positive, strength-based, multitheoretical, and research-based interventions.

Nothing tells the story better than the voices of the students:

Jonathan is a cognitively gifted student who has trouble following the classroom routine and direction, talks back, and generally annoys others. He has attention problems, but he's usually able to make up the work after a lot of fighting and conflict at home, because his parents are so involved in helping him catch up, even at age 10. Jonathan often misses directions and then is seen as noncompliant. When teachers misunderstand him, he shuts down and refuses to follow any directions. He can outlast his parents and teachers in conflicts and argues his side of the story very convincingly. His impulsivity leads him to say and do things that he later regrets. Jonathan is attracted to strong students who often use him as their victim or puppet. His parents see his strengths and cannot understand how he can get himself in so many negative interactions with teachers and peers. He is not being challenged in school and spends most of his elementary school experience in timeout rooms or in the office.

Tanya has been in the foster care system since the age of 4 because her mother was unable to care for her. Although her grandmother wanted to help Tanya, she too was not in a position to care for her because of her own mental health issues. Tanya ruminated about her mother constantly and then sank deeper into a depression. Although there was a period in fourth and fifth grade where Tanya began to establish a good relationship with a teacher, earning passing grades and adhering to teacher direction, she regressed at adolescence. Tanya at times has tried to starve herself, cut herself, and act out sexually. After hospitalization Tanya began to take part in her treatment plan and eventually finished high school. She still struggles with the multitude of people in and out of her life and needs support to transition to the world of work and life outside of school.

Zach struggled to get along with his younger brother and sister; his moods could swing from euphoric happiness, to dark and scary without warning. His mom described Zach as someone with a grenade strapped to his chest: "We never know when that pin is going to come out. There's no telling who will get hurt. He's so unpredictable." Learning the basics like the other children did not happen for Zach. His inability to read, write, complete simple math calculations, and get along with other kids quickly deteriorated into daily classroom mayhem. Zach was taken off the birthday party list. The other parents were afraid to let their children be around them. Prior to Thanksgiving in Zach's first-grade year, the elementary school team pulled the school psychologist, school counselor, special educator, and administrator together and before his mom knew it, Zach was identified as student with an EBD. He continued in adolescence to have troubles that were met by hospitalization, multiple suspensions from school, and trouble with the law. Zach represents the many students with EBD who externalize his behavioral issues or "act out" rather than "act in" his troubles. He has difficulty learning and maintaining relationships. He is a student in need of intervention.

Shannon is an attractive 16-year-old girl from an affluent neighborhood. Shannon has always done well in school but since middle school, she has slowly withdrawn from her family and friends. Her grades have begun to drop and her parents have noticed that her weight has fluctuated a lot. When confronted about the changes, Shannon becomes angry with her mother and storms off to be with her friends, who her mother describes as a "motley crew." The school nurse called recently to say that it had been reported that Shannon was "getting sick" frequently in the bathroom. One of Shannon's friends secretly e-mailed the guidance counselor, concerned that Shannon was cutting herself with a razor. Shannon was briefly hospitalized. Parents have turned to the school for help, only to be told that Shannon is still getting A's and B's, and that mental health needs alone do not qualify Shannon for any services.

In elementary school Charles began to worry and to be oppositional to his parents and teachers. He was worried about the safety of his parents and about his health so much that he could not concentrate on academic or social tasks. He had trouble learning to read and was two grade levels behind his peers. His reading needs were unnoticed until late elementary school, however, because most teachers focused only on his behavioral issues. Charles was frequently absent from school. He had gaps in his learning. In the sixth grade, Charles began to work with a teacher who helped him with individualized reading instruction. He trusted this teacher and began to make progress. Charles' parents sought individual therapy for him and family therapy. He graduated from high school and attended community college. His parents spent a great deal of time helping him accomplish his academic goals. They worked through his difficulties and supported him during his struggles to fit in with his baseball team and his classroom peers. Without early appropriate support he would not have been able to seek higher education and, subsequently, employment.

Students like Zach, Tanya, Jonathan, Shannon, and Charles represent some of the many faces of the children who display a continuum of behavior challenges. Staff and adult perception of social, emotional, and behavioral problems can slow or stop the problem-solving process to intervene early and in meaningful ways, because behavior problems often are seen as being under the control of the child. But, as we learn more about the brain and its functioning, we realize that each individual develops and learns slightly differently and has the ability to learn compensatory strategies. Behavior, emotional, and social skills can be taught. Although the research about behavior lags behind educational achievement research, education can and does make a difference, if that education is done in a way that meets the child's and community's needs. Facilitating behavioral change can be accomplished when the attitude of adults centers on the needs of the student and how the student interacts with her family and community systems, rather than "how we were raised" or our own personal needs.

Change is possible, and there are services, instruction, and interventions available that can aid struggling students.

Understanding emotional and behavioral challenges is in its infancy. Many societies still segregate and are ashamed of persons with an emotional or behavioral disability. Programs in our country today still want to "control" behavior rather than focus on behavioral change and learning. In the future, systems that serve youth must have an integrated approach to service delivery, focus on allowing the child to develop skills for workforce capacity and competence, use data to make decisions, and reach beyond serving students with labeled emotional and behavioral disabilities to those children who are at risk for being children with emotional and behavioral challenges. In this book we will discuss these needs, because now is a great time for the transformation of the way we think about and solve problems in parent-school partnerships. Join us in our quest to improve services for the very talented students who also have emotional and behavioral challenges. If you are looking for hope, this book is for you!

chapter 2

Learning From History

A recent survey found that in the U.S., mental disorders are quite common; 26% of the general population reported that they had symptoms sufficient for diagnosing a mental disorder during the past 12 months. However, many of these cases are mild or will resolve without formal interventions (National Institute of Mental Health [NIMH], 2005).

CHAPTER 1 introduced you to the many faces of talented children who struggle with a continuum of social, emotional, or behavioral problems. Each of these students has experienced emotional and behavioral challenges that have disrupted their lives, affected their families, and interfered with their ability to prosper in school.

Challenging behavior in schools is nothing new. Parents and professionals have been dealing with disruptive behavior for as long as children have been required to go to school. Interestingly, society's response to the problem has been a reflection

Myth	Truth
Children with challenging behaviors have been provided with all of the supports they need to be successful in school.	Children with challenging behaviors have traditionally been excluded from schools.
Funding and providing mental health services is not the responsibility of the school system.	The school system is responsible for providing services that are needed so that students can make meaningful progress, access curriculum, and be prepared to lead independent lives.
Challenging behavior in the classroom is not an issue for most general education teachers.	General education teachers are dealing with more challenging behaviors than they have ever seen before because Response to Intervention (RtI) efforts require long periods of data collection.
Children with challenging behaviors historically have been well provided for by local school systems.	Schools success for children with challenging behaviors has evolved through the grassroots efforts of parents and pioneers in education.
Public education has always protected the rights of all children.	The Education for All Handicapped Children Act of 1975 (PL 94-142) was the first federal law that entitled children with disabilities the right to a free appropriate public education (FAPE) in the least restrictive environment (LRE).
Children with challenging behaviors have low IQs and come from broken homes.	Children with challenging behaviors may be gifted and talented and come from all facets of society.

of the times. This chapter takes a look back at some of the important historical events that have taken place and led us to where we are today. Also, this historical review shows us that now *is* a great time to transform the education of children with social, emotional, and behavioral differences.

This chapter is will address the following questions:

- How have children with challenging behavior historically been served in school?

- How has the education of children with challenging behaviors evolved over time?
- What were the groundbreaking laws and Supreme Court decisions that have helped transform education for children with challenging behaviors?
- How have No Child Left Behind and other laws affected school programs for children with challenging behaviors?

Looking back through the history of the education of children with challenging behavior informs the current understanding that multiple systems must work together to effectively serve children with social, emotional, and behavioral difficulties. The historical view also makes clear why school team discussions about how to intervene and address behavior problems can be so complex. Grassroots efforts have inspired parents and professionals to pursue creative and effective treatment, education, and programming for children who are identified with or at risk for developing emotional and behavioral disorders. And although we have a long way to go, the education of children with emotional or behavioral difficulties has come a long way in a relatively short time.

The battle cry for improved public education makes sense. The United States is producing citizens less able to compete with its foreign neighbors in a global economy. As Europe and Asia begin to dominate the information age, the United States' decreasing ability to produce a well-educated population predicts a scary future, which will require a competent and innovative work force. When contemplating legislation, Congressional discussion about public education has included the premise that public education has been a dismal failure, especially in the major urban areas of this country (Knitzer & Olsen, 1982). In an effort to reform public education, legislation demanding greater accountability from schools, teachers, and students has culminated in robust legislation including the 2004 reauthorization of No Child Left Behind and the Individuals with Disabilities Education Improvement Act, discussed later in the chapter.

The good news is that in less than 100 years, this nation has progressed first in attitude and second in practice so that assumption about segregation is no longer the norm; children with disabilities are entitled to a free appropriate public education (FAPE) in the least restrictive environment (LRE), and the national consciousness has awakened to the realization that there is a relationship between public education and participatory government. Looking back at the legislative history of special education, great progress has been made, but there is still a long way to go.

School systems have struggled for years to find the proper mix of services to support emotionally vulnerable children so that they could succeed in school. Parents and school staff do not often agree with how school success is defined for children with emotional challenges. Many children with serious underlying psychiatric illnesses struggle in school for their entire academic careers. For some children, the ability to be safe (physically and emotionally), tolerate the school day, come home, and participate in family life is considered success.

For other children, managing anxiety while performing at a high level is defined as success. It really depends upon the student and his particular situation. School systems typically define success as it relates to performance on high-stakes testing and rates of graduation. School system personnel will openly say that their job is to educate the child, not provide for his emotional well-being. The "art and craft" in serving these children and creating successful outcomes is tied directly to the instructional and support staff in the building, which starts with the school district leadership and the leadership of individual school administrators.

This chapter is important to school success because it reminds us all of where we have been, which in turn is important for future policy makers and program developers, teachers, parents, and students to understand as the need for innovative programs grows. Going forward while learning from the past is important because the history of educating kids with challenging behaviors should not be repeated.

How Have Children With Challenging Behavior Historically Been Served in School?

Children with emotional and behavioral disorders historically have been educated in one of two ways: (a) completely included in general education with minimal supports and services or (b) totally excluded from the general education classroom. There were many important events and legal decisions that have led us to where we are today. The following section provides some of the major historical events that shaped legislative efforts for children with emotional and behavioral challenges.

Before 1900

In prehistoric times, mental illness was seen as the result of magical beings inhabiting humans that needed spells and rituals or exorcisms by religious leaders. Sometimes, holes would be drilled in the skull of the afflicted person, to let out the spirits responsible for the person's behavior, as evidenced by skulls dating back 10,000 years found in Europe and South America. The first psychiatric text was written during the 20th century BC in Ancient Egypt, which is a location of the first known psychiatric hospital. Centuries later another psychiatric facility was found in Egypt, showing that Egyptians used opiates to induce sleep for dream interpretation, as a way to deliver prayers to gods.

In the 6th century, Judaism viewed mental illness as an expression of sin, and treatment ranged from fasting to self-flagellation. The Islamic view of mental illness was supernatural, but not necessarily evil. Song, dance, and narcotics were used to induce different states of mind. Islamic scholars wrote texts in the 10th century, El-Mansuri and Al-Hawi, including definitions and academic discussion of mental illness. In Europe at the same time, institutions for people with mental illness were feared because of the belief that people were possessed by the devil.

In the Middle Ages, it was commonly thought that demons took up residence in the bodies and souls of certain people. The natural thing to do was make it inhospitable for them exist; hence, all sorts of unpleasant remedies were created to exorcise the spiritual interlopers. Witch-hunting started, along with the movement to segregate people with mental health problems in asylums in the 16th century. By the early 1400s, the first known psychiatric hospital, Bethlehem Royal Hospital (called Bedlam), was founded in London, and by the 1800s, citizens could pay one penny to visit the "insane" "idiots" or "lunatics." Also around this time, the first belief that the person's environment contributed to mental health problems emerged. "Moral management" allowed psychiatric facilities to have beds, pictures on the wall, and more of a home living environment than the penal-like institutions years before. Phrenology introduced study of the shape and size of the brain related to mental health problems.

Jean-Baptiste Pussin and Philippe Pinel literally and figuratively took the shackles off patients, and their studies of different disorders and talk therapy contributed to improving attitudes in other countries, including the United States. At around the same time, a tireless advocate named Dorothea Dix lobbied legislatures across the U.S. and in other countries for the humane treatment of the mentally ill and "feeble minded," and the first U.S. psychiatric hospital was formed in New Jersey.

In the mid-1800s, the Civil War left many military men mentally affected. The public's empathy for their soldiers attracted interest and a soft heart for people with behavior disorders. This occurred in the later decades as well.

1900–1950: Laying the Groundwork for Educational Reform

At the end of the 1800s, in response to the rising number of children being jailed because of behavior problems, the first community mental health clinics were developed, staffed by social workers to provide counseling to students. In 1909, the National Committee for

Mental Hygiene was developed, along with other organizations interested in the education of youth with special needs such as the Council for Exceptional Children (CEC). Elizabeth Farrell founded CEC in 1922, and as its president, adopted goals to forward the interests and rights for education of "special children."

Around this time, White House committees on child welfare were formed, acknowledging the importance of education for youths with behavior problems. All states had compulsory attendance laws by 1918, so children who had been home were required to attend school as never before. By 1922, more multisystem services were being developed in conjunction with the juvenile court systems and this led to the development of the first formal education programs for children with behavior problems (Stullken, 1931).

Educational opportunities for individuals with emotional disturbance were on the decline just prior to World War I. The 1916 Bureau of Census Report indicated that the numbers of children being institutionalized were on the increase because the global conflict overseas resulted in unprecedented numbers of head injuries. Additionally, soldiers were returning from the war with "invisible injuries," emotional and behavioral injuries, caused by the stress of war (Cruickshank, 1967).

The issue of "battle fatigue" has become a popular and troubling subject once again as huge numbers of soldiers are returning from the battlefields of Iraq and Afghanistan suffering from Posttraumatic Stress Disorder (PTSD). Every day there are sad stories in the newspaper and on the Internet about veterans and their struggle to return to civilian life. World War I was important because it served as a turning point in American history. People from all over the United States had willingly and enthusiastically left their families and communities to go to Europe and fight in a very popular war. Like the Civil War, many soldiers returned very different than how they left. This led to a greater understanding of, and compassion for, people with mental health and behavior challenges, and set the stage for the next decades, which brought needed changes to the school systems.

Between 1907 and 1939, forced sterilization in the U.S. led to more than 30,000 sterilizations in almost 30 states, to "purify" the genes away from behavioral and mental disorders (Selden, 2000; Snyder & Mitchell, 2006). By this time, lobotomy, a medical procedure that initially allowed people to forget traumatic events, was common. Electroconvulsive and insulin shock were primary therapies being used along with the frontal lobotomy.

Freud's influence is paramount in the mental health field beginning in the 1930s. His areas of interest included hypnotism, dream analysis, psychoanalysis, and disorders such as Obsessive-Compulsive Disorder. His influence can be seen in modern interventions where the unconscious is believed to motivate behaviors.

Mid-1900s

The American Psychological Association began the national method of classification and diagnosis of behavior and emotional disorders by publishing the first edition of the *Diagnostic and Statistical Manual of Mental Disorders* (*DSM-I*) in 1949. The fourth edition is being used as of the writing of this book, and the fifth edition is being discussed among professional organizations. Diagnoses are discussed in great detail in Chapter 10.

Between the 1930s through the mid-1950s, the first educational programs specifically designed for children with emotional and behavioral disorders were developed (Bullock & Gable, 2006). Loretta Bender, a psychiatrist at New York City's Bellevue Hospital, was responsible for establishing classrooms for students with emotional and behavioral disorders in 1935. Over the next 20 years, across the United States, educational programs for students with challenging behaviors were developed by an innovative group of reform-minded professionals such as Bruno Bettleheim, Fritz Redl and David Wineman, Nicholas Hobbs, and Eli Bowers (Albrecht, 2009).

The inclusion of group therapy within a "structured, psychologically sound environment" (Algozzine, 1977, p. 55) was a fundamental element of a therapeutic milieu (Algozzine, 1977; Redl, 1959; Swap, 1978) that could produce positive changes for children in academic settings. The shift toward the creation of programs that cared for the psychological needs of students through the development of psychologically and emotionally safe treatment environments embedded within the school setting marked a turning point in programming for children with challenging behaviors. An ecological perspective started to more strongly emerge that acknowledged the role of the child's family or community systems and environment in behavior.

Students were either fully included in their neighborhood schools or institutionalized in psychiatric and other separate residential schools. There were only two choices, or "two boxes," for children with challenging behavior. This "two box theory" represented the continuum of services for many years: all or nothing.

1950–1975: Civil Rights and Children With Disabilities

Between World War II and 1975, the collective conscience of America became resolved to legislate equality for all of its citizens. Legislation led to, and continues to lead to, research on mental health issues. The Great Depression, World War I, World War II, and the Korean and Vietnam Wars had left generations of American families and communities forced to deal with large numbers of emotionally and physically wounded individuals. The number and magnitude of people affected by the 45-year period between the Great Depression and the end of the Vietnam War profoundly affected and changed America's attitude toward people with disabilities, specifically children with problem behaviors. At the same time, major changes occurred in the fields of behaviorism, psychiatry, and psychology.

In the 1960s, behaviorists and the scientific community forwarded Applied Behavior Analysis (ABA) as a way to incorporate the philosophies of positive reinforcement and stimulus control. In reaction to a perceived negative emphasis on manipulation of consequences and antecedents in ABA and other methods, the positive behavior supports (PBS) movement unleashed a campaign for its use in the 1980s and 1990s (Baer, Wolf, & Risley, 1987; Carrie, Dunlap, & Horner, 2002; Kutash et al., 2006; Sugai & Horner, 2002).

While the PBS leaders were advertising its use in businesses, medical facilities, schools, and other places, the ABA proponents argued that the PBS methods were too broad and not based in science. To this day, there seems to be a great deal of variation in professional and parent interpretation of ABA, as many believe it is a method of working one-on-one with a child and providing discrete trials and intermittent reinforcement. From our perspective, both movements are important because both apply a problem-solving model that focuses on the individual, a theme that will be continued throughout the chapters that follow. Also, both ways of thinking currently are used in schools.

In the early 1960s, U.S. public images through art and literature painted pictures of horrors of treatment of children and adults in institutions. Deinstitutionalization was a sweeping effort to put people back into the community. At the time, mental hospitals were viewed as the least desirable solution to the problem of mental illness, both from a humane point of view and an economic one. The Community Mental Health Centers Act, signed into law by John F. Kennedy on October 31, 1963, demanded a national system of care to meet the needs of severely and persistently mentally ill (SPMI) individuals and allow for a range of services outside of the hospital. Unfortunately, individuals were not prepared to lead independent lives or take advantage of community-based services. The medical and psychiatric community's strength grew.

At the same time, a movement to the medicalization of the treatment of children with mental health problems emphasized psychiatric, medically based treatments in hospital settings, where the public money allocated was used up for hospital treatment, leaving little for the community-based model that had preceded the medicalization model (Cohen, 1983). The effects of this movement can still be seen in how the insurance, juvenile justice, education, and mental health services systems fund and support school-based programs. Great confusion continues between this community, or school-based, model and the medical model, even at the school level, about who is responsible to provide what school-based service to support school success.

The antipsychiatry movement was led by Thomas Szasz, who wrote *The Myth of Mental Illness* in 1974, which stated that mental illness was not a disease. Proponents contended that mental illness is not medical, but has its roots in social, political, and legal areas. Researchers, writers, and protestors firmly believed that psychiatric illness is purely a social construct, benefitting doctors but not patients.

Riding the coattails of the Civil Rights Movement, the American people spoke through their congressional representatives, and a kinder, more compassionate attitude evolved toward people with differences. As shown in Table 1, the cry for civil rights for people with emotional and behavior challenges were expressed through Supreme Court decisions and federal legislation that was designed to provide rights and protection to all individuals (Bradley, Henderson, & Monfore, 2004; Forness & Kavale, 2000).

1975–Present: An Era of Parental Participation

Building upon the momentum of the previous 45 years, the 94th Congress passed the landmark Education for All Handicapped Children Act of 1975 (EHA). Decades of parent advocacy to transform education for children finally become a reality. For the first time in U.S. history, robust and funded federal legislation was passed designed to protect the educational rights of all children with disabilities.

EHA was the culmination of a powerful grass roots movement of concerned parents and educators that had been gaining momentum and picking up supporters for years. This law was more than a piece of Civil Rights legislation. Beyond access to education programming for children with disabilities, EHA was the first law to federally mandate equal access to a continuum of educational opportunities for all children with disabilities.

Major components of EHA are as follows:

1. the guarantee of a free appropriate public education (FAPE);

Table 1

Supreme Court and Other Legislative Decisions Affecting
Students With Disabilities Before 1975

Supreme Court Case/Legislation	Decisions
Brown v. Board of Education of Topeka (1954)	Considered the first landmark piece of Civil Rights legislation, it is also one of the earliest pieces of federal legislation requiring equal education for all children. To deny children of color or of disability an equal education was a violation of that child's due process rights (Cullinan, Epstein, & Lloyd, 1983).
Elementary and Secondary Education Act (ESEA, 1965)	This law, passed by Congress in 1965, was the first major piece of legislation that required the federal government to subsidize direct services to select populations in public elementary and secondary schools.
PARC v. Commonwealth of Pennsylvania (1971)	The Pennsylvania Association of Retarded Citizens (PARC) represented more than 50,000 children with intellectual disabilities during the 1960s. The PARC contested a Pennsylvania law that permitted local school systems to deny school enrollment to children who had not achieved a mental age of 5 years by the time they would enroll in the first grade (Cullinan et al., 1983; Martin, Martin, & Terman, 1996; Reynolds, 1978; Sage & Burrello, 1994). The consent decree that followed the court case required that the state of Pennsylvania provide full access to a free public education to children with mental retardation up to age 21.
Mills v. Board of Education of the District of Columbia (1972)	Advocates representing seven children between the ages of 8 and 16 with many different mental and behavioral disabilities sued the District of Columbia school system for refusing to enroll or having expelled these students based solely on their disabilities. It was later determined that the District of Columbia schools had denied educational services to approximately 12,000 children with disabilities because they did not have funding available to provide the necessary services. The court ruled that these children were protected under the Fourteenth Amendment, stating children with disabilities could not bear the burden of insufficient funding more heavily than other children (Cullinan et al., 1983; Martin et al., 1996; Reynolds, 1978; Sage & Burrello, 1994).
The Rehabilitation Act of 1973	Section 504 of the Rehabilitation Act of 1973 maintained that any recipient of federal financial assistance (including federal and local agencies) must not discriminate with regard to access to services for people with disabilities. The law also prohibited discrimination in housing, employment, architectural accessibility, other social services, and education (Cullinan et al., 1983; Martin et al., 1996).

2. the development of an Individualized Education Program (IEP) for every child;
3. the right of all parents to participate as equal partners;
4. students with disabilities are to be educated with their non-disabled peers to the extent appropriate;
5. tests and other assessments must be fair, and not discriminate on the basis of race, culture, or disability;
6. due process procedures must be in place to protect the rights of students with disabilities and their parents; and
7. the federal government must provide some funding to states to help offset the costs involved in educating students with disabilities.

Since 1974, EHA has been amended by Congress numerous times. These amendments have expanded the range of children who are entitled to special education and related services and diversified the array of services provided under the law (Luckasson & Smith, 1995). Since 1975, EHA has morphed into the Individuals with Disabilities Education Act and has been reauthorized numerous times. Parent participation and protections for children with interfering behaviors have been enhanced. Figure 1 summarizes important laws affecting children after 1975.

Late 1900s and Early 21st Century

In the 1980s, massive deinstitutionalization and funding cuts took place. These changes led to the closing of many mental hospitals and further reliance on local community care. Many former patients, instead of reintegrating successfully into society or receiving community treatment, became homeless. In 1980, the Mental Health Systems Act was signed into law. It outlined the basics of a national system for mental health community care and treatment. The Americans with Disabilities Act and Individuals with Disabilities Education Act of 1990 continued to spur civil rights of those with emotional, behavioral, and mental disorders.

- 1975: Education for All Handicapped Children Act (EHA): Free and appropriate public education in the least restrictive environment for all children with disabilities

- 1986: Amendments to EHA: Authorized Part C for infants and toddlers

- 1990: Amendments to EHA: Guaranteed that all children with disabilities have available to them a free appropriate public education focusing on special education and related services that are designed to meet their individual needs

- 1997: Individuals with Disabilities Education Act (IDEA): Established framework for current discipline procedures and provided for prevailing party's ability to recover attorneys' fees as a result of dispute resolution actions

- 2004: Individuals with Disabilities Education Improvement Act: Reauthorized IDEA and dramatically changed provisions related to discipline, evaluation, appropriate education, and procedural due process

Figure 1. Important laws affecting children with disabilities since 1975.

The No Child Left Behind Act of 2001 (NCLB) is the nation's most recently passed, and at times most discussed, general education law. It amends the Elementary and Secondary Education Act (ESEA) and has brought big changes to the nation's educational systems. The terms Adequate Yearly Progress (AYP), Response to Intervention, and highly qualified have been added to the educational vocabulary in recent years because of NCLB. Schools and parents around the country sit on the edge of their seats each summer waiting for their children's schools' report cards and test scores to be revealed. Schools in states that have not opted out must meet a defined standard to meet AYP standards. As a result, schools either avoid financial and control consequences or earn financial reward.

Despite being bright, capable students, children with challenging behavior routinely do not perform well compared with their peers (Reid, Gonzalez, Nordness, Trout, & Epstein, 2004). Children in separate classes for students with behavior challenges face particular academic difficulty as a result of NCLB's requirements, because traditionally their education has mainly focused on managing and controlling behavior. Teachers in the field of emotional and behavioral difficulties have been notoriously untrained and have a high burnout rate. NCLB attempts to remedy that with the "highly qualified" requirement; under this requirement, a parent now has a right to know the qualifications of all staff working with her child.

The lack of focus on academics and curriculum acquisition in classrooms designated for challenging behaviors has created a large gap between the achievement of children with behavior challenges and their peers. NCLB requirements also may be contributing to a national problem with teens with challenging behavior dropping out of school altogether—after teens realize that the requirements for a diploma are too difficult without the right type of support.

However, the benefits of NCLB include:

- emphasis on curriculum,
- emphasis on quality curriculum,
- emphasis on quality of instruction,
- emphasis on teacher training, and
- emphasis on quality and closing gaps.

Laws such as No Child Left Behind, and research such as we will explore throughout this book, have further highlighted the lack of teacher preparation for students with challenging behaviors. At the same time, NCLB has led many school districts to the provision of providing services for children for which they may not be equipped or trained to work effectively with children with challenging behaviors. The reduction of separate classrooms has meant that fewer smaller and more structured classroom options are available.

The net result of this has been an increase of numbers of students with interfering behaviors in the general education classroom. And some districts have described either an increase in the suspension of students as an effort to remove students with disruptive behavior, or a resistance of administrators to suspend students in order to make AYP requirements. Overall, the effect of eligibility of NCLB has been a move away from specialized and individualized interventions in separate settings, placing more students with challenging behaviors of all age levels in the community in general. NCLB has failed to improve achievement for children with disabilities (Kauffman & Konold, 2007). The flaw common to NCLB and its predecessors is that there is no one systematic process that will uniformly lead to improved academic achievement for all students.

> Classwork came easy to Jamal. He excelled in every sport he played, and was a good guy to be around. Standardized testing beginning in the third grade found him to be performing at the advanced level. Something happened in middle school. His attitude turned sour, his grades slipped; he became withdrawn and isolated from his friends and family. In January of seventh grade, Jamal got into an argument with a teacher about his cell phone. When the teacher snatched it out of his hand, Jamal jumped up and punched her in her face. Jamal was immediately suspended. Jamal needed the protections of a child with a disability. Because so many schools are using the RtI model for tracking academic performance and behavior, the team had only recently agreed that Jamal should receive targeted interventions as an "at-risk student." Jamal was ultimately sent to the district's alternative school for at-risk kids. There he met and buddied up with a whole new group of friends with whom he got into even more trouble.

Jamal is like many other highly gifted youngsters with challenging behavior who are stuck in general education classes with teachers who don't receive the type of support they need to support his challenging behavior. The students misbehave, the teacher and parents react, and the students react to the adults' reactions. Without the positive behavior supports and interventions explored in this book, the adults and students do the dance of misunderstanding and confusion and together spin further away from the real issue. The effect of failure to identify and appropriately educate children with challenging behavior has been powerful.

Students with challenging behaviors and students with disabilities have not done well on benchmark or high-stakes testing. Many school districts have shifted the focus of their instruction to preparing for the yearly assessments, basically "teaching to the test" and failing to focus on individualized instruction. There is growing resentment for groups of children who fail to meet the standards. The intent of NCLB is to bring a high expectation to all children regardless of income level. The law is designed to bring quality education to all children in schools that must be staffed by highly qualified teachers in an environment where academic standards are high. The curriculum must be challenging, and teachers must change perceptions of students with behavior challenges, as discussed in the next chapter.

Table 2 represents a constitutional recognition that children with challenging behaviors have as much right to a quality education as any other child in the United States. Because litigation is the impetus for scientific progress, these important court cases have not only shaped the legal landscape, but also have contributed to the explosion of understanding that allows us to take hold of the education of children with social, emotional, and behavioral difficulties.

History of Definition

Although the definition of emotional and behavioral disorders or disabilities is fully explored in Chapter 8, a word about how emotional or behavioral problems have been defined is important here. Organizations such as the Council for Exceptional Children, Office of Special Education Programs (OSEP), National Institute on Disability and Rehabilitation Research (NIDRR), National Institute of Mental Health (NIMH), Substance Abuse and Mental Health Services Administration (SAMHSA), Maternal and Child Health Bureau of the Health Resources and Services Administration (HRSA), and National Association of School Psychologists (NASP) have advocated in different ways to change the current definition of emotional disturbance. NASP (2005) supported the definition developed by the

Table 2

Supreme Court Decisions Since 1980 That Have Affected Students With Disabilities

Supreme Court Case	Decisions
Board of Education, Hendrick Hudson Central School District v. Rowley (1982)	The Supreme Court stated that educational programs must be designed to provide "some" educational benefit to children with disabilities. This case is considered the first major challenge to EHA.
Burlington School Committee v. Department of Education of Massachusetts (1985)	The Supreme Court found that a school district that fails to provide a special education student FAPE under IDEA may be required to reimburse the student's parents for private school expenses.
Honig v. Doe (1988)	The Supreme Court decided that a proposed suspension of greater than 10 days is considered a change in placement, which triggers IDEA procedural safeguards.
Schaeffer v. Weast, Superintendent, Montgomery County Public Schools, et al. (2005)	The burden of proof in an administrative hearing challenging the evaluation, identification, IEP contents, or placement of a child with a disability is properly placed upon the party seeking relief, whether that is the disabled child's parents, or the school district.
Forest Grove School District v. T. A. (2009)	The Supreme Court decided that parents of special education students may seek government reimbursement for private school tuition when a public school fails to provide FAPE and the private school placement is appropriate, regardless of whether the child has previously received special education services through the public school system.

National Mental Health and Special Education Coalition, found below:

> Emotional or Behavioral Disorder (EBD) refers to a condition in which behavioral or emotional responses of an individual in school are so different from his/her generally accepted, age appropriate, ethnic or cultural norms that they adversely affect

performance in such areas as self care, social relationships, personal adjustment, academic progress, classroom behavior, or work adjustment. (para. 3)

The past 100 plus years have seen landmark decisions, grassroots movements, and advocacy awareness that have changed understanding, appreciation, and fundamental belief systems regarding educating children with challenging behaviors. The time to transform educational opportunities for children with challenging behaviors has arrived. The great work of pioneers in education along with an explosion of discoveries in neuroscience, evidence-based interventions, and ecological factors have transformed this nation's collective public consciousness to demand that more citizens be productive and self-sufficient. The next chapter will further discuss how perceptions can influence educational decision making, in our quest to discover how best to deliver to children with challenging behaviors an education for success in life.

chapter 3

School Culture and Perception of Challenging Behaviors

A CHILD'S emotions, behaviors, and ability to get along with others are difficult to measure, but easy to perceive. There is no well-defined standard for "normal" behavior; therefore, adult perceptions of a child's challenging behavior become a major factor in how a school team and parents work together to solve behavior problems. The lenses though which we perceive behavior affects how the child's social, emotional, and behavioral skills will be assessed, perceived, and addressed. This chapter explores these important questions, whose answers form the foundation of the journey to school success:

- How do adult perceptions affect how student behaviors are defined, assessed, and addressed?
- How do adult perceptions of student behavior and school culture affect the parent-school partnerships needed for success?

Myth	Truth
Challenging behaviors are the result of poor parenting and poorly disciplined, unaccountable children.	Challenging behavior in school is the result of a complex set of factors (e.g., ecological, medical, neurological, and psychosocial).
School culture is unrelated to school performance, teacher attitudes, and student performance. School culture is just a "feel-good" term that has nothing to do with individual student performance.	School culture is a powerful reinforcer of positive or negative behavior. School culture is the synergy of building leadership, attitudes about children and their ability or inability to learn and be a contributing member of a community.
African Americans and other minority groups receive special education services more than other ethnic groups because they come to school poorly prepared for learning.	Overrepresentation of African Americans and other minority groups in special education is a national issue. Inconsistent special education identification practices, culturally insensitive assessments, inequitable resource allocations, and poor school/home connections contribute to the issue.
Girls do not have as many challenging behaviors as boys.	Girls are underrepresented in special education. Girls are not identified at the same rates as boys because girls will typically "act in" versus "act out" and therefore take longer to be noticed by school officials.
Aggressive, acting out children go to alternative programs for students.	All schools serve children with challenging behaviors. Most children with challenging behaviors can be served successfully with their typical peers in general education classes.
Parents are the primary reason why children with challenging behaviors do not meet with success in school. Parents should leave the decision making to school professionals.	Parents are the true experts when it comes to understanding challenging behavior in their children and play a vital role in their education. The greater the partnership between home and school, the better the outcomes will be for children.

- How do perceptions about economic status, race, gender, and giftedness affect how schools intervene?
- How do parent and student relationships with staff contribute to the overall school culture?
- Why are there so many children from diverse backgrounds in programs for children with challenging behaviors?

Adult Perceptions

The perceptions of parents and professionals affect how children with challenging behaviors are perceived, defined, assessed, and addressed in school. This process is more subjective than any other disability determination process. How an adult perceives and intervenes with a challenging behavior often is a function of her own belief system, formed by her training and personal and professional experiences. It is for this reason that a positive school culture, emphasis on making data-driven decisions, and use of scientifically based methods are important for the school success of children with challenging behavior. Any time a child's team is planning to support the child, the team members must examine their own personal and professional biases or perspectives to fully embrace a data-driven problem-solving model in an open way.

The program culture is hard to measure. Walk into any school and you can "feel" the atmosphere, the climate. School climate may be the single most important programmatic factor that contributes to school success, because the school culture is formed by staff perceptions. In order to make emotional, behavioral, and academic progress, the school must be looking through the lens that allows for collaborative problem solving, understanding of behavior in a way that focuses on skill development, intervention through data-driven decision making, and the belief that children with challenging behavior are capable and worthy.

School culture, and therefore, success for children with emotional and behavioral challenges, is directly related to positive relationships with school staff. The difference maker for a child who is emotionally vulnerable often is the building atmosphere or program. When asked about their school day, elementary and middle school children will rarely talk about what they learned; instead, they like to talk about who was nice and who was mean to them. How much they like or feel welcomed and embraced by a particular teacher is more important to them than their ability to write an essay.

The collection of these good or bad times very often can be the difference from the perspective of the student between school success or failure. School culture is the foundation by which all good things in school may be built. The perception of children, families, the local school, and the community are critical to the development of a positive school culture, and ultimately, critical to a meaningful education for a child (Erickson, 1987).

As seen in Figure 2, differences in perspective can be formed by an educator's training and background, but there also are important perspective differences between educational issues and mental health issues that have been solidified based on the history of policy and legislative action, as we discussed in the last chapter. Although school systems are realizing the need for effective interventions for social, emotional, and behavioral functioning of students, most school districts are not set up to fund or effectively implement services and interventions that traditionally have been seen as irrelevant in the schoolhouse. This perspective difference affects the way that the overall state, local school districts, local schools, and individual educators perceive how to address a child's challenging behavior.

Researchers have recommended the complete transformation of the school system in order to accomplish the integration of needed services and methods to address challenging behavior in a full continuum of school, community, and the other multiple systems surrounding a child, called an Interconnected Systems Approach or Transactional View (Campbell, 2002). Other views framed by Duchnowski and Kutash (2009) include a view that emphasizes mental health or medical orientations or one that incorporates schoolwide positive behavior

Perspective in question	As applied to an educational issue	As applied to a mental health issue
Eligibility for services	IDEA	*DSM-IV-TR*
Theories	Behaviorism, social learning theory	Psychoanalysis, developmental psychology, biological and genetic perspectives, psychopharmacology, cognitive-behavior theories
Focus	Behavior management, behavior control, academic skills	Insight awareness, teaching for skill deficiency, therapy, instruction
Emphasis on prevention	Reactive, less proactive	Prevention and treatment
Systems	Individual factors, child makes behavior choices	Family, school, community, other system factors interacting

Figure 2. How different perspectives play out in educational issues and mental health issues.

intervention supports (PBIS), which we explore in detail in the next chapter.

Teacher Perception of Skills

Even though many children with challenging behavior are bright and have sound academic skills, it is a common belief among teachers and administrators that children with challenging behaviors have low skill levels. This, of course, affects the way that instruction and assessment is delivered, which affects the child's behavior, and the cycle continues to produce less than rigorous instructional practices in the general and special education classroom. There can be resistance to providing interventions if educators perceive that the child is misbehaving due to home-based or internal factors alone. One of the first things a parent can do to help his child with challenging behaviors is to educate as many people as possible that the underlying causes of these invisible disabilities is not just willfulness or bad parenting, but biological and environmental causes.

Perceptions About Socioeconomic Status, Race, Gender, and Giftedness and School Intervention

Socioeconomic Factors

When adults say things like, "Well, what do you expect, he's from the Township neighborhood?" or "What do you expect, he's from the lower income apartments across the railroad tracks?" they are really articulating a bias about the child based on his socioeconomic status (SES). This often is confused with race factors because there is a correlation between race and SES. Adults who think like this or make these statements are really expressing low expectations and blame the child or his parents for his behavior. If the local school system, building administrators, and school staff believe that children with challenging behaviors are bad, poorly parented, and from lower classes, then it is from that perspective that programs will be developed. There is an incorrect assumption that children from poorer neighborhoods are more violent, less motivated, and overall ill-prepared for school, and that assumption can lead to control-oriented staff behaviors, which are not effective. Instead, an ecological approach, one that takes into account the child's environment, family, and community systems, will allow the team to consider the individual factors that contribute to a child's behaviors, which sets the stage for school success.

Research has suggested a relationship between socioeconomic factors and identification as a student with emotional and behavioral disorders (Coutinho & Oswald, 1996). However, there is little empirical evidence to explain why this relationship exists.

Schools in affluent communities have more and better instructional materials than schools in impoverished neighborhoods. Walk through any school in an affluent neighborhood and there will be an amazing collection of the newest classroom technology. Schools in impoverished neighborhood do not have as many community partnerships that offer technology, fundraising opportunities, and student mentors. They are fortunate to have a PTA, let alone a parent organization that is capable of raising money for technology or additional staffing. The difference between schools in terms of instructional materials and equipment affects the school culture and ultimately affects the school's ability to effectively engage all children in learning. There is a relationship between resource allocation and student behavior. The better able a school is to engage their students in learning, the fewer behavior problems will exist.

Race Factors

Overrepresentation of African American, Hispanic, and other minority students in special education has negatively affected school efforts to provide a comparable educational experience for all students. The data on overrepresentation illustrates the problem. For example, according to the U.S. Department of Education (2000), in the 1998–1999 school year, African American students were found to be:

- 2.9 times as likely as White students to be labeled with an intellectual disability,
- 1.9 times as likely to be labeled emotionally disturbed, and
- 1.3 times as likely to be labeled as having a learning disability.

These data have remained static over time (Sullivan et al., 2009) and continue to plague school systems nationally. A recent study found that there were five factors common to all schools identified with disproportionate numbers of minority students receiving special education services:

- *Identification Practices*: Eligibility processes were not the same between schools. Many school IEP teams acknowledged "compassionate coding," or the belief that a student was not learning related to emotional problems and that special education services was the answer, as an influence on identification.

- *Inequitable Resource Allocation*: Instructional materials and interventions were not universally available from school to school.

- *Community Partnerships*: Some schools were better able to develop partnerships with local businesses and other community groups than others.

- *Professional Development*: Inconsistent training opportunities related to cultural diversity were available to staff. Appreciation for cultural differences in language and behavior management (e.g., a discussion on whether the behavior was disturbed or disturbing) needed to be discussed.

- *Awareness*: A number of schools had very low populations of students who were African American. School teams, many who had been intact for many years, did not have experience working with a culturally diverse school population. The "What is normal?" question became a factor in special education eligibility determination processes. School teams routinely have to determine if the differences being observed in learning and behavior are the result of a disability or the result of a child whose learning and behavior does not fit with the type of child the school team is used to seeing on a daily basis.

School staff tends to have lower expectations of their students who are perceived to have or who do have racial, cultural, and socioeconomic differences. If administrators and teachers expect poor behavior and poor academic performance, then that is what they will get. For example, if the unspoken message is that "African American boys have behavior problems" then teachers will unconsciously create the conditions by which students misbehave, believing that the African American boys in their classes really *do* have behavior problems.

The clashing of cultural communication traditions and values contributes to misunderstandings between the predominantly White school personnel and an increasingly diverse student population. These cultural differences combined with pressure to perform academically may be to blame for the increased number of disciplinary issues and subsequent interruptions to instruction being experienced by students. Regardless, the climate is disrupted and the culture of the school becomes defined by the antagonistic relationships between school staff, students, and families.

School leadership and cultural perception. System-level leadership, while very focused on outcomes and the disparities in performance among minority groups, are leery of the systemic politics connected with such a hot-button issue. The problem of overrepresentation of children who are African American in segregated programs is a complex issue. Leadership at the school and district level is a critical factor of any systemic solution to this problem. The level of commitment that school staff and decision makers have in addressing the problem will lead to a long-term and sustainable solution. The issue of overrepresentation of minority youth in special education is often a strategic goal of school systems nationwide. School districts are taking the issue of overrepresentation seriously. Despite that expectation, building principals are sometimes unwelcoming, uninvolved, and disinterested in the process. Their participation in system change efforts may feel coerced and unauthentic. This attitude is not always consistent with the attitudes of their staff, but given the lack of administrative support, staff may feel powerless to make change. Schools that lack administrative support do not report change over time. Conversely, one inner city middle school in a suburb of Washington, DC, that had the highest ratio of overrepresentation in the county sought to aggressively address the problem. The building principal and special education coordinator worked with their School Improvement Team (SIT) to develop an action plan with interim checks along the way to measure progress; they reduced their numbers of over-represented minority students by two thirds between year 1 and year 2 of the project. This school system is no longer considered disproportionate by the Maryland State Department of Education.

Harmful effects of disproportionate identification. The overrepresentation in special education of children who are diverse is a barrier to successful school performance. The disproportionate identification of diverse children has had an effect on their respective community's willingness to trust and maintain a meaningful dialogue with local schools (Harry, 1992). Some of the effects of overrepresentation are listed below:

1. Diverse students in special education are likely to spend more than 60% of their school day outside of general education.
2. Minority students receiving special education spend less time with their typical peers than do their White counterparts (Kearns, Ford, & Linney, 2005).
3. Students who are diverse are less likely to receive services they need.
4. Inappropriate identification leads families to mistrust the school and the school system.
5. Once students are identified to receive special education services, they tend to remain in special education classes longer than is necessary.
6. Once in special education, students are likely to experience a limited, less rigorous curriculum.
7. Students receiving special education services typically are expected not to achieve at the same level as their nondisabled peers. Lower expectations can lead to limited academic and post-high-school opportunities.
8. Students in special education programs are not included in the social fabric of the school community.
9. Overrepresentation can contribute to significant racial separation.

Public schools have been studying and trying to address the issue of overrepresentation for more than 40 years; the problem of overrepresentation continues to be an incendiary topic. School teams often are nervous about directly addressing the issue for fear of being labeled as racist. School systems' attitudes tend to mirror larger societal trends and attitudes. Efforts to address the issue are happening throughout the nation, and while the problem persists, a national dialogue has shined a light on the problem and the movement to reduce overrepresentation of diverse students in special education is underway. There is still a lot of work to be done to solve this important problem.

Gender

There are many more boys receiving special education services than girls in the U.S. Girls in need of special education services remain underidentified because their behaviors tend to be more difficult to identify and understand. Behaviors such as social or relational aggression, depression, or withdrawal are less overt and more difficult to perceive (Callahan, 1994; Kann & Hanna, 2000). Although national data compiled in the Annual Report to Congress on special education is not classified by gender, state data suggest that a large variation in the numbers of girls identified with emotional and behavioral disorders exists (Callahan, 1994; Kann & Hanna, 2000). It should be noted however that the rate of identification for girls begins to increase and reflect that of boys during adolescence (Callahan, 1994; Oswald, Best, Coutinho, & Nagle, 2003).

Approximately 32% of the overall special education population is female (Wagner, Newman, Cameto, & Levine, 2005). There are several possible explanations. Girls mature emotionally and physically more quickly than boys, and boys behave differently in school than girls, thereby making them more likely to be identified with a disability than girls (Harmon, 1992). Other factors contributing to underrepresentation of girls may be the staff's reaction to boys' vs. girls' behavior, biased assessment practices, and gender bias. This idea is supported by the finding that psychiatric hospitals and mental health programs often identify girls' problems before the school system does (Caseau, Luckasson, & Kroth, 1994).

Throughout the special education referral and assessment process, gender role assumptions also have been found to contribute to under-identification (Oswald et al., 2003). Gender role assumptions may be used to protect girls from the special education label, as they will be a minority, and sometimes the only girl in classrooms for students with emotional and behavioral disorders. Gender role assumptions also may be a consideration given that teachers may be more willing to tolerate girls' initial symptoms, such as depression or withdrawal, because of the assumption that "girls will be girls" or that these symptoms are just natural experiences for girls (Rice, Merves, & Srsic, 2009; Salk, 2004). The underidentification of girls for services may be an underlying reason why there is little conceptual or empirical data on school-based interventions for girls with emotional or behavioral disabilities. Needless to say, this underrepresentation and the subsequent lack of appropriate programming for girls is a growing problem in the U.S. Girls typically internalize, act in, and get notice later than their externalizing, acting out male counterparts. For example, many girls develop eating disorders that are more difficult to identify than other problem behaviors.

Aleisha spent a lot of time in the restroom. No one seemed to think it was unusual that she would spend 15 minutes, three times each day in there. It was only after a teacher went into the bathroom, heard strange noises coming from one of the stalls and investigated did school officials realize that Aleisha was making herself sick. Aleisha was a quiet, studious young lady with good grades. She was a bit of a loner and not a member of any particular clique. She had no history of school-related problems, and she seemed to come from a good home. She was essentially invisible. A subsequent in-patient stay at an eating disorder clinic revealed that she was not only bingeing and purging, but also was cutting herself with paper clips during class. It turned out that there was a lot going on with this young lady. After 45 days of in-patient treatment, Aleisha was able to return to school. Challenging behavior is not always easy to spot.

Giftedness

The child who is gifted and has challenging behaviors presents a unique set of issues for parents and professionals. The common perception about children who are gifted is that they are acting out because they are bored and that if they were properly challenged, they would stop misbehaving and live up to their academic potential. The child who is gifted often has a powerful desire to understand the world. He has an emotionally intense personality and tends toward being perfectionist and egocentric. He may ask many questions and often is misunderstood by his peers and the adults around him. In many circumstances, teachers underestimate gifted students' abilities, not fully understanding their talents.

Over time, the gifted student's self-esteem will be affected; he will become isolated, depressed, irritable, and difficult to get along with. He may begin to act out and predictably, the adults will respond to the behavior that they can see. For students who are highly gifted, the acting out behavior may be the result of built-up frustration of not being understood for their exceptional skills. The "snowball" begins to roll downhill; all of sudden, teachers and parents are dealing with challenging behaviors. School success for all children with challenging behaviors is directly connected to our collective ability to appreciate and understand our students' abilities and disabilities and provide educational programming that is capable of meeting the diverse academic and emotional needs of all students. Gifted students must be given the challenging curriculum, advanced pacing, and differentiated instruction they need to be successful in school, along with counseling for their unique social and emotional needs.

Family Factors

The individual student's ecology is a strong factor in his or her cultural considerations. By ecology, we refer to the interaction between the many different environments in a family, including:

1. *Family*: The family performs roles for its members that are important for healthy development and serves as an arbiter

between the child and the rest of the world. Some families resist talking about behaviors. How families perceive behaviors will vary from family to family.

2. *Social Connections*: A family's social connections develop as family members make contact with people in different settings—extended family, social groups, recreation, work, and so on. This network of important relationships reinforces feelings of self-worth and helps children develop their sense of identity and belonging within their family and community.

3. *Community Connections*: A community's formal support networks provide resources for families.

4. *Society*: The society defines the "rules of the road" related to individuals and provides the informal structure, role definition, and cultural expectations for its members.

The next section will discuss how the family, particularly student and parent relationships with staff members, can contribute to the overall school culture.

School Culture

A critically important, yet impossible factor to measure in schools that work with kids with challenging behavior is the ability of the staff to form healthy, trusting relationships with the students. Pulling together the right mix of personalities is tough to do. School success for children with challenging behavior depends upon the positive, healthy, and trusting relationships and their opportunity to be formed, shaped, and reinforced through excellent role models.

The world of services for children with challenging behaviors attracts a variety of interesting, committed, and unique players. The mix of personality, program philosophy, and setting work together to create a programmatic culture that is unique to each building or school corridor. As Rita Ives, a retired professor of special education at The George Washington University liked to say, "programs are people committed to constructive change." Although there is little empirical research that identifies a particular type of personality or personality traits common to staff who work with children with challenging behaviors, there is a general perception that direct care staff who choose to work with children with challenging behaviors bring to the building a belief system grounded in a desire to give back to the community or that they bring to the classroom or program a unique understanding of children borne from their own troubled background.

Starting in the next chapter, and continuing through each of the following chapters, evidence-based and scientifically based methods are explored in depth. These involve the use of methods that have either evidence or scientific research to demonstrate efficacy of interventions and methods for children with challenging behavior. Schools that employ the use of evidence-based methods are more likely to emphasize overall schoolwide interventions, and more likely to implement effective classroom interventions. A school that implements schoolwide and classwide interventions effectively will have the best chance of creating and implementing individual student plans. This follows the structure of the upcoming chapters—schoolwide, classwide, and individual interventions are the heart of positive behavior supports.

Although there is a collection of evidence-based practices that have been shown to be effective with children with mental illness, these practices have rarely found their way into school programs. The research-to-best-practice gap needs to be closed in order to uncover the potential and tap into the talents of children with challenging behavior.

The next chapter will connect this concept to the implementation of schoolwide and classwide interventions. It will explore 10 critical components each school must employ to effectively provide kids with challenging behavior a foundation of positive behavior supports.

Part II

Schools and Classrooms

chapter 4

Schoolwide and Classroom Supports

Universal and Secondary Prevention Programs

WHEN a student is struggling behaviorally in school, specific schoolwide and classroom interventions should be available. Schools should have universal supports and interventions in place to help any student who is failing to follow rules and norms. After these interventions are tried and assessed, plans that are individually tailored to the child's specific needs should be developed. This chapter will discuss effective programming for students with various emotional and behavioral challenges by presenting: (a) a framework of quality indicators for effective programs, (b) a menu of academic and behavioral interventions for classroom interventions, and (c) a list of suggestions for different challenging behaviors. The questions that will be answered are:

- What qualities should I look for in an effective program for students with EBD?

Myth	Truth
If I just wait, the student will "get over" these problems.	The belief that a student will magically outgrow an anxiety, mood, attention, or behavioral disability is no longer acceptable. Early intervention is critical for school success as is *continued* intervention into adolescence.
My child just needs a boot camp atmosphere to "scare him or her straight."	Punishment and suspension have little to no effect on long-term behaviors. Parents should seek a structured, well-managed environment that emphasizes intervention rather than externalized control.
Not telling teachers about the needs of the student will give the student a "fresh start."	School staff should be informed of learning needs and differences. Hiding this information does not aid a student's ability to succeed in school. Meetings where a student's issue is discussed and parents provide suggestions to teachers about "what works" for the student are much more likely to aid home-school collaborations.
Curriculum and data collection will only help after we get the student "settled" behaviorally.	Effective, engaging academic instruction is one of the most effective behavior management tools for all students and should be used in concert with a behavior management program.
Because students with EBD have difficulty working with others, they should be given constant worksheets to "keep them busy" or be allowed to spend the day on behavior, not learning.	Although many students with EBD benefit from breaks in instruction and curricula that help them problem solve and make friends, it is a mistake to assume they cannot learn in cooperative learning settings. Instructional, noncompetitive games can be one effective tool to engage learners as can using technology or active learning strategies.

- What are PBIS and RtI, and how should they be used in schools and classrooms?
- What is the role of academic instruction in the functioning of students with EBD?
- What interventions have been found effective for differing behavioral issues?

Top 10 Critical Quality Indicators for Schoolwide and Classroom Interventions

Understanding the underlying purposes behind behavior is challenging. Psychologists, medical professionals, and educators have been struggling to find out just what causes behavioral differences and what interventions aid behavior change. Although we know that both biology and environment influence behavior, we are just beginning to study effective interventions in large-scale studies in education. Our field has recently begun to experiment and test interventions to determine what works for students with problems with aggression, oppositional behavior, mood, anxiety, and attention. As more research is being conducted, the standards for this research are becoming more rigorous. There are two types of research that are supported: (a) scientifically based research and (b) evidence-based research.

Scientifically based research is research that is more experimental and closely linked to scientific rigor. Scientifically based research uses random assignment to groups, has a control group that does not receive the intervention for comparison, and can be very clearly replicated. Evidence-based research has been studied but is less experimental. Very few scientifically based research studies have been conducted at this point using students with emotional and behavioral challenges. When an intervention is evidence-based or scientifically based we will note it. At the end of the chapter, Tool 4.1 shows how teachers and parents can spot a scientifically based method of research.

The following indicators of effective programs can help guide decision making. We call them our Top 10 Quality Indicators for Schoolwide and Classroom Interventions:

1. A problem-solving framework is used.
2. Intervention is sought early.
3. Consequences are used rather than punishment.
4. Staff is prepared, ethical, and from different disciplines.
5. Language and reading needs are examined.
6. Academics are paramount.
7. Each school has a full continuum of supports in the least restrictive environment.
8. Data drive decisions.
9. Both classroom management tools and behavior change tools are used.
10. Parent partnerships are valued.

In the Tools section of this chapter, we have included a tool (Tool 4.2) detailing these indicators and providing a quick reference-style worksheet for parents and teachers to use when determining if their programs contain these important elements of quality. Each of the indicators is described in more detail below.

Quality Indicator #1: A Problem-Solving Framework Is Used

Response to Intervention (RtI) and positive behavioral intervention supports (PBIS) are two universal systems for use in all schools. They have the potential to help *all* students with their learning and behavior. We call these systems problem-solving frameworks because they provide a structure and a step-by-step process for schools to intervene and collect data on their interventions. These universal group interventions help identify academic and behavioral issues in a positive, systematic way in order to prevent years of failure before disability diagnosis.

RtI. RTI is a problem-solving model that emphasizes: early intervention and prevention of academic and behavior problems, providing more intensive interventions based on more intensive student need, and diagnostic-prescriptive decision making through data collection and teamwork. Interventions are described in terms of tiers, with the most general or universal interventions provided to all children, and more intensive interventions to the children with the greatest needs. Different researchers and schools use different tiered models, but the most common is a three-tier model. The first tier is teaching to the whole group, or universal student body, and assessing student learning through data collection. The second tier is taking the small group of students who did not master the original instruction and designing more in-depth instruction and assessment for them. The third tier is to individualize interventions for any remaining students who are still struggling with the concept. Figure 3 illustrates the core components of RtI.

In the first tier, educators deliver instruction and then assess each individual to see who has mastered the material. So, if students were learning how to tell time using the hour hand, they would receive instruction, and then have to demonstrate with accuracy how to tell the hour. In every group there will be a few students who need more time, more intensive instruction, or another way of being taught the material. These students, the students in Tier II, would be given intensive instruction and then be assessed again. The students who still need differing strategies to master the material would then receive more intensive instruction in Tier III. In this way, RtI seeks to remediate while learning happens rather than waiting until a student fails a subject or a grade and then qualifies for special services. The theory behind RtI is to create a learning community who understands the learning needs of each student and who responds immediately and as a team to these issues (Witt, 2006).

The use of RTI also has implications for the frequency and type of evaluations, including how often behavioral data should be collected. As

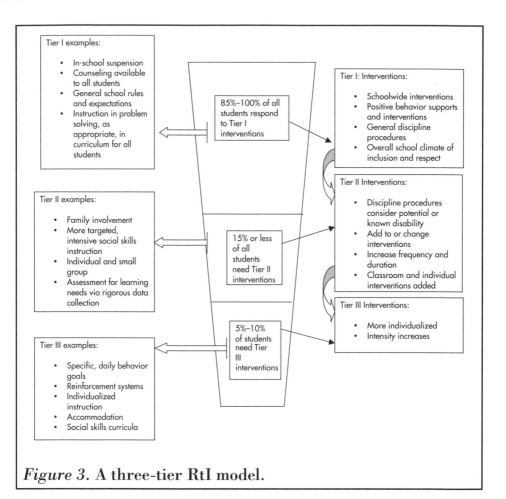

Figure 3. A three-tier RtI model.

shown in Table 3, evaluations become more specific, more individualized, more specialized, and require specialized personnel as students move from universal to individual interventions. Evaluation information, including data collection, is collected while interventions are in place. As you will see, this fits well with the models we present in Chapters 6 and 8.

As shown in Figure 4, when the components of the RtI model are working effectively, schoolwide interventions are available and meet the needs of most students.

PBIS. PBIS has a similar philosophical base to RtI. It was a concept developed by two researchers, Sugai and Horner, from the University of

Table 3

The Three Tiers of Response to Intervention

	TIER I	TIER II	TIER III
What percent of students?	80% to 90% of all students	10% to 15% of students	5% to 10% of students
What are the students' needs or diagnoses?	• Student may or may not have a psychiatric diagnosis that affects her in school • Student may be standing out as not benefitting from general instruction in the regular classroom	• Student may or may not have a diagnosis, but there is some effect of symptoms on performance • Student has not responded to Tier I interventions as expected	• Psychiatric diagnoses whose symptoms significantly affect a child in school • Student with poor behavior and academic performance • Student has not responded to Tier I and II interventions as expected
Teacher qualification or special training	• Standard qualifications • No special training	• More specific qualifications • More specific training	• Need specific qualifications • Specific training necessary • Partnerships with various specialists from different disciplines
Frequency of assessment and data collection	• Approximately 1 to 4 times per month	• Approximately 1 or more times per week	• Approximately 2–3 times per week or daily
Who is involved?	• Grade-based team discussion may occur about student's behavior. • Parent contact when discipline issue; light parent involvement, normal level of staff involvement; home-school systems as expected for all students	• Grade-based team, along with specialists (e.g., behavior specialist, psychologist, consultant) • Parental involvement increases; home-school systems may be put into place on a more intensive level; multidisciplinary team may be involved	• Multidisciplinary team along with grade-based team, as described in Chapter 6 • Specialists, staff with special training and expertise, partner with parents and private providers such as therapists or psychiatrists

Table 3, continued

	TIER I	TIER II	TIER III
Type of evaluation	• Tests required by state, school district, classroom, or individual teacher	• Tests required by Tier I, but more specialized evaluation tools are used, with need for more training and higher skill of examiner • Multidisciplinary team may be involved	• Tests are individualized and formal or standardized • More individualized and specialized than Tier II • Evaluation by multidisciplinary team • Suspected of having or determined to have an emotional disturbance or emotional behavioral disorder
Type of intervention needed	• Universal and scientifically based interventions	• Universal interventions, plus added small group or some short-term or light individual scientifically based interventions • Functional behavior assessment	• Scientifically based instruction, methods, and interventions delivered with fidelity • Functional behavior assessment, with use of specialists, and behavior intervention plan
Type of plan needed	• Schoolwide and classroom-based interventions with a continuum of positive behavior supports	• Schoolwide, classroom-based interventions and some individualization for specific students • behavior intervention plan	• Individualized Education Plan, including behavior intervention plan, with schoolwide and classwide interventions, with accommodations

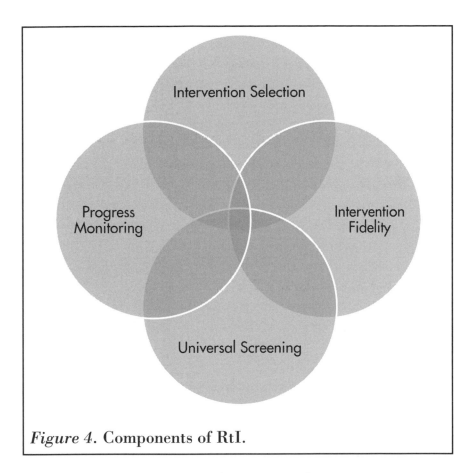

Figure 4. Components of RtI.

Oregon. PBIS is a schoolwide behavior system that creates interventions in steps. The first step is to have schoolwide practices that reinforce positive behaviors to meet the needs of students with challenging behaviors. Through setting up the first step, called universal/primary interventions, the whole school recognizes positive behaviors, giving clear directions as to the expectations of the school and consistently reinforcing school values. The second step designs interventions for students who are still struggling with their behavior after receiving consistent universal intervention. At this level, small-group instruction or social skills groups can be used to help teach the students behaviors. Quick checks on the students during the day also can help support positive behaviors. The final level is for the few students who do not respond to interventions in the first two levels of PBIS. In this third level, assessments of individual behaviors are done and interventions are designed specifically for an individual. For further information, please see the Office of Special Education Programs Technical Assistance Center on Positive Behavioral Intervention and Supports Effective School Interventions' website at http://www.pbis.org. One of the most important parts of using PBIS and RtI is delivering and using the ideas consistently.

Parent Questions. When examining a school and its use of RtI and PBIS, parents should be asking about how students are grouped for instruction, how learning is documented, and what happens when a student does not understand a concept the first time. Other questions include:

- What is done for all students?
- What happens if a student needs more support?
- How is progress documented?
- What individualized interventions have been used in the past to support students?
- What evidence-based or scientifically based methods are being used, and why were they selected for my child?

Quality Indicator #2: Intervention Is Sought Early

When intervention is sought early, parents get help when their children are very young, as soon as a problem is identified. Early intervention is not just for young children, however. As soon as concerning behaviors surface, intervention is needed.

Human development is a complicated process. It is extremely difficult to know when a behavioral issue is just a sign of a temporary stage or when it is a symptom of a more serious issue. Most professionals now agree that early intervention in behavior, as in speech and reading, is most effective in the long run (Guralnick, 2000). Screening tools for behavioral issues are currently being suggested for use in preschool and early elementary school. One of the best-known examples is the First Step to Success program (Walker & Severson, 1990). First Step to Success is a program to identify students at risk for behavioral problems.

Students are screened using teacher rankings and trained observers and then a prescriptive program rewarding behavior is administered in the general education classroom. Students are rewarded for attending to task, getting along with teachers, and developing positive peer relationships. Additionally, home intervention is completed for 6 weeks.

Students with problems expressing themselves behaviorally must be identified early so that a menu of interventions can be individually tailored to meet their needs. Students with behavioral issues rarely "grow out" of their issues. Explicit assessment and intervention strategies must occur as soon as issues are detected. These ideas of early intervention are sometimes new to seasoned professionals. Do not be dissuaded from assessment and action or be complacent with a "wait and see" attitude. Seek assessment and intervention support as early as possible.

Parent Questions. Parents should seek multiple assessments to help them assess an emotional or behavioral issue in order to provide support for their children early. Some questions to ask include:

- What medical issues are surrounding the presenting problem?
- Are there neurochemical issues? Sleep issues? Issues with seizures?
- Are there language or communication issues?
- Is there difficulty with sensory information from the environment or motor issues that affect movement and handwriting?
- Does the student have difficulty reading?

Quality Indicator #3: Consequences Are Used Rather Than Punishment

Another indicator of a quality program is the effective use of rewards and consequences. In order to be effective, programs must avoid punishment and instead have a consistent, predictable structure that outlines "can dos" and "can't dos." Effective schools use many interventions to help each individual. There are built-in rewards and motivations for each student, schoolwide and classwide. Effective programs use consequences rather than punishment. Consequences are logical, natural effects that come from actions. For example, the consequence of not sending out invitations until the day before the event is that people have other plans and don't come to the party.

Punishment is a purposeful action that decreases the likelihood of the behavior being repeated. It is not "bad," but it has been associated with shame and humiliation so professionals prefer to teach people to use consequences to manage behavior. If one does not send out party invitations until the day before the event and another person then forbids the party host any social activity for a month—that is punishment. Punishment often leaves a person feeling helpless and not in control and sets up an "us" versus "you" condition. Consequences should be determined as clearly as possible before an infraction occurs and should be linked to a logical result rather than a painful process. For example, if a student does not complete his or her writing project during language arts then it would make sense that he or she would have to complete it during free time as a consequence.

Finding effective programming for students with behavioral disabilities can be difficult because the natural response to troubling behaviors often is the *wrong* response. When faced with opposition, defiance, fatigue, or anxiety we all mirror the behavior in front of us or flee physically or psychologically from the situation (Long, Long, & Whitson, 2009). If a student is oppositional or directly challenges the authority of an adult the automatic response often is counteraggression. Parents and teachers will hear themselves say, "Yes, you will," or "Because I said so," or " I will make you listen." Students who are aggressive tend to be defiant when asked to complete tasks. This defiance generally continues until the adult ceases to demand anything from the student. The child or adolescent wears down the adult, and then the student is left with not completing the task. This produces more difficulty because it reinforces to the student that adult requests are optional. The natural course of response is not the correct one!

Similarly, when a student is self-injurious or so depressed that all he or she wants to do is sleep, the adult's natural response is to "let the student off the hook." We sometimes try to engage the student for a short period of time but then begin to feel futile. We tend to mirror the hopelessness in front of us (Long et al., 2009). Instead of reacting in this way, adults must hear the feelings and emotions of the students, clearly communicate the expectation, and then remind the students of the consequences in order to facilitate behavioral change. Teachers and staff members who feel ineffective and stressed often use punishment rather than other strategies to induce behavioral change. They do what is natural unless there is a philosophy of the program to correct these false assumptions. Some are sarcastic, yell, or take away every privilege students can possibly enjoy instead of seeking creative and respectful solutions.

Parent Questions. When examining a program or classroom for students with emotional and behavioral challenges parents should examine the use of punishment within the program. Questions to ask include:

- How do the adults interface with the students?
- Are administrators visible and accessible?
- Are there multiple interventions used or is every problem responded to by timeout or suspension?
- Are students involved in the rule making of the program or are they just expected to listen and obey?
- Is there specific training for staff regarding crisis situations?
- Is there specific training for students on social skills?
- How long does the program leave a student in timeout?

Parents also should ask about the use of timeout, exclusion, or physical restraint in order to see if the program relies too heavily on these intensive, punitive interventions.

Quality Indicator #4: Staff Is Prepared, Ethical and From Different Disciplines

There are many staffing situations that can affect the learning of all students, especially students with behavioral challenges who need staff with advanced skills. In order to help students with behavioral challenges learn and progress, staff must be qualified to deliver services. There are documented shortages across the country of special educators qualified to teach students with emotional and behavioral challenges. When a person is licensed, it assumes that he or she is familiar with the ethical guidelines. Ethical dilemmas are so common in education and mental health that just being a good person is not enough! Professionals need documented training on how to keep personal feelings from clouding judgment and how to handle confidential information and situations. In addition, there are few educators who have experience working with this population and who have passed the content competencies required to be considered a highly qualified teacher. Parents should inquire about the percentage of staff who have advanced degrees and a state license in a relevant area of study.

Some programs use rotating substitutes who do not have any professional teaching credentials to serve students for long periods of time. These unqualified personnel are wonderful people, but they often do not understand curriculum and learning. In order to begin to solve the mix of content and expertise in individualizing instruction, some states have a general education teacher and a special education teacher team-teach in one class. This can work well, but can be problematic if both teachers do not choose to work together, if the content teacher is unwilling to accommodate different learning styles or assessments from students, or if the special education teacher does not individualize instruction during the process.

Program constancy, together with a strength-based philosophy, provides the basis for the strongest programs. Students with various emotional and behavioral challenges can need academic support, behavioral support, mental health support, and the services of occupational and speech and language therapy. The role of related services personnel in schools is critical. Professionals who are qualified in speech and language therapy, occupational therapy, social work, or psychology should spend adequate time with individual students, as well as be part of the school team that creates interventions.

Parent Questions. Parents should ask about the content knowledge of teachers especially at the middle school level and beyond, including:

- Is one teacher being expected to know chemistry, biology, physics, and social studies?
- How can you be sure the staff knows the content that students need to learn?
- How can you be sure that the educator who knows the content will also know how to modify lessons to accommodate learning and behavioral differences?

Helpful information also can be found when asking about the turnover rates of teachers, clinicians, and support staff. One question to ask includes:

- Is the program in constant flux as new teachers are hired, burned out, and replaced by novices?

Finally, parents should seek to understand the culture of collaboration in a program:

- Are there professionals available to meet the many differing needs of the student?
- How do the professionals work together?
- For how much time do the professionals interact directly with the student?
- How will you know these services are being provided?

Quality Indicator #5: Language and Reading Needs Are Examined

As we learn more and more about the brain, behavior, and learning, there appears to be a correlation between language, reading, and behavior. Many students with emotional and behavioral challenges have language problems and reading difficulties. According to one study (Nelson, Benner, & Cheney, 2005), about 70% of students in the sample with EBD had a speech or language delay. Young children with behavior challenges also may have a language base for their behaviors. Additionally, researchers are now exploring the connection between dyslexia, the largest category of reading disabilities, and students with EBD (Rescorla, Ross, & McClure, 2007). Usually professionals are so concerned about the behavior of a student that they often neglect to screen students for their needs in receptive and expressive language, phonemic awareness, and reading comprehension.

It is easy to understand that a student who has trouble learning to read may misbehave rather than face his difficulty. Reading and literacy skills are important to consider when hypothesizing about reasons for student behavior and when designing intervention plans. Also, weaknesses in expressive language, receptive language, and pragmatic language can contribute to or cause behavior problems. In order to ensure that students with social, emotional, and behavioral needs are receiving proper academic and behavioral programming, parents and teachers should make sure that each student with a suspected behavioral difficulty receives a screening for language and reading. Effective programs consider the needs of the whole child and try to assess the underlying cause or causes for the emotional or behavioral problem. Effective programs have more than one reading program to meet the diverse needs of youth. Effective schools also understand the language-literacy-behavior connection.

Parent Questions. Parents should ask about the particular reading programs that are being used in the school and about the time and structure of reading instruction. A scientifically based research report from the National Reading Panel has emphasized effective practices that aid reading (Shanahan, 2006). The findings guide instruction through highlighting practices that should be taught to students. Reading instruction should include: (a) phonemic awareness or distinguishing between sounds; (b) systematic phonics instruction; (c) reading aloud, rereading, and one-to-one feedback to improve fluency; (d) vocabulary or word meaning instruction; and (e) comprehension strategies that gradually have the student take responsibility for using multiple strategies (Shanahan, 2006).

Parents should ask some of the following questions:

- What reading programs are you using in this school?
- How often is reading assessed?
- Are all of the components of reading included in instruction?
- How does the speech-language pathologist serve students with challenging behaviors for the school, in specific classes, and for individual students?

Quality Indicator #6: Academics Are Paramount

In recent years, professionals in the field of EBD often have been more interested in "managing" or "controlling" the behavior of students rather than student learning. In the past 10 years, however, more publications have emerged noting the academic performance and needs of students with emotional and behavioral challenges. Students with EBD have varying levels of IQ from high to low and need to be challenged and engaged. Effective programs use a curriculum to guide instruction and have assessments and activities tied to this curriculum. Teachers should be able to discuss the units that will be presented in each subject area, and these units should correlate with the general education curriculum and then be *individualized* to the needs of the student. While learning the curriculum, students with emotional and behavioral challenges should have their learning needs considered. Effective programs make appropriate accommodations and modifications for each individual student, and directly instruct the social, behavioral, and emotional skills through a curriculum with standards-based student evaluation methods.

Learning Strategies. How do students learn best? Many researchers have tried to study what makes some students more successful in school. One promising avenue of research related to students with learning and emotional and behavioral challenges is the Strategic Instruction Model at the University of Kansas. These learning strategies are research-based ways to help make an individual more active in the learning process. The strategy is direct and explicitly taught. The strategies researched to be effective by Deshler and his colleagues at the University of Kansas follow a good lesson plan format, with the use of curriculum-based measurement procedures:

1. The strategy is introduced, with instruction about the importance of the strategy. Student participation in developing enthusiasm and goals for learning the strategy is important. Pretest data are taken.
2. The strategy is memorized and practiced. Baseline data is collected and charted.
3. The student uses the strategy with guidance from the teacher or adult. Data are collected and charted.
4. The student uses the strategy independently. Data are collected and charted.
5. The student and teacher review and a postassessment is given.
6. The student uses the strategy in different ways for generalization, and data are collected and charted.

Special teacher training and certification generally is required. Parent and student involvement is critical, and there are routines for both to be involved in the strategy instruction. Strategies for academic, behavioral, and study skills have been developed. For more information about strategies related to reading, storing, and remembering, see the University of Kansas Center for Research and Learning at http://kucrl.org.

Homework. Homework should be at the independent level of the student. Many parents of students with disabilities spend many hours trying to help their child complete homework. Research shows that homework at the frustration level does not improve student achievement. In fact, parental efforts to engage in battles for nightly assignments can result in worse behavior at school. Teachers of children with troubling behavior also can tend toward not assigning any homework, because collecting, assigning, and giving feedback on homework assignments can be a task in itself. Parents need to check in with their child's teachers and school to answer important questions about homework and other academic assignments. A listing of good questions to ask is included in the Tool 4.3 at the end of this chapter. This list also includes questions for parents to gauge their level of interaction with their children on homework and what may be causing frustration to occur around homework time.

Parent Questions. Parents should ask to see the curriculum, along with asking the following questions:

- How will the curriculum be individualized for the student?
- What assessments are used to measure learning?
- How often will these assessments be used?
- What happens if a student is absent or is unavailable for learning during instruction?
- How will academics be modified and adjusted?
- What accommodations will be made to support learning?
- What measures are used to evaluate progress in the curriculum?
- Do students have available to them the same courses that their nondisabled peers can access?

Quality Indicator #7: Each School Has a Full Continuum of Supports in the Least Restrictive Environment

A child should not have to move to a different school in order to receive positive behavior supports. So often, however, a child is faced with this situation because the class with a structured behavior program is at a different school, or there is no psychologist to provide counseling at the child's current school. If each school has a continuum of positive behavior supports, each school ideally would have a number of both special education and general education classrooms and staff ready to provide small-group instruction, individualized services, and even a full schoolwide continuum of the interventions listed later in this chapter. In such an ideal situation, a child would receive interventions based on need and without regard to school-based resources.

The concept of "restrictiveness" comes from a history in the field of education, as described in Chapter 2, where people with disabilities were restricted from accessing community resources. The more specialized and separated a classroom or program generally the more restrictive it is seen to be. For example, if a ninth-grade classroom has only four students with disabilities, one special educator, two teacher aides, and has a 10-minute interval reward system, it would be very different from the regular classroom, so it would be considered more restrictive than the general classroom.

The multidisciplinary team decides the child's placement and services. These should be delivered in a setting that allows the child to be in his regular classroom, as long as the child is making meaningful progress on his goals and in the curriculum. A child with challenging behaviors that interfere with learning should be seen as a child with a disability and should be protected under federal and state laws.

Least restrictive environment is more fully explored in Chapter 9 on individual learning plans. The setting described in a child's 504 Plan, behavior intervention plan, or Individualized Education Program should be a setting where the child will make meaningful progress, and generally access a free appropriate public education.

Parent Questions. Some questions for parents to ask regarding least restrictive environment include:

- What are the placement options for my child?
- How does the school district comply with the requirement to provide a continuum of services?
- Are the alternative schools in this district used to provide services in this continuum?
- How will the school evaluate the proper environment for my child?

Quality Indicator #8: Data Drive Decisions

Effective programs are increasingly using data to monitor student progress and school programming. Pertaining to students with social, emotional, and behavioral challenges, it is imperative that daily, weekly, and monthly behavioral data are collected. Programs should be able to tell whether or not a student is making progress behaviorally. Goals should be set for students based upon their individual needs. Then data should be collected, analyzed, and used for programming decisions. Data collection, or lack of data collection, is one of the most seminal issues in education, and one of the most important issues for parents. Therefore, we detail data collection in Chapters 6 and 7.

If a daily point sheet is being used to tally points earned for selected positive behaviors, these point sheets can be analyzed monthly to see individual trends and classroom trends. There also are types of behavioral recording that can be used to analyze patterns of behavior (see the Tools section of this chapter for worksheets on these types of behavior records).

Effective programs also use data to monitor student learning. Using the state standardized tests is one way to analyze learning. They are especially helpful to see if there were certain subjects or concepts where a majority of students score low, so that improvements in teaching in that grade can be made. These once-a-year tests are not enough, however. Best practice suggests that curriculum-based measures, or data that collect evidence on how students are doing on a particular concept in the curriculum, are real-time assessments that can drive instruction. Portfolio and work samples for learning concepts also show student learning. Many believe that testing students with emotional and behavioral challenges is unduly stressful. Although not always comfortable, assessments must drive the learning process. Additionally, assessments that are game based or that are given orally or on the computer can have different results than traditional paper-and-pencil tests. Systems of data assessment exist that are helpful to programs. The Northwest Evaluation System Measures of Academic Progress is a curriculum-based way for programs to monitor student progress in the curriculum. This system gives educators specific information for each student about where he is performing relative to the curriculum (Walter, 2006).

Parent Questions. When visiting a school, one should ask about the collection of data, including:

- When are data collected to monitor academic and behavior progress?

- Is there a sample behavior tracking sheet that is available?
- Does the staff meet to discuss patterns in behavioral data and instructional data?

Quality Indicator #9: Both Classroom Management Tools and Behavior Change Tools Are Used

There is an old saying that, "If all you have is a hammer, everything looks like a nail." Limited knowledge of classroom management and behavioral change tools limits our responses to students. Too frequently in the history of services to students with disabilities, professionals have let their theoretical and philosophical beliefs limit their use of interventions. You may hear: "Go to timeout," "You just lost recess," "Go to the principal's office," or "He has problems at home." Or you would see only therapy or point sheets used in a program. Now, it is generally accepted that there are interventions from various traditions that work in combination to support the management of behavior and the facilitation of behavioral change. Effective programs use many types of interventions in order to best individualize services. There are two main types of interventions that are used: interventions that manage behavior and interventions that change behavior. Teachers must be able to use both types of interventions. They must be able to manage the group and also use interventions that challenge students to change their behaviors.

A Menu of Interventions: What Are Group Management Techniques? General teacher education stresses the importance of classroom management as a tool for helping students learn. Classroom management and consistency is very important in teaching students with emotional and behavioral challenges. The following sections detail important features of an effective classroom for students with emotional and behavioral challenges. These interventions do not change behavior but they do help manage behavior. These ideas align with the Institute of Educational Studies' recommendation for scientifically based interventions (Epstein, Atkins, Cullinan, Kutash, & Weaver, 2008).

1. A detailed schedule is posted and reviewed with students daily.

2. Rules are created with the students and are posted. Rewards and consequences are clearly understood and reinforced by the teacher and the administration. There are opportunities for students to earn privileges as a group and individually. There are consequences for being off task, for not being cooperative, for leaving the classroom, for destroying property, and for not respecting peers, but the emphasis is on the positive.

3. Routines for lining up, turning in work, resolving disagreements, earning free time, using computers, answering teacher questions, and homework are established, taught, and practiced until mastered.

4. Easily understood objectives are posted for each lesson. Expectations for behavior are posted and restated before every activity.

5. There is a clear agenda detailing how each lesson will be structured so students can tell what is coming next. There is attention to how transitions are made.

6. There are opportunities to be praised and to be successful in academic and social capacities.

7. There are opportunities for the group of staff and students to discuss classroom climate and other issues.

Specific Group Management Techniques. Once an effective classroom is established there are specific tools educators can use to keep the classroom running effectively, including surface management techniques. In addition, there are principles from the behaviorist school of thought on positive reinforcement and token economies that can help manage a class.

Surface management techniques. The following techniques can be used in enforcing group or classroom behavior:

- *Planned ignoring:* In this strategy, the adult purposefully ignores a behavior. This is effective when you know the behavior will go away if ignored. In this strategy, the adult refuses to acknowledge or comment on the behavior and instead discusses something else. Never use this if the student is teasing another student.

- *Signal interference:* We all remember the "look" a teacher could give us to show that we were not complying with rules. In this strategy, a signal is developed to redirect a student or remind the student of a rule. This is helpful when you want to redirect the behavior but do not want to have a lengthy argument about why the student is doing something.

- *Proximity control:* In this strategy, the adult uses his or her body to move closer to the person who is having a problem. Sometimes moving closer to one student while still talking to the whole group helps diffuse talking or minor disruptions.

- *Involvement in the interest relationship:* Students with behavioral challenges sometimes lose interest more quickly in lessons or activities than typical students. Recent brain and learning research suggests that the brain responds better with shorter bursts of information and changes in the environment to keep interest.

- *Tension decontamination through humor:* Humor, without sarcasm, can help relieve the pent-up emotions of a stressful situation for students and adults. Sarcasm is not appropriate humor because it usually is at someone's expense.

- *Hurdle help:* In this strategy, frustration is avoided when the adult helps a student start an assignment or do something difficult or unfamiliar. When an adult lends the student help it gives confidence to the student. A hazard of this strategy is that the student will only start a task or do something challenging when given help. In order to be effective, this strategy must be slowly faded over time.

- *Removal of seductive objects:* Have you ever tried to concentrate on one thing but been so distracted by something else in the environment that you haven't completed your original task? In this strategy, the adult purposely removes objects that would

distract a student or would be so enticing the student would
get into trouble.

- *Antiseptic bouncing:* In this strategy, the adult sends a student
  on an errand or task to remove him from a situation that seems
  to be escalating. Some teachers send a note to another teacher
  or have the student deliver something in order to thwart a
  potential problem in the classroom.

Other group management techniques. Many group management
techniques are critiqued because they rely on reinforcement. We have
often heard teachers say, "Why should I reward that positive behavior?
The student should just do what is expected!" Although we agree that
sometimes schools and teachers rely too much on reward or consequence in their intervention style, we still see the role of motivation
in our society as important. We work at jobs for satisfaction, but also
for a paycheck! As long as rewards are only part of the management
process rather than the whole program, they are effective. Below is a
list of management techniques that can be used in the classroom to
help manage student behavior:

- *Positive reinforcement:* The old saying that "You catch more flies
  with honey than vinegar" is true in practice and is supported in
  behavioral research. In order to change behavior it is *imperative* that teachers and parents focus on the "good" behavior and
  reinforce it through verbal praise, stickers, earning privileges,
  and other "rewards." You may think you are already doing this;
  however, studies of teacher behavior have shown that praise
  often is not used correctly. When praise is used specifically,
  correctly, authentically, and often enough, it can be a very
  effective behavior management and change tool (Epstein et
  al., 2008). Try to offer three genuine positives (don't make
  them up!) for every one correction. Be sure to stress that students choose to earn or not to earn privileges—they don't "lose"
  them and you don't take them!
- *Token economies:* Many programs for students with challenging

behaviors use a token economy to help manage the behavior of students. A token economy, like our societal economy, creates reinforcements for positive behaviors by having students earn points throughout the day. In a token economy, students have an individual point sheet where they are earning points for positive behaviors throughout the school day. Often these point sheets are tied to having successful days that tie into a school store or prize box or a culminating earned activity at the end of the week. Token economies do work for some students although school staff and parents should pay particular attention to potential problems: (a) not all staff award points for the same behaviors in the same way; (b) some staff focus on taking away points, which leads to power struggles rather than a reward of positive behaviors; (c) when a student has a problem early in the day and knows he cannot earn a successful day then the system does not work; (d) the earning of points becomes the focus of the entire academic and behavioral program; or (e) some students just don't respond to earning things or praise and need another type of intervention.

- *Level systems:* When a program uses a token economy, it often uses level systems to accompany it. Students need to earn points, to have successful days, and to earn levels of privileges. In some programs, for example, students at the most basic level have to be escorted places within the school whereas students who earn the higher level can be trusted to walk to the restroom or do an errand without an adult escort. One major issue with level systems is the small minority of students who never leave the basic level. If a student never earns enough successful days to earn a new level, the staff must recognize this and develop a new plan to help "hook" the student into the group and the school. Another flaw in level systems is a focus on the negative. It does not take many bad moments for a child to lose all of her points for a given day and have to start over. It is important that these systems function in such a way as to help students maintain hope.

- *Behavior contracts:* When done correctly, behavior contracts can help an individual earn something that is special to her through working on one behavior. A behavior contract is a written agreement between a student and an adult that clearly records a positive, specific behavior and then details a pre-determined reward. For example, if a student is working on raising her hand before talking, a behavior contract could say that when the student raises her hand before talking 10 times, she earns 10 minutes of free time on the computer. Some key elements of behavior contracts are: (a) the student is interested in the reward, (b) the contract can be fulfilled easily in a short amount of time, and (c) that only one behavior at a time is recorded and other behaviors the student does do not influence the success of the contract.

- *Self-monitoring:* Self-monitoring is the process of helping each student check and assess his own behavior when prompted. For example, if a student has problems with attention, there would be a timer or a signal from the teacher every few minutes where the student would stop and assess whether he was on task. Through having a student check his own behavior, the student becomes more involved in the behavior change process.

- *Service learning:* One promising intervention for many students is service learning, where students are actively involved in projects that serve the community. Often these are real tasks or needs in the community where students can be empowered to use their strengths to make a difference. Students are involved in planning, implementing, and evaluating their projects and can be coached through the experience.

Behavior change techniques and programs. Many schools and programs are so worried about the management of a classroom and the management of the behaviors of students that they often forget that management tools *do not change behavior.* There are separate tools that help facilitate a change in behavior. These behavioral change techniques are imperative to changing behavioral patterns, regardless of the setting:

- *Cognitive-behavioral think sheets and workbooks:* Recent research in psychology and medicine have found that cognitive-behavioral therapy, a therapy that examines and challenges thinking errors, has helped people with various emotional and behavioral disabilities. Parents and teachers can use some of these ideas through accessing workbooks and think sheets that help the student either (a) learn triggers, (b) brainstorm alternate options to a behavior, (c) learn the problem-solving process, or (d) reflect on his behaviors to help learn alternative strategies.

- *Social skills instruction:* The research on social skills instruction has mixed results on its efficacy with students with emotional and behavioral challenges. Students do need explicit instruction on how to interact successfully with others; however, isolated instruction that is not generalizable or reinforced consistently throughout the day has not proved successful. Successful programs use a curriculum, are reinforced schoolwide, and have students practice new skills in realistic situations.

- *Metacognitive strategies:* Advances in neuroscience show that some skills are slow to develop in the prefrontal cortex for children and adolescents. In order to aid students with executive functioning (i.e., planning, decision making), there are metacognitive strategies that help students learn to be organized and follow a specific procedure for problem solving.

- *Life Space Crisis Intervention:* One way teachers and staff can help students think about their behavior is through talking to students. One specific training, Life Space Crisis Intervention, helps students see their role in their behavior through exposing students to one of the six underlying patterns of behavior: (a) refusing to see reality, (b) displaced anger, (c) poor social skills,

(d) getting "set up" by other students, (e) feeling too much guilt or trying to punish self, or (f) refusal to feel guilt. The staff can learn this way of talking to students and can help students recognize the behavioral pattern that impedes their growth.

- *Wrap-around services:* Many of the longitudinal studies of students with emotional and behavioral challenges have examined a wrap-around approach. A wrap-around approach is a whole-child approach that helps the family, the school, and the community in their involvement with the child. Family counseling and support often is a component of a wrap-around service. One way educators can utilize the principles of the wrap-around approach is to try to connect with the family, the school social worker, or the afterschool program to help develop a communication system to support the student. Wrap-around services where community agencies, including the school system, work together to provide services for children with social, emotional, and behavioral disorders would be an example of a Tier III intervention for a child in need of a very high level of in-home services, residential placement, or respite support, where caregivers other than parents provide some level of care. Whatever the case, parents, guardians, and agency representatives must work together to provide the most appropriate, evidence-based methods possible.

Parent Questions. Questions for parents to ask regarding classroom management and behavioral change tools include the following:
- What methods and interventions does the school or classroom use to change behavior? To manage behavior?
- How are the interventions provided in the classroom, in the overall school, and for individual students?
- What is the process when the school needs added training, interventions, or resources to provide a wide range of interventions?
- How will my child's progress be evaluated?

Quality Indicator #10: Parent Partnerships Are Valued

Research supports the common sense idea that parent partnerships improve performance and behavior. Parents and educators must collaborate in sometimes challenging situations. Often parent-educator trust is lost, and there is finger pointing between parents and the school. The following suggested strategies for working with behavioral challenges may help daily interactions with students. It should be noted, however, that these strategies help support the medication and mental health treatment strategies developed by a team of professionals.

One of the most underutilized tools in working with challenging youth is home-school collaboration. In order to best work together schools and families should:

- Avoid the blame game.
- Have a system of communication between home and school. Be determined to communicate positive as well as negative information.
- Seek outside help when necessary. Schools should be able to offer support to teachers and educational advocates, and assessments by relevant outside professionals can help families know how to ask for the right services and supports for their children.

Parents and school teams must work together generally, but when students are showing problematic behavior, that partnership becomes even more critical. When children struggle, it is an emotional situation for parents. Tool 4.4 at the end of this chapter suggests ways to intervene for children who show anxious, depressed, oppositional, or aggressive behaviors.

Parent Questions. When understanding how parent-school partnerships are formed, parent will want to ask questions such as:

- Does the school have a parent liaison, or who is responsible for interfacing with parents?
- What is the school philosophy about parent-school partnerships?

- What are the expectations for parents at the school and how can parents support the school programs?

Schoolwide and Classwide Supports

Schools that can put into place a blanket of positive behavior support throughout the school will have the best chance of creating effective classroom interventions. A national survey related to school-based mental health services showed that boys in school struggled with aggression and disruptive behavior, while girls struggled with anxiety and adjustment. A vast majority of schools reported about a fifth of the whole school population received mental health services (Walter, 2006). When schoolwide and classwide interventions are available to every child and used correctly, the need to design individualized plans should decrease. It is still necessary, however, to design individual plans. So, the next chapter will examine discipline problems, both schoolwide and at the individual level. The following chapter then discusses the importance of evaluating the individual child's strengths and needs in order to design and implement effective individual plans.

Tool 4.1
How to Spot a Scientifically Based Method

Some interventions or methods have evidence to back them up, but others actually have a scientific basis to show their effectiveness. To find out if a certain program, curriculum, intervention, therapy, or other method meets this rigorous standard, use this checklist.

Circle answer that applies:
1. Is there research that supports effectiveness?

    Yes   No   Unknown

2. On which populations of students has the intervention been proven to work?

    Like My Child   Not Like My Child

3. How frequently and for what period of time must the intervention be used in order for fidelity of implementation to be satisfied?

    Long Enough   Not Long Enough

4. What trainings must be completed before someone can implement the intervention? List these in the child's individual plan.

5. Does the intervention contain a data collection system by which progress may continuously be monitored?

    Yes   No

Evaluations, methods, interventions, and strategies must be scientifically based. This is a more rigorous standard than an evidence-based standard. Evidence-based methods are those that have some information about the intervention's efficacy, while scientifically sound interventions are scientifically based. Use this checklist to assure that evaluations, schoolwide interventions, or individual positive behavior supports, interventions, and strategies meet the rigorous criteria for scientifically based research (U.S. Department of Education, 2000, p. 46576):

❏ Research is objective, reliable, and valid and includes "rigorous, systematic, and objective procedures" that shows information about education activities and programs.

❏ Research "employs systematic, empirical methods" that use observation or experiments to prove effectiveness.

❏ Data is collected rigorously, and data is adequate to test the hypothesis and confirm conclusions.

❏ Valid and reliable data is collected over multiple times, and shows the same results, even when different observers, examiners, investigators or measurements are used.

❏ A scientific method is employed, including experimental or quasiexperimental designs where different conditions are used with appropriate controls. A preference for random-assignment experiments or experiments using with-condition or cross-condition controls is noted.

❏ Studies can be replicated, or offer enough detail about the experiments so that another scientist can build systematically on the findings of the research.

❏ Research has been accepted by peer-reviewed journal, or a panel of independent experts.

Tool 4.2
Top 10 Quality Indicators Worksheet

Academics Are Paramount
- Is a curriculum used?
- How will the curriculum be individualized?
- What assessments are used to measure learning?
- What happens when a student is absent or unavailable for learning?
- What accommodations will be used to support learning?

Language and Reading Needs Are Examined
- What reading programs are used?
- How often is reading assessed and how?
- Are phonics, fluency, vocabulary, and comprehension addressed?

The Staff Is Professionally Prepared and From Different Disciplines
- What is the staff turnover every year?
- Are there experts in speech and language therapy, occupational therapy, and psychology/social work?
- How much time do these professionals spend with students? With staff?
- How will you know these services are being provided?

Punishment Is Rarely Used in the Program
- How do the adults interact with the students?
- Are multiple interventions used or is everything timeout or suspension?
- Is there specific training for students on social skills?
- How long are students in timeout?

Intervention Is Sought Early
- Is there a wait and see attitude?
- What are the surrounding other issues such as sleep issues? Speech and communication issues? Sensory Issues? Handwriting issues? Issues with reading or frustration?
- Has assessment been sought early?

An RtI and PBIS Framework Is Used
- How are students grouped for instruction?
- What happens when a student does not understand the first time?
- How is progress (academic and behavior) documented?
- What are your interventions for the universal, secondary, and tertiary levels of PBIS?

Parent Partnerships Are Paramount

- Does the school have a parent liaison?
- What is the school philosophy about parent-school partnerships?
- What are the expectations for parents at the school and how can parents support the school programs?

Both Classroom Management Tools and Behavior Change Tools Are Used

- Does the program use a variety of management tools such as positive reinforcement, token economy, level systems, behavioral contracts, self monitoring, or service learning?
- Does the program use any behavior change tools such as cognitive-behavioral therapies, social skills instruction, metacognitive strategies, or Life Space Crisis Intervention?
- What is the attitude about changing behavior?

Data Drive Decisions

- When are data collected to monitor academic and behavior progress?
- Is there a sample behavior tracking sheet available?
- Do staff meet to discuss patterns in data and instructional data?

Each School Has a Full Continuum of Supports

- What are the placement options for my child?
- How does the school district comply with the requirement to provide a continuum of services?
- Are the alternative schools in this district used to provide services?
- How will the school evaluate the proper environment for my child?

Tool 4.3

Questions on Homework and Academics for Parents

- How long does the school expect your child to work on homework overall and by subject?

- Is the modification of homework specifically spelled out on the IEP?

- Are you providing accommodations while working on homework (e.g., writing for your child, reading to your child) that are not being used in the classroom?

- Is your child misbehaving during homework time? What is the cause or function of the misbehavior—homework is too difficult, time for homework needs adjusting, location and structure for homework time needs adjusting?

- Have you considered a peer tutor or older child or other tutor to remove any power struggle around homework time?

- Does your child know what the homework expectation is, and is there an effective way for him to record the homework?

- Does your child need an extra set of texts at home or online texts to help manage materials?

- Does the child's homework reflect his own work and show his skill level to the teacher?

- What is the curriculum and where can I find it?

- How will the curriculum be individualized for the student?

- What assessments are used to measure learning?

- How often will these assessments be used?

- What happens if a student is absent or is unavailable for learning during instruction?

- How will academics be modified and adjusted?

- What accommodations will be made to support learning?

- What reading programs are you using in this school?

- How often is reading assessed?

- Are all of the components of reading included in instruction?

Tool 4.4

Suggestions for Parents to Manage Difficult Behaviors

Suggestions for Helping Children Who Show Oppositional Behaviors

1. Refuse to battle with a student or use a "passionate" voice. Sometimes students who are oppositional enjoy seeing someone get upset and act out their own anger. Be sure that you state and restate the rule and refuse to engage in a power struggle.

2. Use forced choices. Just as you would not ask a 2-year-old child, "What do you want to do?" you should not ask all open-ended questions to a person who is being oppositional. It is often more effective to ask the person to choose from a list of options.

3. State the direction and walk away or change the subject to avoid the battle.

4. Plan ahead for times you know will be difficult and elicit a plan for handling situations with the student *before* the situation occurs. For example, if the student hates writing and homework time requires writing, set up a plan with the student on the weekend to deal with writing assignments. Write the plan down and post it so that you can point to the plan rather than discuss the plan.

5. Reward the student for any compliance you see or when he or she follows a direction the first time asked.

6. Build in times where the student can choose an activity or the way he or she does an activity so that the whole day is not spent getting the student to comply with adults.

7. Focus on the child's strengths. Develop talents and abilities, including hobbies and activities in areas of interest.

8. Drive while looking forward, not in the rearview mirror. Take each day as a new day, resisting the temptation to hold onto the previous days' violations.

9. Integrate movement into your child's day. This can be a simple as after-dinner walks as a family, shooting hoops for 10 minutes after school, time on a trampoline, or tickle time for young children. Giving students responsibilities they can enjoy that also involve movement, such as walking or playing with a family pet, can help them release their emotions before homework time.

10. Refuse to fight about homework.

Suggestions for Helping Children Who Show Anxious Behaviors
1. Keep the discussion present oriented. Ask the student to focus on immediate next steps he or she can control.
2. Use and reinforce relaxation techniques.
3. Build in coping strategies to keep student from catastrophizing events.

Suggestions for Helping Children Who Show Depressed Behaviors
1. Recognize the pain of depression so that you don't react impulsively to things and events that shouldn't be upsetting.
2. Think of some action you can help the student achieve—by involving her in a task for others or setting a small goal and achieving it, you help lessen the rumination in her thinking.
3. Support regular exercise.
4. Promote regular sleep hygiene—regular bedtime routines and sleeping hours.

Suggestions for Helping Children Who Show
Passive-Aggressive Behaviors
1. Recognize the effects of passive-aggressive behavior on you and do not react with anger to a "set up."
2. Help the student to express his anger in healthy ways.
3. Wonder aloud at the reasons that are propelling the behavior and let the child ponder the intent of his or her action. For example, if a child is purposely whispering when the adult is trying to hear his or her answer, the adult could say, "I wonder why you are speaking so quietly. I wonder if you are really feeling angry and hoping to see me get angry."

chapter 5 Discipline

ALL of us likely have at least one story from school about being disciplined or seeing a peer disciplined by a school official. Not much has changed about discipline over the years, in that children are still being suspended from school. School responses to a student's challenging behavior vary greatly. Fortunately, there is monitoring of the disciplinary actions by federal and state offices, and some common disciplinary actions are being questioned for their effect on academic achievement. Alternative schools are being used for discipline removals, and the staggering drop-out rates for children with behavior problems show that we are not effectively disciplining our youth. There will be consequences in our communities. Although we have come a long way in understanding disruptive behavior, public

Myth	Truth
Students who need discipline should be expelled from school; suspensions work for kids who get into trouble at school.	Suspension has been shown not to change behavior.
A statement like, "I don't want to live anymore" is no big deal.	Suicide is the third leading cause of death among high school students and the second leading cause of death in college students. Talk about suicide should always be taken seriously, and not be met with discipline.
Discipline is the parents' fault and responsibility.	Parents often need support in forming a partnership with school. When behaviors interfere with learning, the child may have an educational disability.
Mental illness is not real and cannot be treated.	Mental disorders are as easy to diagnose as asthma, diabetes, and cancer with a range of effective treatments for most conditions.
Even if a child has an emotional or behavioral disorder, she should be disciplined like everyone else.	A child with a condition or educational disability affecting learning or behavior is protected by a process called "manifestation determination."
Troubled youth just need more discipline.	Discipline alone is not shown to improve behavior.

schools have yet to develop a comprehensive set of child-centered early intervention practices that work.

This chapter is important because it is the most significant incidents of suspension, expulsion, restraint, or exclusion that we most want to prevent; incidents where people can get hurt are the most serious, and the effects of violence ripple through a community. Regardless of diagnosis, evaluations, and school or individual plans, a child may be acting out in a way that demands the adults in charge manage or control the child's behavior. In many cases, these behaviors are aggressive, violent, and self-destructive, often forcing treatment providers to take extreme measure to keep students and everyone around them safe.

Therefore, this chapter will answer the following questions:

1. What are alternative schools, and when can a child be placed there?
2. Under what conditions are seclusion, exclusion, suspension, or expulsion used and effective?
3. When can physical restraints be used at school?
4. How does discipline change for students with disabilities?
5. What are current legislative efforts to reform seclusion and restraint practices?

Negative Effects of Removal From School

When children are out of school, parents may have to miss work to stay home with them or meet with the school, and older students can cause problems while unsupervised all day. Research has shown that in-school suspension is an ineffective means of dealing with challenging behavior, yet removals and in-school suspensions are still being used to remove unwanted behaviors from the schoolhouse for a short time (Dickinson & Miller, 2006). And it's common knowledge that suspension actually can reinforce undesired behavior, because the child successfully avoids tasks or problems that caused the suspension in the first place.

Students who are being suspended out of school, have earned detentions or in-school suspensions, have been asked to leave class to go to the hallway or administrator's office, or have been instructed to go to timeout are the children who have a high level of impact on the learning of all children. The amount of time that teachers spend managing minor infractions, refocusing students' attention, and addressing more serious behavior cumulatively impacts the learning environment for all children. Suspension, removal from the classroom, and generally removing the child further and further from the school community is the standard, general reaction of most schools. This is because, for the vast majority of children, the threat of suspension is enough to prevent behavior problems.

The most common behaviors that result in disciplinary action are usually externalizing behaviors, which include:

- arguing,
- noncompliance,
- elopement,
- verbal aggression,
- physical aggression,
- property destruction,
- use or possession of drugs on school property,
- use or possession of weapons on school property, and
- threats.

Ignoring teachers, refusing to follow teacher direction, negative verbal interactions with peers and teachers, and physical aggression are common externalizing behaviors that require attention in schools (Passaro, Moon, Wiest, & Wong, 2004). School systems use a "progressive discipline" approach when dealing with behavior that disrupts the learning environment. Discipline procedures are clearly used schoolwide, classwide, and for individual students.

Students who display externalizing behaviors are more likely to receive disciplinary actions than students who display internalizing behaviors. Common internalizing behaviors include:

- withdrawal,
- isolation,
- secret self-harm,
- eating disorders, and
- tuning others out.

Disciplinary procedures universally used by school systems include:

- verbal warnings,

- timeout,
- loss of privileges,
- office visits to see administrators,
- calls to parent or parent conferences,
- lunch detention,
- loss of recess (part/whole),
- afterschool detention,
- in-school suspension,
- out-of-school suspension (short- and long-term), and
- expulsion.

Suspension and Expulsion

Several studies have confirmed that the time an expelled child spends away from school increases the chance that child will drop out and wind up in the criminal justice system, according to a January 2010 study from the Advancement Project, a legal action group. (Chen, 2010, para. 21)

Students who disrupt the learning environment can expect to be dealt with swiftly and decisively in America's public schools. School systems across the country have adopted "zero tolerance" policies for dealing with disruptive students, often relying on predetermined one-size-fits-all disciplinary policies and procedures.

This hard line approach has been met with overwhelming support by most Americans. A byproduct of the zero tolerance movement has been the frequent elimination of common sense. For example, in October 2009, a 6-year-old Cub Scout from Delaware brought his favorite camping utensil to school to use when eating lunch, which was misperceived as a weapon. The child's school system initially suspended the first grader for 45 days and ordered that he be educated in an alternative program for children with behavior disorders for 45 days. The national and international response convinced administrators to encourage classroom staff to manage behavior within the classroom as a first step.

A Continuum of Positive Behavior Support Responses

Schoolwide and classwide discipline options usually are used freely with students with challenging behavior, as we discussed in the last chapter. Examples of Tier I, or universal interventions, which are said to work for a great majority of students, may include surface management techniques such as moving a seat, having the student remain indoors during recess, giving lunch detention, or, when all else fails, having the student serve an afterschool or Saturday detention. The more serious infractions of school rules or habitual acts of noncompliance may result in afterschool detention. The aforementioned disciplinary interventions are the most frequently used methods for responding to disruptive behavior; however, school systems across the U.S. turn to suspension and expulsion for the most serious behavioral infractions. Most public school programs use a philosophy of removal in concentric circles outside the student, further and further from the group, as behaviors increase in frequency, duration, or severity.

It seems unlikely that schools would continue to use suspensions when they have been shown to be ineffective, but the research on suspension and expulsion strongly indicates that those interventions do not change student behavior. Children who are suspended often are unsupervised during their time out of school, fall further behind academically, and more importantly become increasingly disengaged from learning, thereby making them more at risk for continued problems in school.

Reasons for Suspension

Short-term suspension (removal from school for up to 10 consecutive days) may occur for one or a combination of reasons:
- continued willful disobedience (occurs when there has been accumulation of violations of school rules over time without a positive change in behavior in response to other, nonexclusionary behavior interventions);
- disrespectful behavior toward staff;

- physical or verbal aggression toward staff or other students;
- property destruction;
- possession of a weapon on school grounds (students can be suspended from school if charged with weapons or drug possession outside of school);
- possession of illegal substances;
- excessive tardiness or absenteeism; and
- out of location or elopement (Children with challenging behaviors will frequently leave their assigned area without permission. This behavior is referred to as being "out of area." When a student runs from the classroom and out of the building it typically is referred to as elopement.).

Alternative Schools

Misbehavior in America's public schools has been a problem since public education became compulsory across the nation in 1918. School systems traditionally have had limited tolerance for chronically misbehaving youth. When phone calls home, parent conferences, lunch and afterschool detentions, and out-of-school suspensions have failed to get the student's attention, many school systems have turned to alternative schools as the remedy. Alternative programs are considered for children who are at risk for continued school failure and require a nontraditional approach. These programs used to be called "reform schools" and were originally developed to teach troubled and delinquent students how to fit into and contribute to society. Today's alternative school programs are located in a building separate from a comprehensive school program. These programs are highly structured and follow behavior-modification principles. The students in these schools usually carry point sheets, are rewarded or punished for their behaviors, participate in group counseling, and are closely monitored by school staff throughout the day. Students are never unsupervised.

Enrollment in an alternative school is the last stop for many students. Failure to follow the rules in an alternative school often results in permanent expulsion from the school system. Class size is often two thirds the size of a traditional classroom and the staff may receive professional development in alternative teaching methodologies and behavior management.

Alternative schools can be rough places. These programs serve the school system's most disruptive youth, many of whom are not identified with an educational disability. Many of these students are already involved with the criminal justice system, have drug and alcohol problems, and have long histories of out-of-control behavior. Maintaining safety in the building is a daily priority for school staff. In an effort to save money, many school districts have combined their alternative programs and their special education programs into one facility. This model fails children. The combination of needs and the social dynamics created by the merging of at-risk students and children with learning disabilities creates an explosive school environment in which educational achievement happens accidentally.

Physical Restraint

Physical restraint is one of the most controversial topics related to students with challenging behaviors. Poorly trained staff, not enough staff, and super aggressive and violent situations have led to serious injuries and deaths in facilities nationwide. On a daily basis students are being physically restrained by building staff. The overuse of hands-on interventions by school staff is a national issue. Stories of children being grabbed and forcibly moved or held awkwardly for failure or refusal to follow school rules is a problem that won't go away. Property destruction, student and staff injuries, and, in several highly publicized and tragic situations, student deaths have occurred. It seems that when educators run out of options to manage challenging behavior, they resort to going "hands on."

By the time a child with challenging behaviors has been restrained, she likely has experienced many different types of interventions multiple times. We are in a very dynamic time regarding the use of physical restraint. As previously stated, the laws around its use are changing. Many states have developed regulations specifically forbidding physical restraint and seclusion altogether. A tour of residential treatment centers in Maryland found that many former seclusion rooms have turned into small, windowless offices for university interns. That being said, alternative programs, day and residential treatment programs, and some school districts continue to use physical restraint.

The Joint Commission on the Accreditation of Health Organizations (JCAHO, 2002) defined physical restraint as "the direct application of physical force to a person with or without the individual's permission to restrict his/her freedom of movement. The physical force may be human, mechanical devices, or a combination thereof" (p. 2). Students may occasionally go into crisis. A crisis is an event where a child loses control emotionally and may become physically aggressive and/or combative. Examples of crises that may lead to physical restraint include:

- two or more students fighting,
- an unprovoked physical attack on a student or staff person,
- verbally aggressive or threatening behavior,
- extreme destruction of property,
- self-injurious behavior (student cutting self or behaving in a dangerous manner), and
- elopement (leaving an assigned area without staff permission).

The topic of physical restraint is a hot-button issue. Nationally there have been many deaths and serious injuries sustained by children who have been improperly restrained. There are many physical restraint curricula and techniques marketed across the globe, all designed to teach treatment professionals how to "therapeutically" manage out-of-control behavior. Despite federal, state, and local regulations mandating their use, ongoing staff development, and accountability systems, children and staff are being hurt and killed due to improper restraint and violent behaviors at an alarming rate.

This type of situation happens several times per day in treatment facilities around the country. Many schools and behavioral health systems are modifying their physical restraint protocols. An incident occurred in Maryland in 2006 where a student was restrained face down in a situation similar to the one above. During the "hold," staff observed that he had stopped breathing. Attempts to resuscitate him failed and he died. The medical examiner later determined that he died from positional asphyxia. This occurs when compression to the rib cage prevents the lungs from being able to inhale or exhale, ultimately leading to an inability to breathe, and cardiac arrest. This type of situation is the leading cause of death or serious injury in restraints.

Beyond the physical injuries to students and staff and the property destruction associated with physical restraint is the emotional and/or psychological damage that is the result of physical restraint. Children with emotional and behavioral disorders often come from chaotic living situations in which physical and sexual abuse have been a part of their lives. Physical restraint can lead to Posttraumatic Stress Disorder (PTSD) responses in students and staff over time. The repeated use of physical force to contain and control a person's ability to move freely is an intensely intimate experience. The misuse of this intervention can "push the bruise" or recreate trauma for children and exacerbate preexisting emotional issues, which ultimately will not support healing.

The use of physical restraint will always be present to some degree. Children will go into crisis and there will be a need to keep them and everyone around them safe. To simply outlaw the use of physical restraint would be irresponsible. It must be the option of last resort. All staff must receive preservice and biannual in-service training in the proper and humane use of physical restraint. Program administrators

Jesse did not like it when he felt that the school staff was "messing with him." It did not matter who it was, male or female. There were going to be problems if someone told Jesse to do something he didn't want to do. During lunch, Jesse forgot to throw his trash out and one of the staff members assigned to lunchroom duty politely asked Jesse to clean up his area. Jesse just stared at him. The staff member asked Jesse if he had heard him. The students became quiet and moved away from Jesse. They knew the drill. Jesse said, "I'm not throwing that [stuff] away. That's what people like you are paid to do." The staff person, a former police officer, squared up with Jesse, folded his arms, took a deep breath, and moved imperceptibly closer to the boy and said "Jesse, I'm not going to ask you again to throw your trash away." The staff person spoke to Jesse softly; regardless, Jesse felt cornered and threatened. The guy was big and had an imposing presence. Backing down was not an option at this point. In an instant Jesse flung his arm across the dining room table, hurling his trash against the wall; he lowered his shoulder and smashed into the staff person, sending him flying into the salad bar. Another staff member who was observing the showdown called for "all available staff" on her two-way radio, and jumped into the mix with two staff members who had been walking by the cafeteria. A melee broke out between Jesse and the four staff persons. Jesse was big, strong, and in full-on rage mode. The staff tried to use their crisis management "take down" techniques, only to be tossed around. Finally, the "crisis team" arrived, and took Jesse to the ground and held him there while he screamed and struggled. A nurse arrived to oversee the situation and after determining that Jesse could not settle down on his own, administered 500mg of Benadryl by needle into his right buttocks. After about 10 minutes, Jesse got drowsy and was escorted to a quiet room where he promptly fell asleep. In the fracas, he had cut his chin, probably from hitting the floor, and fractured two ribs. He was taken by ambulance to the local emergency room, treated, and sent back to the school.

must strive to embed this intervention within a framework of positive behavior supports; the focus on the training should be as follows:

- careful selection and screening of staff for their appropriateness to work with children;
- preservice training prior to their contact with children;
- use in conjunction with a positive behavior supports system-wide orientation to behavior management;
- verbal de-escalation and the use of therapeutic language;
- in-service training that requires demonstrated mastery of all behavior management interventions (verbal de-escalation techniques and physical interventions); and

- accountability systems that randomly and routinely review behavior management data.

Physical Restraint and Seclusion: Outrage to Action

The management of out-of-control behavior has resulted in countless injuries to children and staff. A recent spate of deaths and serious injuries in juvenile facilities has led Congress to introduce legislation designed to reduce the use of physical restraint and seclusion in schools and other programs. The Preventing Harmful Restraint and Seclusion in Schools Act was introduced to Congress by George Miller of California and Cathy McMorris Rodgers of Washington. The foundation of the legislation is rooted in the belief that the inappropriate physical restraint and seclusion of children in public and private schools has resulted in severe injuries, psychological trauma, and death. The act reinforces the belief that all children, regardless of where they are educated, have the right to be treated humanely, respectfully, and free from physical or emotional abuse. Staff should never use physical restraint and seclusion as disciplinary interventions and all staff should be trained in the use of positive behavior interventions and other evidence-based interventions.

This bill is expected to be signed into law by President Obama in 2010 and is designed to mandate minimum safety standards to prevent abusive restraint and seclusion in schools across the nation. After 2 years, states will be required to have their own policies in place. It would apply to public schools, private schools, and preschools receiving federal education support. The legislation would:

- limit physical restraint and locked-door seclusion, allowing these interventions only when there is imminent danger of injury, and only when used by trained staff;
- outlaw mechanical restraints, such as strapping kids to chairs, and prohibit restraints that restrict respiration;
- require schools to contact parents or guardians after seclusion or restraint occurs;
- encourage states to provide professional development to pro-

tect students and prevent the need for seclusion and restraint; and

- improve accountability and enforcement resources to prevent future abuse.

This legislation is an important first step in "legislating safety" for children with challenging behaviors. All too often the triggering event that leads to seclusion or physical restraint is a misperceived interaction that quickly escalates into an out-of-control situation between children and adults. In far too many situations, after the adults have unpiled from atop one another, the injured have been treated, the parents and agencies have been notified, and the administrators and clinicians have conducted their investigations into what happened, it often is found that the adult response did not fit the situation.

Students With Disabilities and Discipline

This section applies to children who are at risk in regular classrooms and to children already eligible for special education, as described in Chapter 8. A child is suspected of having a disability just by demonstrating behaviors that interfere with his own and others' learning. Students identified to receive special education and related services often have long track records of disciplinary removals. In fact, the disciplinary removal data used by school IEP teams play an important role in the special education eligibility process.

What the Law Says Regarding Students With Disabilities and Suspension and Expulsion

When students are suspended over and over, they are said to be experiencing a change of placement because the student is missing so much specialized instruction. The 1988 *Honig v. Doe* Supreme Court case limited local school systems from suspending children with disabilities in excess of 10 school days per year. Prior to 1988, it was not unusual for children with disabilities, especially students with emotional or behavioral disabilities, to be suspended from school in excess of 30 days per year. The Supreme Court ruled that school removals in excess of 10 days per year constituted a change in the student's placement.

Only a multidisciplinary team (discussed in the next chapter) can change a student's placement, so the repeated suspensions or recommendation for expulsion require the school team to consider the child's disability and its effect on the behavior. Or, in the case of a child who has not yet been identified, but who is at risk and experiencing some challenges, the child should still not be removed for more than 10 school days because he would be known to have a suspected educational disability, and therefore, entitled to the protections of IDEA.

For children with challenging behavior, legal protections are in place to prevent repeated removals from school that basically equate to a change of placement; although all schools follow generally similar schoolwide policies, when it comes to the discipline of children with more-challenging-than-typical-behaviors, special rules apply.

Children with disabilities may be treated like any other student when it comes to behavior to a point. School systems are required to follow certain procedural steps when a student with a disability is suspended or removed from instruction for more than the equivalent of 10 days. After that time, the school system must convene a *manifestation determination process* to determine whether the behavior that resulted in the disciplinary removal was related to the student's disability.

The manifestation determination process must answer the following questions with a "yes" or a "no" answer. Only one of the questions may be answered yes for the behavior to be considered a manifestation of disability:

- "Was the conduct in question caused by, or had a direct and substantial relationship to, the child's disability?
- Was the conduct in question the direct result of the local education agency's failure to implement the IEP?" (IDEA, 2004, p. 118).

In the event that the manifestation determination process determines that the behavior *was* a result of the student's disability, then the student must be allowed to return to school without serving the remainder of the suspension. In the event that the behavior is not determined to be a manifestation of disability, then the student may serve the remainder of the suspension. Students with disabilities continue to be protected under IDEA when they are suspended from school. They must continue to receive special education services during the time that they are suspended from school.

Expulsion for Students With Disabilities

A school system may place a child in an appropriate Interim Alternative Educational Setting (IAES) when the child requires a long-term suspension or exclusion from school. A child with a disability may be placed in an IAES for up to 45 school days (not calendar days). An IAES is defined as a "setting other than the student's current placement that enables the student to continue to participate in the general curriculum and progress toward meeting the goals set in his or her IEP" (Weinfeld & Davis, 2008, p. 122). The IAES must allow the student to participate in the general education curriculum, although in another setting.

There are three exceptions to the rules regarding the manifestation process. If one of the "big three" behaviors is committed, then the school system has the legal authority to suspend or expel the student from school in the same manner that they would a student without a disability. A child with a disability may be removed or suspended indefinitely from school just like the child without a disability if he or she has been found to have committed one of the following three behaviors:

- *Possession of a dangerous weapon:* The U.S. Department of Education (2006) defined a dangerous weapon as:

  > a weapon, device, instrument, material or substance, animate or inanimate, that is used for, or is readily capable of, causing death or serious bodily injury, except that such term does not include a pocket knife with a blade less than 2.5 inches in length. (p. 46723)

- *Possession or distribution of illegal substances:* The second exception relates to the possession or distribution of illegal substances or drugs or attempts to purchase or distribute a controlled substance, while at school, on school grounds, or at a school-sponsored activity.
- *Serious bodily injury:* The third exception relates to situations in which a student with a disability causes serious bodily injury to another person while at school, on school grounds, or while attending a school-sponsored activity.

Seclusion

The Joint Commission (2002) defined *seclusion* as "the involuntary confinement of a child/youth in a room in a Covered Facility, whether alone or with staff supervision, in a manner that prevents the child/youth from leaving" (p. 3). Children in day school, residential treatment, and in-patient psychiatric facilities may find themselves in a seclusion room if they behave in a manner that is determined to be unsafe to themselves or others. The child who attacks other students or staff, or destroys property and cannot calm down on his own often ends up in seclusion.

Discipline is one of the most important issues in schools. When a child needs an individual plan, schoolwide and classwide discipline may not be enough to support the child's behavior and achievement.

Individual plans are created from evaluation, so the next chapter fully explores how to effectively evaluate a child's emotional, social, and behavioral strengths and needs.

Part III

The Individual Child

chapter 6

Evaluating Emotions and Behaviors

EVALUATING emotions and behaviors usually brings to mind a picture of a child being tested by a psychologist or educator, after which a report is written and shared with the parent and school team. The reports may be put into the child's folder and not used as an integral part of instruction. Or, a team may complete a functional analysis of behavior, but in a way that is not integrated into instruction or not revisited to inform instruction. The way we evaluate a child's strengths and needs forms the foundation for instruction, and what we know is that there is a need to transform the instruction of kids with challenging behaviors. Therefore, we believe there is a need to transform the way we evaluate a child when she demonstrates behaviors that interfere with her and others' learning, called *interfering behaviors*.

The structure and tools provided in this chapter

Myth	Truth
When parents ask for an assessment, the school district has to do it.	When parents ask for an assessment, the school district must consider the request and give the parent a response in writing if the evaluation is refused. That notice should tell the parent why the multidisciplinary team (MDT) decided not to evaluate, what information or reports were used to make the decision, and what information was considered.
School districts have to implement my son's private doctor's or therapist's recommendations.	School districts do not have to accept the recommendation from a privately obtained evaluation.
There is a 60-day timeline for reevaluation.	Timelines for reevaluations vary from state to state.
Calling the school principal should be enough to get the school to evaluate my child.	Parents must consent in writing to assessments and this consent starts timelines. The MDT will decide which evaluations are needed, then seek parent consent.

will allow parents to partner with educators for effective evaluation of social, emotional, or behavioral areas. Reading this chapter will guide parents and educators in the evaluation process and answer the following questions:

- What is evaluation, what are the purposes of evaluation, and how does the evaluation process work?
- How do perspective and bias affect the way we conduct evaluations for children?
- What are legal issues for evaluation?
- What is the role of the parent and child in the evaluation process?

Evaluating emotion and behavior is difficult and complex because there is no one valid, standardized way of measuring behaviors or emotions, and also, there is a wide range of "normal" behavior. Assessment

Table 4

The Differences Between Evaluation and Assessment

Assessment	Evaluation
Collecting data	Analyzing the data
Gathering information	Reviewing information
Testing	Testing not necessary
Numbers, facts	Systematic investigation
Provides evidence	Opinions, analysis of facts
Quantitative	Makes judgment, analyzes value

of social, emotional, and behavioral needs also is difficult because evaluation can be subjective and differ by perspective. By gathering data and analyzing that data to figure out the best possible explanation for behavior, the parents and school team apply science and art using a variety of tools. This and the next chapter will help the child's school team and parents evaluate a child's needs effectively, which can be a challenging task (Kern & Hilt, 2004).

What Is Evaluation?

Evaluation is the process of making decisions about a child's school program through analysis of data and evidence collected by parents and school staff. Evaluation and instruction are two sides of one hand; evaluation is not important without intervention, and vice versa. If a teacher teaches without evaluating her children's needs, or evaluates the children without instructing them, then education is useless.

Most parents and educators think that evaluation and assessment mean the same thing when, in fact, there are important differences. The difference in terms is important to understand, as reflected in Table 4. We will use the term *evaluation* to mean the collection, interpretation, and analysis of information to make instructional decisions.

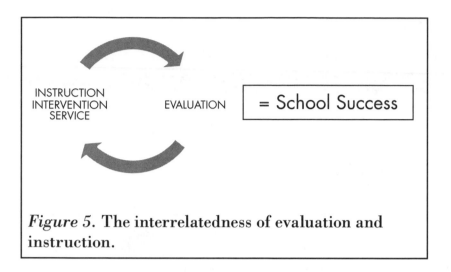

Figure 5. The interrelatedness of evaluation and instruction.

When a parent requests an evaluation, she will be the most effective advocate for her child if she is aware of the difference between these terms and how the evaluation process works.

What Are the Purposes of Evaluation?

Evaluations should help identify, select, and implement interventions or methods for instruction. Evaluation is only important if it helps determine the right interventions, as shown in Figure 5.

Purposes of evaluation include:
- diagnosis;
- identification of disability;
- to rule out other problems;
- documentation of current functioning, compared with peers;
- recommendation for further assessment;
- defining frequency, duration, and intensity of challenging behaviors;
- understanding the reasons for behavior;
- development of a successful school program;
- recommendations for academic and behavioral interventions;
- recommendations for eligibility for special education;

- analysis of progress in the curriculum or toward individual goals;
- recommendations for eligibility for accommodation or services;
- recommendations for reduction in services or interventions;
- recommendations for additional or different services or inter ventions; and
- recommendations for scientifically based methods.

Who Conducts the Evaluation?

Meet the multidisciplinary team (MDT). Called by many names from school to school, the multidisciplinary team is a group of professionals from multiple areas of expertise, or disciplines, and this group conducts evaluations in the school districts. Each of these professionals is responsible for interpreting, administering, and conducting evaluations, and advising others on their areas of expertise.

> **Legal Tip**
>
> Required members of the MDT who want to be excused from the meeting must get both the parent's and district's written consent, and submit a report with their recommendation before the meeting.

As shown in Figure 6, the MDT can involve many individuals. All members of the MDT are important when discussing what types of evaluations to do, how the evaluations should be done, and when considering how evaluations will help develop a child's school program. In the current and perhaps outdated paradigm, the school psychologist usually is seen as the expert on the team who can administer, discuss, and interpret psychological evaluations. In the new paradigm we set forth in this chapter, the members of the team, with the parents, should work together to develop a comprehensive evaluation plan and execute it and conduct ongoing reviews and revisions based on data. Parents are a critical part of evaluation of behavior and should not be left out of the evaluation process.

Figure 6. **Multidisciplinary team members.**

Legal Tip

School districts must *consider* any information provided by a parent; just because a private evaluation report provided by a parent contains a specific recommendation does not mean that the district must do what the private examiner recommends.

Choosing the right examiner. Parents should consider different factors when selecting private, and to the greatest extent possible, school district examiners, including the following:

- cost, payment plans, or reimbursable costs for evaluation;
- personality and rapport with child;

- philosophy of behavior intervention or shared perspective about the child;
- willingness to participate in MDT meetings;
- use of tools and techniques that the school district uses and will accept;
- quality and comprehensiveness: record review, gathering information from multiple sources;
- ability to evaluate the child in the language and form necessary;
- ability to use both formal and informal tools, including classroom observation and/or use of rating scales across different settings; and
- skill and ability to involve the school team in the evaluation process.

There are pros and cons a parent should consider when deciding to allow the MDT to conduct the evaluations, whether to obtain the evaluations privately, or a combination of both. See Tool 6.1 for a list of pros and cons to consider when selecting the right examiner.

Differences school to school. The differences between schools is a real factor that can change perceptions of the MDT. This can be seen when five different multidisciplinary teams study the same child, and come up with five different evaluation plans. When resources are either plentiful or tight, differences from school to school can affect evaluation processes. The reality is that there are vast differences that mostly depend on the financial prowess, resources, and location of the school system or local community.

The members of the MDT may have different perspectives about the causes for or ways to support behavior. Members of the MDT also may have limitations on the type of tests that can be administered, or may have varying degrees of understanding of evaluation processes, methods, and tools. This can affect team dynamics, which can create inconsistency in procedures. School districts usually have a process in place to determine what tests will be purchased and used by the MDT.

Regardless of a particular school's lack of resources, it is critical that the MDT evaluate a child fairly, properly, and comprehensively.

> Josef is a student whose school does not have a lot of resources. The guidance counselor is not there full time, and there is no behavior support, social worker, or additional support staff at the school. From classroom to classroom, teachers employ their own behavior systems, and the only schoolwide program rewards students of the month. Suspension or sending students to the administrator's office for discipline are the most common discipline techniques. Josef is sent to the office at least once a day. His classroom removals and out-of-school suspensions are affecting his schoolwork, and when he comes back to school, his teachers remind him of work to be completed, but little else.
>
> On the other side of the state, Javier's school employs a wide range of behavior supports, and the teachers all directly teach social skills through group-building activities. A multiple intelligences, strength-based approach is seen throughout the school, including understanding of people who learn differently. Javier is demonstrating challenging behavior, and his school team has met several times, involving his parents and school counselor. When Javier breaks rules, he engages in problem-solving sessions afterward to prevent future problems. In-school detention focuses on teaching material missed and includes direct instruction of problem-solving skills. Javier's mother communicates with his teachers and counselor on a regular basis.

Philosophy or beliefs about behavior can be different from team member to team member, and parents may view behaviors differently than school team members. Further, different schools, or different teams within the same school, can make different conclusions about the same child. It is widely understood that adult perception and expectation for challenging behavior can influence how teachers teach and how children learn. This variability between and within schools obviously can affect how data collection, teaching methods, and services are determined and implemented. This underscores why the evaluation process, shown in Figure 7, is so important. Fair, objective, and thorough evaluation through sound data collection can reduce variability between schools and reduce the effect of perception, judgment, and unfair treatment of children with challenging behavior.

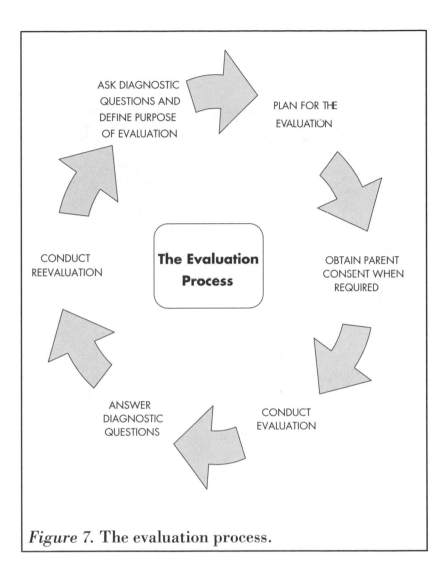

Figure 7. The evaluation process.

The Evaluation Process

One of the most critical steps in the evaluation process is planning for evaluations and formulating the right diagnostic questions.
Evaluation planning leads the team to decisions about what tests the
child will take, what rating scales will be used, what problems will be
assessed, what specialists need to be involved, what special consider-

ations the child needs, and how parents and private therapists or other private providers will be involved. Tool 6.2 provides a list of questions to ask when planning for an evaluation.

> **Legal Tip**
>
> IDEA requires the initial evaluation to be conducted within 60 calendar days of parent consent (signature), but states can form their own timelines. Subsequent evaluations are subject to state regulations' timelines. Schools can take a parent to a hearing to force evaluations, but schools cannot take a parent to a hearing to force special education.

Parental Participation

Parents are critical partners with the school in the evaluation process. Parents are the first natural teachers and evaluators of the child's behavior. Gaining parent insight and perspective into a child's emotional or behavioral functioning is critical, and a parent must be a part of the entire evaluation process, not just one or a few stages. Parents may need training or counseling to understand the nature of the child's disability, how to work with the school for the child's progress, or how home-based behaviors may be affecting a child at school. One of the biggest mistakes the team can make is to diminish the importance of parental input or to fail to include parents in each aspect of the evaluation process, especially the functional behavior assessment (FBA). When working with parents, educators should remember that:

- parents can ask to review a formal test before it is used with a child,
- schools should make alternate ways for parents to participate with the school team,
- schools should explain fully the reasons for testing and gain parent consent, and
- parental input should be included in the evaluation.

Legal Tip

Parents are broadly defined under IDEA and can include guardians. A parent can be anyone who is responsible for caring for a child. When a child lives in a group home or other publicly funded place, the public agency representatives should not be seen as parents, unless designated as a parent surrogate.

Perspective and Bias

Evaluating emotions and behaviors is far from a science; it is more like an art that uses a lot of science and scientific principles in the best way we currently understand. Evaluations form the basis for any schoolwide or individual behavior plans, service, or intervention, so it is critical that evaluations are done in a way that is fair, impartial, and based on data, and can be used for making effective teaching recommendations. One test or tool or piece of information should never be used to evaluate a child's behavior. Evaluation should focus on what can be done to improve the behavior. Evaluation should include use of sound and reliable ways to discover and document a child's strengths, needs, and current levels of performance.

IDEA is one of several sources that require unbiased, fair, and impartial evaluation. The American Psychological Association, publishers of different tests, professional organizations, states, and school districts also have requirements for evaluation that strive to minimize the effect of human bias or perspective through the evaluation process. Barriers can include the persistent perception of incorrect motive for behavior, incorrect instruction, lack of training, and invisible attitudes that affect team and evaluation dynamics. Scientists have been studying features of evaluation, and in particular, have been interested in the bias inherent in evaluations of social, emotional, and behavioral functioning of children for many decades. Yet, there are very few scientifically based evaluation methods available to assess social, emotional, and behavioral concerns (U.S. Department of Education, 2008).

The range of human behavior and emotions is so vast and variable that perceptions, biases, circumstances, environments, and attitudes can affect how adults see or perceive a child's behavior. How the child perceives his own behavior, his environment, and his support systems also is important. When behavior problems interfere with learning, belief systems, perceptions, attitudes, and emotional factors are at play. Troubling behaviors often are upsetting to parents and educators, and adults may have different perceptions about a child's behavior, such as that a child is intentionally disrupting education or that a parent's lack of support is causing the problem to get worse. These perceptions may affect adult motivation to view the evaluation process as a problem-solving process. This cycle is relevant to the MDT, which works with the parents through the evaluation process. To help the child improve his behavior and, therefore, his academic success, it is imperative that the team and parents join together through a problem-solving perspective, which starts with an effective evaluation process.

Unlike other educational problems, challenging behaviors and social-emotional difficulties often cause emotions from the school team and parents that can cloud how the team engages in collecting information about the behaviors. Much of the time, the conversation about behavior leads to a conversation about the child's behavior at home, and the team engages in a more personal discussion about emotions and behavior, which can be uncomfortable. There often is unfortunately a strained or poor dynamic of mistrust if a child's school program is not working or if the child is not receiving the right kind of intervention. If the school team believes that the behavior is intentional or manipulative, and that the reason the child is misbehaving is due to poor parenting or being spoiled, the team will make different decisions about evaluation than another team who may believe that a child's diagnosed conduct or mood problem must be treated through counseling, teaching of skills, and implementation of positive behavior supports.

Confirmation bias also may affect how the team plans for and conducts evaluations. The idea is that we predetermine a conclusion, and then only test and accept information that agrees with our predetermined conclusion (Grobman, 2008). For example, if a teacher believes that a child is incapable of developing and maintaining relationships, then the teacher may only collect information to prove that. Or, if a teacher believes that a child is unmotivated, she may believe she is seeing behavior caused by a motivation problem within the child that is out of her reach. When the MDT discusses the child using an FBA, testing the hypothesis is vulnerable to confirmation bias. If a team collects data under an incorrect hypothesis about behavior due to biases, team members may overlook data that does not fit their ideas.

> Jeremy has been mouthing off to his teachers for months. When he cursed at the principal, the team met with his parent. At the meeting, each teacher took turns discussing how pervasive his "smartmouthing" is, recanting stories through the year of how he constantly talks back. Mrs. Wysdome, Jeremy's mom, told the teachers that she thinks he is frustrated and has an undiagnosed reading problem. After data collection, the team met again. The behavior specialist from the district reported that the "mouthing" or "talking back" behavior was seen one time per week, over a 3-month time period. The teachers and parent then agreed to conduct a reading assessment. It showed reading problems. So, the behaviors the teachers thought were pervasive turned out to not be happening that often. It was Jeremy's grumbly personality and academic struggles to which the teachers were really responding.

Formal Versus Informal Evaluation

The differences between informal and formal evaluations lie in how the tools are developed, how they are administered, how they are scored, the qualifications of examiners, and how the results are reported. The following sections describe some of the various types of evaluations a child with EBD may be given.

Neurological and Psychological Evaluation

The most common types of neurological and psychological evaluations used by schools are cognitive or IQ tests and projective or personality tests.

Cognitive or IQ tests. School psychologists focus on school system processes that guide them in evaluation. School psychologists also are obligated under ethics and training requirements of their state and professional associations. A neuropsychologist is a psychologist who has special training in the brain and biological factors. The most common psychological tests are aptitude, cognitive, or intelligence tests. These tests are designed to measure (Weinfeld & Davis, 2008):

- how a child processes information;
- the child's response to feelings or emotional triggers;
- cognitive strengths and areas of need;
- attention and concentration needs;
- visual motor skills;
- verbal problem-solving skills;
- levels of depression, anxiety, and other emotional responses;
- executive functioning skills such as task initiation, flexibility in problem solving, making transitions or shifting, working memory, and task completion; and
- short- and long-term memory.

Like some standardized tests, intelligence or cognitive tests are given individually. The examiner gives a series of subtests to the child, from writing tasks, to verbal tasks, to visual perceptual tasks, using a variety of tasks to score the child. The child responds in any number of ways to the test items—by pointing, discussing, calculating, writing, or clicking a mouse. The examiner's manual and the examiner's training show the examiner when to start testing and when to stop testing. The manual tells the examiner how to set up the testing room, how to document unusual circumstances, how to give directions, score and interpret the number of correct items, and how to interpret scores.

Projective or personality tests. Projective tests were developed by psychologists who believed that unconscious (id, ego, superego) forces are at play, and the subconscious is below the surface and should be uncovered. These tests are said to "project" the subject's personality onto the test through responses to pictures, inkblots, or other stimuli. Examiners use nondirected questioning and ask the child to respond

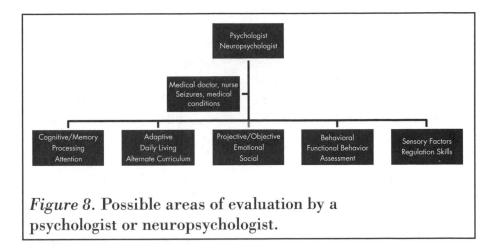

Figure 8. Possible areas of evaluation by a
psychologist or neuropsychologist.

to incomplete sentences or pictures. Other projective tests incorporate
drawing or storytelling tasks.

Without a very high level of training, however, examiners delving
into a child's personality or motivation can be detrimental, especially
when the conclusions of the examiners are incorrect. There can be problems with the incorrect interpretation of projective tests, or overreliance
on the examiner's interpretation, so these instruments should be very
carefully considered when used to evaluate a child's social, emotional, or
behavioral needs. Also, in the past, and even currently, psychological and
other tests are subject to being used incorrectly. For example, these tests
have been used as the only test that pigeonholes a student into segregated
programs. Findings on a particular test can be interpreted differently
depending on the training, perspective, and skill of the evaluator. It's
not the test you use, but how you use the test you've got!

Evaluation by the psychologist can include different areas, as
shown in Figure 8.

Achievement and Language:
Curriculum-Based Measurement

For children with challenging behavior, achievement testing is
important because the behavior likely has a relationship with academic

skills or demand. The behaviors may be affecting the child academically, or the academic problems can be contributing to the behavior. When considering the functional assessment of a child's challenging behavior, the team and parent should understand the demands of the curriculum, and supplement formal achievement evaluation with curriculum-based assessments. Recent research has shown that there is a link between literacy and language and behavior (Hyter, Rogers-Adkinson, Self, Simmons, & Jantz, 2001; Nippold, 1993; Nippold, Mansfield, Billow, & Tomblin, 2009; Spira, Bracken, & Fischel, 2005). Not only should the MDT consider reading and other academic evaluations, but it should consider whether the expertise of a speech-language pathologist is needed to understand the behavior and to develop a proper, useful functional assessment of behavior.

Occupational Therapy Evaluations

School-based occupational therapists can play an important role in the evaluation of a child's social, emotional, and behavioral skills (American Occupational Therapy Association, 2009). Because troubled youths have difficulty participating in the classroom and in the workplace, the occupational therapist can be involved in evaluating a child's needs for the purpose of recommending appropriate school-based services. The American Occupational Therapy Association (2008) acknowledged the need for occupational therapists to partner with the school to provide services for students who are either eligible for special education, or children who are at risk of being identified with an EBD. The evaluation, therefore, should focus on the child's strengths and needs with respect to mental, emotional, relaxation, and social skills needed for the child to effectively perform an occupation (Quake-Rapp, Miller, Ananthan, & Chiu, 2008). An MDT should convene to plan and conduct curriculum-based and functional behavior evaluations.

Trend Away From Formal Testing

Although formal psychological and other evaluations still play a major role in most school-based multidisciplinary teams, there is a trend that emphasizes a functional, curriculum-based way to effectively evaluate behavior. Problem-solving models such as Response to Intervention and positive behavior supports mirror the evaluation process, as long as one's framework about evaluation is that it is a problem-solving process that is ongoing. Informal methods are being used to a much greater extent, and this trend has allowed for an opportunity to view evaluation of behavior in a different way. The FBA is scientifically sound and yields valid information about a child's behavior that informs the development of schoolwide, classwide, and individual interventions. Unfortunately, the FBA has can be seen as a tedious, burdensome task that has little meaning for students, parents, and educators.

The next chapter invites educators and parents to view the FBA in a new way. Unleashing the power of the FBA means that the whole team and parents partner to follow the steps prescribed in the next chapter.

Tool 6.1

Pros and Cons of Private and Public Evaluation

	PROS	CONS
Private Evaluation	Parents select the examiner; parents interface with the examiner through the evaluation process and may be able to express concern or family history more freely; parents can review results before giving them to the school system; evaluators may select from a wide variety of sound assessments.	Expense to parents; no guarantee that the school system will accept the findings; school systems may still want to conduct their own evaluations; private evaluators may not be familiar with school system process; proficiency of examiner is important; school system may not approve of an assessment tool that has been used.
Public Evaluation	They are free; school systems are more likely to accept their own findings; various members on the MDT can more easily consult with one another; the examiner may be familiar with the child and vice versa; public evaluations are equally practical.	Parental involvement may take more work and effort on the part of the parent; examiners may not be qualified and it may be difficult for parents to know qualifications; school system examiners may consult with one another and reach a decision before discussion with parent; evaluation tools and tests may not be available because the school system has not purchased a test; examiners may have pressure from the school system due to directives or trends; school system may only choose which assessment to administer from a narrow list of tools that they have approved.

Note. Reprinted with permission from *Special Needs Advocacy Resource Book*, by R. Weinfeld and M. Davis, 2008, p. 98. Copyright 2008 by Prufrock Press.

Tool 6.2
Questions to Ask When Planning for the Evaluation

- Which evaluation tools will be used to collect information?
- What does the test measure and what groups of students was it tested on (standardization sample)?
- Why are different evaluations being conducted?
- What are the diagnostic questions the evaluation will answer?
- Which educational disabilities does the team suspect?
- What is the definition of any disability suspected?
- Have the parents signed consent for evaluations, after being fully informed?
- Who will conduct evaluations?
- What other information does the team need to answer diagnostic questions?

chapter 7

Functional Behavior Assessment

THIS chapter invites educators and parents to take on the transformation of the evaluation process by effectively using a functional analysis of behavior as an ongoing problem-solving approach, where instruction is integrated, and a scientific method is applied. We predict that, with teacher training and understanding of how effective it can be, the functional behavior assessment (FBA) structure will be better utilized for children who are at risk of developing, or are known to have, emotional or behavioral disabilities.

This chapter will explore these questions:

- What is functional behavior assessment?
- What special factors should be considered when evaluating a child?
- How should the parent and school team work together for an effective FBA?

Myth	Truth
If I disagree with my child's FBA, there is nothing I can do.	As long as a parent understands his rights, he may ask for an Independent Education Evaluation at public expense for FBA.
The FBA will work to help my child right away after it is developed.	The intervention plan that flows from the FBA may need to be revised to see a behavior change over time.
The FBA does not need to involve the parents or behaviors that happen at home.	The FBA should be conducted with full parental partnership, including behaviors seen at home and in the community.
The FBA is a test that is given, and the report is filed in the student folder.	The FBA is a group problem-solving process that is ongoing and involves continuous progress monitoring.
The FBA is not required.	The FBA is required for serious discipline issues and whenever behaviors are part of a child's suspected or known disability.
There is no approved format for the FBA.	The FBA should include all parts researched to be effective.

The FBA can be a powerful and productive way to view and analyze behaviors. An FBA is a problem-solving activity done by an MDT in close collaboration with a parent. Any child whose behavior is interfering with learning should be considered for this informal assessment. The FBA takes into account the individual and his relationship to the environment and systems in which he lives, with consideration toward individual factors that make an individual unique. The FBA is different from other assessments in that there is no examiner and there is no test or testing sessions. A team and parents conducting the FBA will meet often, collaborate closely, and partner in each step of the FBA.

The FBA process too often is misunderstood and misused by the MDT. Unfortunately, functional assessment of behavior varies widely from school to school, and is not effectively utilized by school teams. Although there has been an explosion of information and research in this area, school districts are not yet efficiently using a functional way to evaluate behavior. This is not surprising because there is no standard format for the FBA and no defined way to conduct it. However, there is a longstanding body of knowledge about how the FBA, using positive behavior supports, methods, and interventions, should take place as a result of data collection. So in some ways, this problem-solving activity has been a longstanding best practice that has been misused and underutilized. Also, too often the FBA is completed by one or two people, and presented to the parent in a meeting. Instead, the parent should be involved in each of the stages of the assessment. The purposes of the FBA include to:

- define how serious the behavior is and how it affects learning;
- quantify with data how long the behavior lasts, when it occurs, and under what condition it occurs;
- find out what sustains the behavior;
- discover why the behavior is occurring; and
- inform the development of the intervention or instruction.

Functional behavior assessment has been defined by different states as "the systematic process of gathering information to guide development of an effective and efficient behavior intervention plan for the problem behavior" (Maryland State Department of Education, 2009, p. 9). When the team effectively works together, includes the parents, and the FBA is done well, the behavior intervention plan will put into place the right interventions. An effective FBA puts the team and parents in the best position to develop a behavior plan that will really work.

The following steps should be included in a successful FBA and are detailed in the sections that follow:

- Define the behavior:
  - Define and analyze the interfering behaviors
  - Document the discussions
  - Develop observable definitions of 2–3 targeted behaviors

- Develop a hypothesis:
  - Generate hypotheses about functions or causes of behaviors
  - Generate hypotheses about what is happening before and after behavior that may be supporting or reinforcing behavior
  - Analyze whether the behavior is due to a skill deficit, a performance deficit, or both
  - Consider individual factors that may contribute to the behavior

- Conduct the intervention with fidelity:
  - Generate a behavior intervention plan (see Chapter 9)
  - Determine interventions to start immediately
  - Use the performance on the interventions as part of the assessment

- Collect data:
  - Collect data to test the hypotheses
  - Decide who will collect data
  - Decide how to collect data
  - Gather data collection tools

- Reflection:
  - Assess whether the hypotheses were correct based on data
  - Assess whether the interventions are effective based on data
  - Reflect on the previous steps and fill in gaps
  - Plan to revise the individual plan, if warranted

- Revision:
  - Revise behavior intervention plan, IEP, or 504 Plan
  - Revise data collection systems
  - Continue or change interventions
  - Collect ongoing data and plan to review or revise as needed

- Repeat the process

Tool 7.1, found at the end of this chapter, provides a worksheet that can be used to document each step of the FBA process.

Define the Behavior

An interfering behavior is one that interferes with the child's learning and the learning of others. The idea behind a well-developed FBA is to discover what factors affect a child's interfering behavior, why the child is displaying the behavior, and to bring a group of professionals with parents together in a problem-solving, data-gathering activity that will likely lead to the development of an individual student plan. But first, the behavior must be defined, discussed, and analyzed. The way the behavior is defined sets the stage for the rest of the FBA.

Defining the problem is the first step in further evaluation of any problems, whether a child is showing behaviors that are oppositional, defiant, withdrawn, aggressive, or disruptive.

For example, Matthew is a gifted 11-year-old who frequently argues with adults and refuses to follow directions. To his parents, this is disrespectful behavior that he uses to get his own way. To teachers, Matthew appears unmotivated and disinterested. To an outside observer, it's a communication problem; Matthew may be trying to express his feelings, but does not know how. What actually happens usually is different from perspectives and opinions about what happened. Different perspectives on the same behavior will lead to different ways to describe or express behavior; it is important to define the behavior in observable and measurable terms.

How Matthew's behaviors are defined will determine which members of the MDT will evaluate him and what tests will be used. If depression is suspected, or part of how the child's behavior is described, then the team may elect to use different rating scales than if the behavior is defined as defiant behavior. Descriptive terms such as depressed or defiant should be avoided for this reason. Defining the behavior is mostly about using language that is observable, specific, and measurable. Nock and Kurtz (2005) gave a correct example of the proper way to define behaviors: "the number of times Johnnie kicks a classmate' satisfies the observable criterion, while 'the number of times Johnnie gets angry' does not" (p. 362).

Some degree of challenging behaviors in children is normal. Some degree of almost any behavior in humans is normal. So, we must consider the child's age and the overall behavior expectations of her peers. But we also must consider whether the type and degree of behavior will respond to interventions so the child is served with the right match of type and intensity of interventions. Also, tolerance per teacher or family varies tremendously, so teacher and parent perspective must be considered when analyzing information provided by different individuals (Schwarz, 2004).

Dominique's wry, sarcastic sense of humor has helped her to survive the losses in her life. She tries to use it, however, when teachers are trying to correct her behavior, or when parents are making her do chores. She has been suspended this year for fighting (another female student looked at her and mumbled something), mouthing off to teachers, leaving the classroom, refusing to follow directions, and a variety of other smaller infractions have landed her in the "school support center," the district's in-school suspension program. She cannot complete the stack of work piling up. When she goes to class, the conflict with the other girl starts all over again. Girls are whispering about her. She can't find her notebook and drops her pens on the floor. She hears more snickering. She is failing the class and did not do the project that was due today. As the bell rings, her teacher tries to stop her to discuss her behavior, and mark her point sheet. Dominique tears up the point sheet, tells the teacher to leave her alone, and storms out of the classroom. The next day, the teacher sends her immediately to the office where an administrator calls her mother for the 18th time so far this year—it's only November!

Frame the behavior in a positive, objective way. Humans like to make meaning out of events. What means something to one person means something else to another person. Lack of eye contact can mean boredom or, in some cultures, respect. When preparing to collect data, the MDT should remember the idea that teachers and parents look for behaviors as they are defined. If the rule is to walk in the hallway, then

Correct Description	Incorrect Description
Puts head down on desk during directions	Unmotivated behavior
Yells, "I hate you!" after given a direction	Manipulative behavior
Comments under breath toward teacher	Disrespectful behavior
Walks out of class and slams the door	Explosive behavior

Figure 9. How behaviors should be defined.

teachers are likely to look for and praise walking in the hallway. But if the rule is framed as "don't run," the teachers will more likely look for running behavior and issue a consequence. It is important to define the behavior in positive, observable terms, so that evaluation tools will collect the right kind of information. Figure 9 provides examples of the common, incorrect ways behaviors are defined and the more specific, correct ways they should be defined.

So, instead of targeting unmotivated, manipulative, disrespectful, or explosive behavior, the MDT should strive to target the specific, measurable behavior in the evaluation process. The way the team frames the behavior will affect the way that evaluations are completed, and may ultimately affect the interventions and school plan.

Develop the Hypothesis

There are three aspects of behavior about which the team and parent form hypotheses, which are then confirmed or refuted based on data. The hypothesis stage of the assessment is a three-prong question; the MDT must consider:

1. whether the target behavior is happening because of a skill deficit or performance deficit;
2. what functions the target behavior serves for the child; and
3. whether there are other factors that affect the child's target behaviors.

The Hypothesis, Prong 1: Skill Deficit or Performance Deficit?

The team must understand whether a child knows how to perform the desired behavior. A child will not stop calling out or annoying his peers if he does not know how to inhibit his behavior, employ waiting skills, or enter a conversation appropriately. It will not matter how great the reward system and how often he is rewarded for good behavior—if the child does not know how to perform the behavior or skill, a behavior intervention plan will not make a difference.

The team is looking for problems with the child's academic and behavioral skill level or performance. The reason for this is that if a child does not know how to perform a skill, it won't matter whether a behavior system is put into place to improve the skill. A common question is whether a child "can't do" or "won't do" a task (Duhon et al., 2005). This is a critical question because it can change how a teacher or parent views the child's behavior. Also, a problem-solving approach for behavior often uncovers an academic problem, which can lead to a reanalysis of the behavior, and hopefully, the addition of academic interventions. The team may conclude that the problem is a learning problem, not a behavior problem. That kind of shift allows a team to understand the child's behavior as a skill deficit. When the child's reading or writing skills do not match the task, the child is more likely to exhibit challenging behavior. Or, a study of "explosive" behavior may reveal frustration due to lack of a social skill. That type of skill deficit is common, as well as deficits in executive functioning, self-calming skills, regulation skills, or attention skills. We have found that the majority of behavior problems relate to a skill deficit, and when a student is taught the correct skill, the behavior will diminish.

When the behavior is seen as a performance deficit, the child knows how to interact with others, but has difficulty using the skill in the classroom, playground, or locker room. Reasons for performance deficits can include lack of understanding of how to use the skill in a different environment; interference by emotion, attention, or sensory response;

or failure of the child to understand the importance of using the skill. If a performance deficit is uncovered through the FBA, the MDT and parent would craft a different intervention than if a skill deficit is found.

Austin has been suspended 4 times for fighting, with a total of 9 days of suspension, and it's only February. Austin is the bright kid who wants to have friends, but is isolated at school. In class, he is the first to blurt out something off topic, and he doesn't seem to follow what the teacher is saying. There are a few peers Austin constantly looks at, for too long a time, and these peers interpret this as confrontational behavior. So, in the hallway, peers push or threaten Austin, and he fights back, receiving in- and out-of-school suspensions, after which he is behind in classwork and further behind in peer relations. Austin's school team conducts an FBA and discovers that Austin does not know how his behaviors annoy others, and does not have a problem-solving strategy for understanding the succession of behaviors. Through direct instruction in a social skills class, with emphasis on the use of his new skills in the classroom, Austin develops skills to interact with his peers.

The Hypothesis, Prong 2: Functions of Behaviors

The function of a behavior is the purpose that the behavior serves. The FBA process assumes that all behavior serves a purpose, and that the factors that occur before (antecedents), during, and after (consequences) the behavior can be manipulated to improve or diminish behavior. As stated by the Maryland State Department of Education (2009), "Any behavior of an individual is typically characterized as being a practical and efficient act to accomplish a desired purpose" (p. 10). The FBA is designed to understand behavior in the context of its functions or purposes. It is a group activity that involves meeting, collecting data, and analyzing and discussing implications, while changing instructional factors, collecting more data, and identifying instructional and behavior interventions. There are well-known, established functions for human behavior:

- *To get something:* Some behavior occurs to get attention, approval, or love. Other behaviors occur to get a tangible reward. So, the function of a behavior can be to get an emotion or to get a tangible object.

- *To avoid something:* Behaviors can occur to avoid disapproval, to avoid responsibility, or to avoid conflict. Other behaviors can occur to avoid a consequence, such as going to work with a cold to avoid a day off without pay. Children display interfering behaviors at times to avoid schoolwork that is too difficult!
- *To regulate the body:* Some behaviors relate to the body's internal state. For example, some behaviors occur for sensory stimulation, which could be included in the discussion above about getting something. Self-stimulating behaviors can be used to regulate the body and gain a sense of peace.
- *To express or communicate something:* Behaviors also can occur for the purpose of communication of an idea, thought, feeling, or attitude. If this is a concern, the MDT may include a speech-language pathologist.

The Hypothesis, Prong 3: Other Factors

Other factors can affect a child's behavior, including the following:
- regulation and executive functioning skills,
- instructional level of materials,
- teacher skill,
- teacher and student personality and style match (or mismatch),
- family involvement,
- medical or health issues,
- language or communication issues, and
- sensory and motor functioning.

Discussion about these should be included within prongs 1 and 2. For example, a student may have a medical problem that contributes to behavior, which would not be appropriately addressed by a reward system. If students are not challenged, or the work is too difficult, just the mismatch of instructional level alone can cause behavior problems (Burns & Dean, 2005; Gettinger & Seibert, 2002; National Association of School Psychologists, 2005).

Conduct the Intervention With Fidelity

When an intervention is provided with fidelity, the intervention is applied in the way it was researched to work. For example, the use of praise is researched to work, but only when a teacher or parent uses praise specifically, immediately, and at regular intervals. If that way is not followed, the strategy will likely not work. Similarly, behavior systems, reading programs, or any academic or behavioral intervention must be provided with fidelity. Otherwise, the intervention will likely not be useful in helping parents and educators assist students in meeting goals.

Educators should be innovative, creative, and use the child's strengths and abilities to tailor interventions to meet the child's needs. The child should be involved, to the extent appropriate, in designing the intervention through the FBA. Choosing motivating reinforcement is not the only reason to involve the child. If the child is showing resistance to the intervention, behaviorally, or via lack of progress through data, the team should intensify the intervention, and assure it is being delivered the way it was intended by trained and highly qualified staff. Keeping the child at the center of the process is key to success.

Collect Data

The definition of behavior, the hypothesis, the intervention, the reflection, and the revision all rely on data to inform the MDT and parent whether the behavior is getting better, worse, or remaining the same, so that the team and parent can make educational decisions. Data, therefore, is an element of evaluation whose importance cannot be underestimated. The team and parent will need to understand the various ways soft and hard data should be collected in a meaningful way. The next section explores other informal methods of evaluation, where we present some of these data collection methods. However, due to the individualized nature of the need for data collection for the

- Checklists
- Rating scales
- Observation
- Record review
- Behavior while testing
- Interview (e.g., parent, student, provider, teachers)
- Curriculum-based measurement
- Strategic instruction model
- Behavior ratings
- Daily behavior contracts
- Discussion
- Quiz or classroom test
- Computer-based intervention
- Inventories
- Portfolio assessment
- Intervention programs with data collection inherent
- Work samples
- Hard data
- Soft data
- Criterion-based assessment

Figure 10. **Various types of informal data collection tools.**

FBA, the team may find that the data collection tools need to be developed by the team. Therefore, the MDT may require the participation of a specialist in data analysis. Tool 6.2 can be used to record multiple types of data for data collection.

Figure 10 shows the variety of informal tools available to the MDT as it conducts evaluation of a child's behavior. The FBA will utilize any number of these and consider formal evaluations together with informal tools.

Given the data-involved nature of an effective FBA, the FBA requires a number of various data gathering tools. Data collection tools should yield data that can be analyzed for a variety of reasons, including whether a child is making meaningful progress in the curriculum. These tools can be integrated into the child's IEP, Behavior Intervention Plan (BIP), or 504 Plan, or for other purposes such as progress monitoring. The data analysis is the heart of the evaluation process. When data are collected, they should reflect sound scientific techniques. Therefore, sometimes specialists or experts are used to collaborate with the MDT process. To measure progress effectively, soft and hard data collection tools can be individually adapted to meet a child's needs. Soft data is narrative, while hard data is quantitative. Hard data uses numbers and soft data uses words. Both should be considered using a variety of tools.

Observation

Observation is the most common form of data gathering used by parents and educators alike. Observations can vary in structure, purpose, form, and conclusion. Potential pitfalls of evaluation include: observer bias, altering the environment, limited time, observers making incorrect conclusions based on observation, and overall inconsistency of approach. The observer is either familiar to the students and participating in instruction, or not providing instruction and not typically part of the classroom. Observation can be conducted in a way that collects valid and reliable information by:

- assuring that observation includes data,
- comparing observation data with other sources of information,
- rating the behavior observed on same scale used by multiple observers,
- using both rating and narrative approaches (hard and soft data),
- collecting data about the child and his peers for comparison purposes, and
- scheduling and conducting the observation as unobtrusively as possible.

Online Resources/Use of Technology

At http://www.interventioncentral.com, parents and educators can find online data collection and data charting devices and ideas. This is just one way technology can be used to collect data. The following site has a variety of links to resources for parents: http://www.nichcy.org/Pages/behavassess.aspx. The National Association of School Psychologists' website (http://www.nasponline.org) also provides multiple resources for parents.

Record Reviews

Parents and educators should carefully attend to and regularly review a child's records. A parent often finds information in the child's record she has not seen before, such as observations, comments about behavior, or other notes about the child. Also, educators can use the record as a sort of portfolio assessment, if the record is maintained and organized in collaboration with the parent. Records are vital because written documentation forms the basis of a child's progress, and information used to develop an effective plan for the child is found within a child's records. If it did not happen in writing, it is as if it didn't happen! If documentation is organized clearly within a child's record, the information in the record will be effectively used in the evaluation process.

Interviews

Like observations, interviews are routinely used by teachers and administrators when they talk with a parent on the phone, in a conference, or at a meeting. In a structured interview, the interviewer uses a consistent way to rate the interviewee's responses and develops questions before the interview. Interviews should allow the responder to answer questions quantitatively (where a score is given) and qualitatively (where a narrative response can be provided). Technology can be used effectively for a variety of purposes in interviews. Video conferencing, meeting online, and various types of phone conference calls can now be used, recorded, and played back. A good example of a parent interview form can be found at http://www.parentsrteacherstoo.com/BehaviorAssessment.pdf.

Rating Scales and Checklists

Rating scales and checklists vary widely in their purposes, validity, reliability, and uses. Rating scales and checklists are inventories given to the student, his teachers, his parents, and other informers to attempt to quantify the seriousness of the behavior and the frequency of duration of behaviors. It is not unusual for children to minimize their own social-emotional concerns, and a sound scale or checklist will adjust and account for that. Some rating scales are well standardized, but others are informal and yield limited information that can be used to compare a child to his peers across the country. Scales and checklists should be provided to a variety of informants, and the results should be seen as only one of many sources of information about a child's behavioral or emotional needs. Some rating scales are specifically designed to help with diagnosing emotional disturbance, attention problems, autism, or other conditions, and can be used with children with challenging behavior if there is a diagnostic question about the educational disability or diagnosis.

Portfolio or Work Sample Assessment.

Problem-solving sessions, essays, PowerPoint presentations, role-plays, social activity videos, audio recordings of phone calls or discussions, and myriad other creative techniques can be used to create a work sample portfolio. This portfolio can be specific to individual student goals. It should be based on the social skills or other curriculum being used or based on goals set for the child by the team and parents through an individual student plan.

Social Interaction Data, Social Mapping

Social skills mapping can show peer-to-peer interactions in a visual and data-driven way. Social skills anchor charts (Ontario Ministry of Education, 2005) can be used to show students how social skills look and sound. These behaviors can be easily tracked in an observation form or checklist.

Use of A-B-C

Some FBA frameworks have used the ABC charting of behaviors to inform the team and parent about the reasons for behavior and the things that occur after the behavior that maintain the behavior. A stands for antecedent, B for behavior, and C for consequence.

> The morning warm-up is too difficult for Suzanne. Each morning, faced by a new warm-up on the board, she feels panic. She fumbles to get out her pencil and starts to copy the board. But like every morning, copying makes her angry and frustrated. "I just can't do this! I am so stupid!" she thinks. She starts to call out, get out of her seat, and generally disrupt the classroom until the teacher sends her to the guidance counselor's office. While there, Suzanne happily eats cookies and talks with the counselor for about 20 minutes. When she walks back to class, the teacher is usually leading a class discussion, in which Suzanne happily participates.

Simply put, if the child gets to go to the beloved counselor and eat a cookie after misbehaving, the team may reveal that the trip to the counselor and cookie reinforce the undesired behavior, and this maintains or increases behavior. The team may decide to put a skill training program into place, set goals for success, and allow the trip to the counselor to occur after a goal is met, to reward the desired behavior. This simple example highlights that if there is a simple and connected relationship between antecedent, behavior, and consequence, the ABC method of collecting information may be effective. However, much of the time, behavior is more complex than a simple immediate antecedent, behavior, and consequence sequence. When ABC charting is effective, it is used along with other sources of information to plan for school success.

Curriculum-Based Measurement

Curriculum and assessment are two sides of one hand. When conducted correctly, curriculum-based measurement (CBM) is always a good idea for kids with challenging behaviors. The main problem with curriculum-based measurement is that very few educators understand how to do it in the way it has been researched to work. Another problem is that, for social behavioral skills, schools must be using a social skills curriculum or behavioral curriculum to properly conduct CBM. Curriculum-based measurement is a specific way of using probes or small curriculum-related quizzes for formative (ongoing) assessment of how well a child is learning curriculum. CBM, when used properly, graphs student progress, and can yield information that not only highlights a child's weaknesses, but also his strengths and interests. The child is involved with setting goals for success, and collecting and graphing data. In this way, CBM can advance the child's self-awareness, self-advocacy, and self-determination.

Reflection

This step of the FBA requires the team members and parents to meet or otherwise discuss the results of the first four steps. This reflection of the behavior, hypothesis, intervention, and data collection stages allows the team to refine definitions of behavior, hypotheses, or make recommendations for different interventions. Therefore, this stage also should include a review of the BIP, IEP, or 504 Plan. If there is an informal plan in place, the team will review it as well. Follow-up, persons responsible, and discussion should be documented and include answers to these questions:

- Was the team correct in identifying the behaviors that interfere with learning?
- Are additional behaviors seen?
- Is the behavior defined correctly?
- Were all three parts of the hypothesis correct?
- Is there a need for a different intervention or adjustments in the intervention?
- Are there any additional areas for reflection before revising the plans?

Revision

Either the evaluations or the interventions are revised during this stage. The team revises the FBA, the individual student plan, or the student evaluation plan. Sometimes, this process generates discussion about the need for additional information. Once the team and parent are satis-fied with the reflection of the FBA, the team should review the entire evaluation process, and consider the need for reevaluation as needed. In the reflection stage, the team may consider reevaluation in the context of to what extent the original diagnostic questions were answered.

Legal Tip

Reevaluation discussion must occur every 3 years. But reevaluation can occur up to one time per year or more often if the school district and parent agree.

The next chapter is about how evaluations are used to make deci-sions as to whether or not a child qualifies for an individual student plan for services, accommodation, and special instruction techniques.

Tool 7.1
A Successful FBA Worksheet

Team Members: _____

_____

_____

Steps to a Successful Functional Behavior Assessment

Step 1: The Behavior—Analyze It!

Multidisciplinary Team Actions:

- Define and analyze the interfering behaviors:
- Target Behavior 1: _____
- Target Behavior 2: _____
- Target Behavior 3: _____

Step 2: The Hypothesis—Develop It!

Multidisciplinary Team Actions:

- Hypothesis for Behavior 1: _____

  _____

- Hypothesis Part 1/3: Skill Deficit or performance deficit, or both, and why? _____

  _____

- Hypothesis Part 2/3: Function of behavior? Circle and explain:

  - To get something _____
  - To avoid something_____
  - Internal or sensory factors _____
  - To communicate something_____

- Hypothesis Part 3/3: What are other factors to consider? Circle and explain:

Regulation and executive functioning skills	Instructional level of materials	Teacher skill	Teacher and student personality and style match
Family involvement	Medical or health issues	Language and communication needs	Sensory and motor functioning

_____

_____

_____

The Intervention—Do It With Fidelity!

Multidisciplinary Team Actions:

- ❏ Generate behavior intervention plan. (See Chapter 9)
- ❏ Determine interventions to start now, per behavior intervention plan
- ❏ Use the performance on the intervention as part of the assessment

The Data—Collect It!

Multidisciplinary Team Actions:

- Who will collect the data?_____
- How will they collect the data?_____
  - ❏ Data collection tools gathered
  - ❏ Data are collected

The Reflection—Mirror It!

Multidisciplinary Team Actions:

- Were the hypotheses correct, based on data? What else should be done?

_____

_____

- Were the interventions effective, based on data? What else should be done? _____

    _____   _____

- Reflect on the previous steps. What gaps need to be filled?

    _____

    _____

- How should the individual plan be revised? _____

    _____

The Revision—Change it!

Multidisciplinary Team Actions:

- ❏ Revise BIP, IEP, or 504 Plan
- ❏ Revise data collection systems
- ❏ Continue or change interventions
- ❏ Ongoing—collect data and plan to review or revise as needed

Tool 7.2
Data Collection Tool

Identifying Information:

Name: _____

Date of birth: _____   Grade: _____

School attending: _____

Age: _____   ID number (when applicable): _____

Date of evaluation: _____   Date of report: _____

Reason for Referral:

Why is the assessment being conducted? _____

_____

_____

Background Information:

Previous assessment results: _____

_____

_____

Educational history: _____

_____

_____

School functioning: _____

_____

_____

Birth and developmental history: _____

_____

_____

Diagnoses and special education eligibility decisions: _____

_____

_____

Current school program information: _____

_____

_____

Tests/Tools Administered:

Record review completed by: _____

Notes on record review: _____

_____

_____

Names of formal assessments: _____

_____

_____

Names of informal assessments: _____

_____

_____

Interviews completed with: _____

_____

_____

Notes on interviews: _____

_____

_____

Behavioral Observations/Testing Behaviors:

Describe testing behaviors (including statements of attention to task, concentration, behaviors when more difficult items were presented, how the child responded to examiner, how the child followed directions, and any unusual behaviors noted):

_____

_____

_____

_____

Statement of Validity:

Given testing behaviors, did the results derived appear to adequately reflect current performance? Create a statement expressing this:

_____

_____

_____

_____

Examples:
"Therefore, these results are judged to be a valid and reliable reflection of the student's functioning."
"The following results appear to reflect John's level of academic achievement at this time."

Results of Testing:

Name each test and subtest administered: _____

_____

_____

What did the subtests measure? _____

_____

_____

Describe strengths and weaknesses of the tests: _____

_____

_____

Describe examples of errors made: _____

_____

_____

Student's standard scores and percentile rank: _____

_____   _____

_____

What do the scores mean (average, below average, deficient, above average,

superior range of functioning)? _____

_____

_____

Describe performance on each subtest separately: _____

_____

_____

Summary:

Based on the testing results, what are the student's strengths and needs? _____

_____

_____

_____

Recommendations:

What do you recommend to address areas of need? This is the section to include strategies, accommodations, modifications, and recommended instructional interventions.

_____

_____

_____

This report should be signed and dated. Score print outs should be attached. Raw scores and protocols should be made available.

chapter 8 Eligibility

Qualifying for Services

AFTER a child is thoroughly evaluated, the school team and parents decide if she is eligible for, or qualifies for, special services, instruction, or accommodation. Eligibility usually results in the development of an IEP or 504 Plan.

This chapter covers the following topics:

- What is eligibility and why is it important?
- How are eligibility determinations made?
- What is the role of the parent and other members of the MDT in determining a child's eligibility?
- What special factors need to be considered for eligibility decisions?

Eligibility decisions are made after an evaluation process, which we explored in the previous chapters. So, eligibility is the stage of the special education process after evaluations, but before development of

Myth	Truth
The socially maladjusted child has Conduct Disorder and does not feel badly for his actions.	The child with EBD is usually indiscernible from his counterparts who are socially maladjusted. There is no test or criteria to distinguish social maladjustment.
Eligibility is not that important; as long as the child is eligible, he will get all he needs.	When a child is eligible as a child with EBD or emotional disability, there is still a stigma and achievement gap associated with that disability.
Schools cannot provide special education and related services if achievement scores are in the average range.	Students with EBD have a wide range of academic needs, from gifted to below grade level.
If the child hasn't failed every class, she shouldn't be eligible for special education or related services.	Report cards alone cannot be used to determine a child's eligibility. Teams must consider how much support a child requires after school when determining if the child qualifies for services.

individual student plans, as shown below. As a result of eligibility, an individual plan should be developed to address the child's areas of need.

What Is Eligibility and Why Is It Important?

Eligibility secures the child's legal right to accommodations, special education services, supplementary aides, or related services. Eligibility decisions are important because they can shape how others view the child, and eligibility decisions can affect the child's school program and placement. The eligibility decision is important because it also can affect how parts of the child's individual plan or program are written. An eligibility process can be seen as the process of unlocking the keys to a child's learning needs and define her educational disability, or the condition that is affecting her learning.

Eligibility is the official designation of a right to a meaningful and free appropriate public education (FAPE). When a child receives FAPE, the child makes progress in the curriculum and makes significant progress on any goals set out in the individual student plan. The child is learning the skills he needs to be an independent adult—getting along with others, managing emotions, and generally performing well in a group. Eligibility in the area of emotional and behavioral needs can be complex and subjective; therefore, we cannot emphasize enough the importance of making eligibility decisions based on sound, valid, and reliable data. Different teams could make different eligibility determinations for the same student, demonstrating how perspectives and judgments from school to school or team to team can affect team decisions.

What Laws Govern Eligibility Decisions?

At least four major laws apply in determining a child's eligibility, as shown in Figure 11. Of these laws, the IDEA contains the disability definition most broadly used in schools, so it will be discussed first. States that have agreed with the federal definition below have kept it as state law, while other states have adopted their own definitions of EBD. In many ways, IDEA (2004) frames how FAPE should be provided, and the other laws then follow that framework.

Eligibility Under IDEA

IDEA requires three conditions to be met for eligibility for the IEP, as shown in Figure 12. As seen in this three-part eligibility question, whether a child meets the state or federal definition for emotional disturbance, emotional disability, emotional behavioral disorder, or another disability in your state is key to the team's decision. Not only must a child

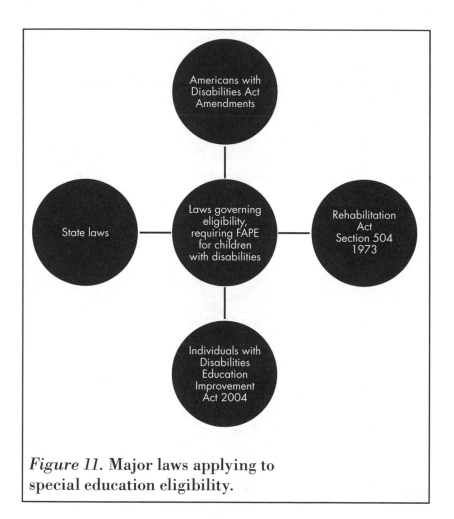

Figure 11. Major laws applying to special education eligibility.

meet the federally or state-defined disability definition, there must also be an adverse effect of the disability on the child's learning, *and* the child must require special education. Only when a team answers each of these questions in Figure 12 with "yes" will the IEP be developed.

Three steps to understanding eligibility include the following:

1. Understand where the eligibility stage fits in with the whole process, and understand the eligibility questions in Figure 12.
2. Understand that diagnoses are different from disabilities.

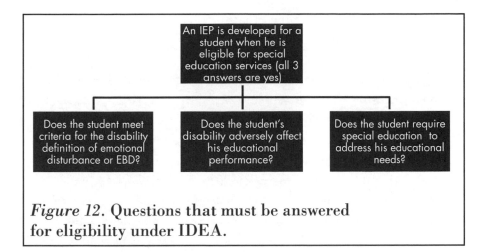

Figure 12. Questions that must be answered for eligibility under IDEA.

3. Understand legal definitions from your state and the federal definition:

> *Emotional disturbance* means a condition exhibiting one or more of the following characteristics over a long period of time and to a marked degree that adversely affects a child's educational performance:
>   1. An inability to learn that cannot be explained by intellectual, sensory, or health factors;
>   2. An inability to build or maintain satisfactory interpersonal relationships with peers and teachers;
>   3. Inappropriate types of behavior or feelings under normal circumstances;
>   4. A general pervasive mood of unhappiness or depression; and
>   5. A tendency to develop physical symptoms or fears associated with personal or school problems.

Emotional disturbance also includes schizophrenia. The term does not apply to children who are socially maladjusted, unless it is determined that they have an emotional disturbance. (IDEA, 2004, p. 46756)

There has been much debate over this federal definition of emotional disturbance, and its application across the nation. Although about 14%, or more than 6.5 million children around the U.S., receive special education, children with emotional disabilities account for less than 1% of these children (U.S. Department of Education, 2008). Considering that some estimate that 20% of children have a diagnosable mental health disorder and about 10% of all children have problems that interfere with functioning at home, school, or community, it is easy to see that there is a vast underserving of kids with challenging behaviors under this definition (Genshaft, 2009).

Diagnosis or disability? There is a difference between diagnoses and disability. For educational purposes, the disability (or applicable state definition) is the important definition, not the diagnosis, with important exceptions for schizophrenia and possibly depression. Although a diagnosis of Conduct Disorder, anxiety, or Oppositional Defiant Disorder can help the team discover the correct educational disability definition, the team will focus on the disability defined by IDEA and whether there is an effect of the disability in the classroom where special education instruction is needed.

Severity and duration of challenging behavior. The following criteria set up in IDEA (2004) must be met: *"Emotional disturbance means a condition exhibiting one or more of the following characteristics over a long period of time and to a marked degree that adversely affects a child's educational performance"* (p. 46756). The first part of the definition is not specific, so "over a long period of time and to a marked degree" often is a topic of debate among the MDT. Some states have adopted a guideline of 6 months, while others have determined this criteria on a case-by-case basis. State regulations should be consulted for individual states.

Sensory, intellectual, and other health factors. This exclusionary criteria must be met for emotional disturbance eligibility. This prong of the definition relates to a child's inability to learn and explores reasons other than emotional disturbance why a child may be showing interfering behaviors. An FBA should fully explore each of these factors to determine the cause of or the function of a child's behavior, because the behaviors may be due to other factors, not an emotional disturbance. Intellectual, sensory, or other health factors can exclude a child from being eligible under emotional disturbance. Students who melt down during a fire drill or have difficulty managing sensory experiences such as visual, auditory, tactile, gustatory, olfactory, and other internal factors may not qualify for services as student with an emotional disturbance. Sensory factors may lead an MDT to consider a child's challenging and troubling behaviors to be due to autism.

I Iealth factors that cause interfering behavior may exclude a child from being eligible for services under IDEA. Health factors can be considered under a different disability category called Other Health Impairment. If a child has limited intellectual ability and poor adaptive, functional skills, that child's challenging behavior may be caused by intellectual disabilities, not emotional disturbance.

Giftedness. The needs of a child with a behavioral or emotional condition who also is cognitively disabled is clearly different from the needs of a child who is cognitively highly gifted. When a child is cognitively gifted, the giftedness may in some ways mask the child's social, emotional, or behavioral needs. Children who are cognitively gifted can show unique social and emotional profiles. Although children with low cognitive skills can display problem behaviors, the child who is highly gifted also may display problem behaviors. The giftedness may, however, allow a child to express himself differently, so the evaluation of children who are known to be highly gifted should include someone who is an expert in this special consideration.

Relationships, inappropriate behavior, moods, and somatism. Only one of the following must be met for eligibility under emotional disturbance:

- *Build and maintain relationships:* Failure to develop and maintain relationships is part of the definition of emotional disturbance. Because children can fail to develop relationships for many reasons, and because there is a wide range of perception about what a "good" relationship is, this criteria has potentially wide applications. As will be seen in the next section, some states have tried to better define this criteria, but many states also have retained the federal definition.

> Sherry is a sixth grader who has trouble making and keeping friends. She sits alone at lunch, and she rarely sees other children from school after the day ends. In afterschool activities, she has conflicts with peers and, sometimes, even adults. Sherry is starting to refuse to go to school some days. She feels like an emotional refugee, an outsider. Her parents have tried medications, therapy, and counseling, but nothing seems to work.

- *Inappropriate behavior and feelings in normal situations:* This prong of the disability definition has been widely debated and considered across many MDTs. Human behavior can be appropriate in one situation and not in another. Children with emotional disturbance who qualify because of this criteria may laugh when other children get hurt, verbally abuse a teacher after she gives directions for a long-term project, or display emotions or behaviors that are out of the norm. But the norm is very broad, and children, like all people, can display inappropriate behavior under normal circumstances. So, this criteria in particular must be at a marked degree, over a long period of time, resistant to interventions, and evaluated properly before being considered for a child's eligibility determination.
- *Mood of unhappiness or depression:* Perhaps the easiest criteria of emotional disturbance for the MDT to understand is the description of a child with a pervasive mood of unhappiness or constant state of depression. Depression may or may not be diagnosed for a child to meet this criteria. A child who is grieving or experiencing trauma may or may not be considered to be eligible for emotional disturbance.

Max is a highly cognitively gifted 11-year-old who used to love skateboarding and playing video games with friends. Since the beginning of the school year, Max has been observed frequently putting his head on his desk or sitting in class with his hood over his head, and Max has a general way of grunting when others talk with him. In groups in the classroom, Max sits with his arms crossed and his body turned from the group. When he does say something, it is usually brilliant. The psychologist's rating scales do not indicate Max thinks he is feeling depressed; he just wants all of the adults to "get out of his business."

- *Somatization:* If the child goes to the nurse often, complaining of physical symptoms, although she has no medical condition, she may be experiencing fears or physical symptoms associated with personal or school problems. This physical pain associated with emotional conditions is called somatization. When a child has physical pain or fears because of emotional or behavioral problems, this can be a factor in determining a child's eligibility under IDEA. A child who experiences this will make many trips to the nurse or doctor, with no physical problem found. Headaches and stomachaches are common, as well as aches in different parts of the body.

The school nurse knows Justin well, because Justin visits her at least twice a week. He has stomachaches and just doesn't feel well. His mother has to come pick him up some afternoons. He goes to the family doctor who cannot see anything of concern, medically speaking. Justin talks about his feelings of frustration at school. A visit to the doctor reveals that Justin is experiencing somatic complaints related to worry, stress, and overall feelings of failure.

Schizophrenia. Schizophrenia is usually a very serious brain disorder that has various symptoms that can be frightening to others. Schizophrenia is found across genders, races, cultures, and parts of the world. Behaviors seen include disorganized speech, bizarre behavior, poor reality-based thinking, psychosis, delusions, and social isolation or withdrawal. Children with schizophrenia should be considered children eligible for services as children with emotional disturbance (Done, Crow, Johnstone, & Sacker, 1994; Spearing, 2002).

Social maladjustment exclusion. The exclusion of children described as socially maladjusted has been one of the most contentious elements of the debate about the definition of emotional disturbance. Interestingly, the five criteria used in the federal definition came from a study in which children were selected due to challenging behavior (Bower, 1982). Children with an inability to build and maintain relationships with peers and adults seem to by definition be socially maladjusted. Testimony before Congress (Keeping Families Together Act, 2003) by Tammy Seltzer, of the Bazelton Center for Mental Health Law, suggested the problems inherent with the social maladjustment criteria for eligibility:

> Something is obviously wrong when the U.S. Surgeon estimates that nationwide five percent of all school-aged children have mental disorders and "extreme functional impairment" and 11 percent have mental disorders with "significant functional impairment" while, for more than two decades, the national rate of students identified with emotional disturbance under IDEA hovered just under one percent. By 2001, the rate of identification under IDEA had fallen to 0.74 percent. Data suggest that schools may be failing to correctly identify four fifths of children with mental or emotional disorders serious enough to adversely affect their educational performance. The federal definition—due to its vague language, undefined terms and inappropriate criteria—leads to significant under-identification of children with emotional disturbance. The exclusion of children on the basis of "social maladjustment"—an ambiguous distinction with no basis in research—contributes to the fact that many children who need special education services are failing to qualify for them under IDEA.

In practice, there are no reliable tools that distinguish students with EBD from those who are socially maladjusted. Many advocates argue that children with these behaviors should qualify for services under the IDEA definition of emotional disturbance, not be excluded from services.

Some scientists have even determined that the exclusionary factors for emotional disabilities are not logical, because there does not seem to be any test, evaluation tool, or criteria that reliably distinguishes children from each group. The debate has been ongoing for decades. Some believe that the definitions must be clarified, while others believe that eligibility should be determined based on student need. Currently, there is no definition of social maladjustment, and this is an area of great concern for child advocates, parents, and educators alike (Smith, 2007).

Eligibility Under Section 504 Rehabilitation Act

Children with social, emotional, and behavioral disorders can receive special services, accommodation, and instruction under IDEA. Or, children may receive special services and instruction under the Rehabilitation Act of 1973. Children eligible under IDEA are entitled to a written plan called the IEP, while children eligible under the Rehabilitation Act are entitled to a written plan called a 504 Plan. There is no exact definition for a disability under the Rehabilitation Act, however. Instead, the Rehabilitation Act states that people with a physical or mental impairment must receive needed accommodation, instruction, or services in order to have full access to programs that receive public funding, like public education. A mental impairment can be defined in a number of ways, and includes any condition or impairment that affects the individual's ability to perform major life functions, such as learning. Therefore, a mental health diagnosis, condition, or other disabling syndrome can qualify a child for a 504 Plan.

A child who is eligible under the Rehabilitation Act should be seen as a child who is entitled to FAPE, and he would be protected under IDEA in that he would be a child who would have a suspected disability. In other words, if a child has a condition that makes him eligible to receive a 504 Plan, it is likely that he also would be eligible under IDEA for an IEP. School teams may perceive that the child's condition does not affect him in the classroom as much as IDEA requires and may develop a 504 Plan first. This allows the school staff and parents to gather data on how the child responds to interventions before determining if the child is eligible under the IDEA and state definitions discussed in the beginning of this chapter.

Influence of No Child Left Behind (NCLB)

Although a child cannot become eligible for services because of an educational disability under NCLB (2001), the law has influenced how the school team makes eligibility decisions. NCLB has been in place for a number of years, but was reauthorized and strengthened in 2004 to include funding for schools that make Adequate Yearly Progress (AYP) through the use of high-stakes testing, among other requirements. As we explored in Chapter 2, the law has changed the way that school districts are identifying children who are eligible for special services, including testing accommodations.

NCLB has forced schools to examine schoolwide and child-specific methods that are evidence-based and proven to work with children with challenging behavior. In the Response to Intervention (RtI) model under NCLB, interventions should be provided as soon as challenging behaviors are seen or when children are at risk for developing behavior problems. The result of this increased monitoring has been that either more or fewer students are qualifying for special services, depending on the district.

On one hand, it has opened up services that are available to all children; on the other hand, NCLB has resulted in a resistance to the identification of children with educational disabilities in favor of the use of other, general interventions. In fact, a potential pitfall of the use of RtI is a delay in the timely and proper identification of children who need more intensive services or school placement (Fuchs, 2007; Wehby, Lane, & Falk, 2009).

Eligibility Under the Americans With Disabilities Act Amendments Act (ADAAA)

In 2008, the ADAAA expanded the definitions for eligibility purposes, and this increased the number of eligible people with disabilities who are entitled to receive services under the Rehabilitation Act and IDEA. All of these laws strive to protect eligible students who have challenging behaviors and therefore who may be entitled to services and FAPE. These laws also protect children who are at risk of developing more serious behaviors. From preschools to college campuses, early intervention is understood to be key in the school success of kids with challenging behaviors.

The ADA and the ADAAA require that persons with disabilities who are impaired in performing a major life function receive necessary accommodations, supports, services, or instruction. Although the list of major life activities does not specify behaviors or emotions, these difficulties can definitely be said to affect learning, thinking, working, concentrating, and communicating, among others. When social, emotional, and behavioral factors interfere with a child's ability to learn or perform in the classroom, eligibility should be explored under different legal umbrellas. ADA is relevant to school-aged children in that it protects all people with disabilities; children who are eligible for special services, accommodation, or instruction under the Rehabilitation Act or IDEA also would be protected as people with disabilities under the ADA. This represents a big change in the way school districts have seen eligibility requirements, and therefore, it represents an opportunity for school districts to identify and serve previously ineligible children with social, emotional, and behavioral difficulties.

State Definitions

As if it weren't confusing enough to have subjective federal guidelines, states also may add to the confusion by employing different definitions of EBD. For example, Wisconsin attempts to clarify the duration and severity of behaviors and has developed a checklist of behaviors for an emotional behavioral disability (Wisconsin Department of Public Instruction, 2009). In Georgia, the main characteristics of the federal disability are in place, but the disorder is labeled as an emotional and behavioral disorder, not an emotional disturbance. Georgia added exclusionary factors, stating,

> A child whose values and/or behavior are in conflict with the school, home or community or who has been adjudicated through the courts or other involvement with correctional agencies is neither automatically eligible for nor excluded from EBD placement. Classroom behavior problems and social problems, e.g., delinquency and drug abuse, or a diagnosis of conduct disorder do not automatically fulfill the requirements for eligibility for placement. (Georgia Department of Education, n.d., p. 2)

Search for your state's regulations for special education eligibility for emotional disturbance at sites such as http://www.nectac.org/sec619/stateregs.asp or at your State Department of Education website.

What if the Team Determines the Child Is Not Eligible?

If a child is not found to be eligible, this does not mean that she cannot receive services and special accommodations. However, without a written plan such as an IEP or 504 Plan, there is little or no accountability, and documentation of the agreement reached between school district and parents can be vague. Without eligibility, there is no legal entitlement for services.

Without an eligibility decision, the IEP or the 504 Plan will not be developed, and the MDT stops. It is therefore critical that parents and educators understand how eligibility decisions are made in relation to the special education process. A parent should understand his rights to appeal a decision with which he disagrees. If the team determines that the child is not eligible for services at Stage 4, the child returns to Stages 1, 2, and 3, including referral back to the MDT for consideration of general interventions that are available to other students in the school building.

> Alicia is an eighth grader who has been suspended multiple times, mostly for "insubordination." Her mother brought a letter from the doctor to the school saying that Alicia has been diagnosed with ADHD. Alicia is personable, but when someone does something she thinks is unfair, she either mouths off to staff, swears, or leaves the classroom. The school refuses to evaluate Alicia because the teachers say that when Alicia is present and calm, she can do the work, and she earns A's on the work she does. When the teachers talk among themselves, they think that Alicia should be on medication and that the parent is not doing her part. Alicia has many incomplete assignments, but the school says that she simply has to make up the work. The team refuses to find Alicia eligible for services, and in fact, has refused to do any evaluation. Despite more than 20 days of suspension from school, the school district does not find her eligible for services.

Alicia's example highlights how educators and parents struggle with understanding federal, state, and local guidelines, laws, and procedures that govern how a child's program is developed. Often, teachers are not the decision makers; allocation of resources in the school district can be hampered by many factors such as top-down policy making, lack of programs to support eligible children, lack of support from administration, or failure to view challenging behavior in a way that deserves eligibility for services.

In Alicia's case, if the parent understood how to document the effect of Alicia's possible educational disability and spoke the correct "language" with the team, Alicia would have a better chance of being properly evaluated, and likely become eligible for special education and related services. When Alicia's parent hired an expert to help her that is exactly what happened. The question for Alicia's team was: What factors interfere most with Alicia's ability to learn? She is a very bright student, but her attention and regulation deficits affected her in the classroom, affected her relationships, and were major factors in her challenging behavior, so Alicia was found eligible under the primary disability of Other Health Impairment and a secondary disability of emotional disturbance.

Involving Parents

Even the most savvy parents and experienced educators often do not know the disability definitions, how to evaluate a child, and how to effectively navigate the process to obtain services and school placement for children with EBD. We have found that parents typically are not aware of even the basic eligibility requirements. Tool 8.1 provides parents with information they need to understand their child's eligibility for special education.

For parents, eligibility determinations can be the most emotional stage of the special education process. Parents also may be concerned or afraid of what the decisions will mean for the child's future. Other parents are relieved because they have been seeking eligibility for some time, and the decision means that the child can now receive the special education he needs. Sometimes, parents are resistant to the child being labeled at all, and many parents have a negative reaction to the term *emotional disturbance*. Family cultures and attitudes are powerful factors to consider while moving through the IEP process.

When parents and educators are collaborating successfully, eligibility decisions include openly sharing information. That information should be used for the next stage of the process: development of the individual student plan. If decision making is child centered, data driven, informed, and caring and considerate, the parent and school will be set up for success as an individual plan is developed.

Tool 8.1

A Guide to Understanding Eligibility for Parents

The parent who understands how her state defines emotional and behavior problems or disorders will also have the best chance of working effectively with the school team. However, because the eligibility criteria can be interpreted in different ways, there are times that the parent and team do not see the behavioral or emotional needs of the child in the same way. Parents must provide consent for special education services to be given to their children

Questions a parent could ask to be prepared for an eligibility discussion include the following:

- Have I (the parent) seen in writing the school district's defining characteristics definitions of eligibility criteria?

- Have I been advised of my rights as a parent?

- Have I been involved in all discussions about eligibility for my child?

- Have I understood the threshold for the school district in regards to agreeing readily vs. resisting providing services?

- Have I, the parent, provided the district with sufficient and correct amount and type of information?

- Do I know the value of cooperating and collaborating with the district, despite disagreements?

chapter 9

Individual Plans

F O R a number of students, schoolwide and classwide interventions are not enough, even with the provision of small-group and some individual instruction. Some students may be receiving a number of accommodations from a teacher who is differentiating the content, process, and product, while integrating instruction of social and emotional curricula. A number of students will still need a more detailed analysis of their social, emotional, and behavioral needs, followed by an individual plan. Therefore, this chapter is about how plans are developed to meet an individual child's social, emotional, and behavioral needs.

The best start to an effective individual behavior plan is excellent teaching, where children show learning through products that can be analyzed by the MDT. Individual plans will be used in concert with the schoolwide and classwide interventions

Myth	Truth
The regular classroom setting is appropriate for all students.	Each student should be considered individually for placement in a setting removed from the regular or general classroom.
Behavior contracts and level systems are behavior change methods.	Behavior contracts and level systems have limited success rates.
The IEP is a living, breathing document that can be changed at any time.	The IEP can be changed without a meeting if the parent and school provide written consent. If a child needs a service, and that need is shown through evaluation, the service should be listed in the IEP and how often the service will be provided, how long, and by who must be clearly understood.
Removal from the general classroom setting should only be done when accommodations and modification in the regular classroom do not meet student needs.	Counseling, staff training, and other professional development for regular classroom teachers is not available at all schools.
A child has to fail before receiving an individual plan.	Response to Intervention problem solving should be used to intervene early, so a child can respond to evidence-based methods.

that we discussed in Chapter 4, but the individual plan will be more uniquely tailored to meet a child's specific needs.

The foundation for all successful plans is a comprehensive evaluation, as we discussed in Chapter 6. So, if you are teaching or parenting a child with challenging behavior, and would like to develop a school plan, first assure that evaluations are complete, consider all of the child's needs, and compile baseline data to inform the development of a plan. Designing and implementing an individual student plan can be a multifaceted problem-solving process, time consuming, and revealing. It may require the involvement of specialists, both within and outside of the school district, and it always requires the expertise of parents.

If a child's individual program or plan is written appropriately, she is much more likely to be successful in school. She is being successful if she is accessing the curriculum, making meaningful progress, and receiving benefit from her program. The major question is: What type of plan is right for any specific child?

Therefore, this chapter will answer these questions:

- What factors are relevant to developing meaningful individual plans?
- What is a behavior intervention plan (BIP) and how should it be developed?
- How can a beneficial and meaningful Individualized Education Program (IEP) be developed?
- How can a 504 Plan be written in a meaningful way?
- What possible roadblocks surround the development of student plans?
- What are the factors relevant to developing meaningful individual plans?

Relevant Factors

Whether your child has an IEP, BIP, 504 Plan, or other informal plan, there are three factors important to its development:

- the ability of the plan to support generalization across settings;
- teaching skills from the curriculum, including a social skills and behavior curriculum; and
- providing adjustments for the individual child.

Although there are many interrelated factors that influence how effective a plan can be to improving school success, the most important aspect of developing an individual plan is its meaningfulness to the child. Depending on the age and developmental level of the child, she should be involved with, agree to, and participate in developing and carrying out the individual plan. Individual student plans should:

- be based on proper evaluation of behavior, including an FBA;
- include scientifically based, or at least evidence-based, positive behavior supports, methods, and interventions;
- define goals, along with or in conjunction with the IEP goals, if any;
- incorporate how progress will be monitored;
- include data collection tools;
- assure instruction for emotional, behavioral, or social skills is based on a curriculum;
- be individualized and include parents;
- include specific present levels of performance;
- be multimodal, both proactive and reactive;
- be meaningful to the child;
- include meaningful accommodations;
- consider necessary related or supplementary services; and
- be at the child's instructional level—not too easy and not too difficult.

Tool 9.1 can be used in multidisciplinary meetings by parents and educators to assure all elements of the plan have been considered. The framework of the individual student plan includes great instruction, schoolwide and classwide behavior management and change quality indicators from Chapter 4, and an MDT's perspective that the child's behavior requires problem solving. In other words, a successful individual plan to address behavior should be informed by the topics covered so far in this book.

The Individualized Education Program (IEP)

The first type of formal plan we will discuss is the Individualized Education Program (or Plan, depending on the language used in your district), commonly called the IEP. The IEP is developed within 30 days after the multidisciplinary team has decided that the child is eligible for a plan under IDEA. We are discussing the IEP first because it is the most well-defined plan and contains many aspects commonly considered by the 504 Plan. Also, the IEP contains specific requirements that should be used as a template for other types of plans.

Who Develops the IEP?

The MDT, including the parent, develops a school success plan, including an IEP. The MDT, through the development of the IEP, decides which services, accommodations, goals, and placement the child will receive for all parts of the IEP. Tool 9.2 includes a checklist for parents to consider when taking part in the MDT's development of the individual student plan.

What Is the IEP?

The IEP is a document that spells out everything a child needs because of his educational disability or emotional behavioral disorder. There are 10 legally required parts of the IEP as defined by Weinfeld and Davis (2008), and shown in Figure 13. Each part interacts with the others, and together, delivers a beneficial, meaningful education to a child with a disability.

Part 1 of the IEP: Identifying information. This section includes the child's name, address, and contact information for the parents. It usually contains an identification number and identifies the child's disability.

Part 2 of the IEP: Present levels of academic achievement and functional performance. This foundational part of the IEP documents a child's strengths, his needs, and areas that are affected by his emotional or behavior disability. Parents who want to speak the school district lingo may use the acronym PLOP (present level of performance) to describe this part of the IEP. The PLOP of the IEP is like the foundation for the house (the IEP) that is about to be built. Each area that affects a child such as regulation skills, communication skills, social skills, reading skills, follow-

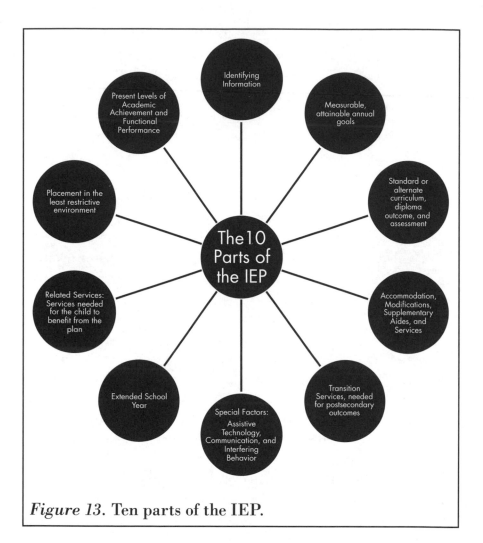

Figure 13. Ten parts of the IEP.

ing directions, peer relations, organization skills, or other areas identified by evaluations are included in the PLOP. This part, therefore, starts the threads in the IEP—from identification of needs, to recommendations for a program, service, or type of instruction—that will be woven through the different sections to ultimately recommend a school placement and services. Parents and educators should be sure each area of need or concern is listed, so that later in the IEP, the child's needs are considered for each area in the PLOP that affects educational performance.

This PLOP of the IEP documents a child's:

- *Strengths:* Kids with challenging behaviors often are creative, and this section of the PLOP can be used to identify a child's interests or abilities, both those related to school and those related to future goals. It also can recognize a child's giftedness and show under what circumstances a child shines. For example, this section might read, "Louis attends to tasks better when the environmental distractions are limited. When he has at least one break each half hour and opportunities to talk with the teacher privately when he's having problems with his peers, he is able to remain on task to complete 85% of his writing assignments."

- *Parental concerns:* Parents can write this section before the meeting to help the team understand their concerns. These can include answers to questions like, "What could the school do to help my child succeed?" "What would I like to see in place for my child's counseling needs?" or "What is a specific program I'd like my child to be part of?" For example, this section might read, "We think Kenny needs a smaller classroom setting where there is a counselor on site all of the time. Kenny needs an intensive reading program because his behaviors get worse when he is frustrated with his reading problems."

- *Academic needs, including study skills:* Study skill problems are usual for children with challenging behaviors, no matter the age. Study skills can be learned, and should be included if needed in the PLOP section. Executive functioning, attention, and other regulation difficulties can contribute to the behavior and academic failure of students. Remember that classroom performance does not have to be related only to poor reading, writing, and math skills—organization, attention, and memory can affect a child's academic performance as well. For example, this section may read, "Shelly has difficulty organizing her writing, coming up with ideas for writing prompts, editing her writing, and typing final drafts. She gets frustrated and will rip up her paper or refuse to write at least one time per each daily 90-minute language arts block."

- *Instructional level:* Educators who teach kids with challenging behaviors often do not use classroom or individual strategies, including adjusting the instructional level of materials (Penno, Frank, & Wacker, 2000). A large number of behavior problems could be avoided if the teacher understood the child's instruction grade level and used materials that were adjusted to the child's instructional levels (Gettinger & Seibert, 2002). A task or materials at the child's level of frustration should not be used. Independent-level materials should be used for independent practices, leisure or enjoyment, when new material is being introduced, or for repetition or reminders. For example, the PLOP section, under reading, may state, "When new information is being introduced, provide independent-level reading material for Jordan, at no higher than the 4.5 grade readability level, to prevent frustration."

- *Functional and classroom performance:* There are times when kids with challenging behaviors are capable of performing the grade-level academic demand, but because of challenging behaviors, the child may have a performance deficit. This performance deficit can be identified when the team conducts a thorough and correct FBA and includes the parents. Part of the analysis of behavior should include whether the behavior is due to a skill deficit or a performance deficit. This "can't do" versus "won't do" question is part of the FBA (see Chapter 7). For example, the PLOP section, under math, may read, "Desiree can recite the steps to solving problems, but when under real or perceived stress, she may not use her problem-solving skills. This affects her educationally because time is needed outside the classroom for her to regain a calm demeanor and successfully generate solutions to the problem."

- *Results of current evaluation:* If you remember the formal and informal evaluation discussion we had in Chapter 6, you will know the types of data sources that should be used to document the results of both formal and informal testing, including classroom-based information. Specialists' reports and recommendations can be included here. The same data tools used to monitor progress can be listed in this part of the IEP to form baseline functioning against which future goals will be measured. Data from informal assessment can be individualized, detailed, and informative. However, continued teacher training and parent training is needed. For example, under the "Social Skills" section of present levels of academic achievement and functional performance, Sherri's scores were:

Test or Tool	Score	Description
Test of Pragmatic Language	79	Low, well below average. (Average is 90–109)
Social Mapping	1 out of 15 interactions were initiated by Sherri	Below age expectation. Average for class is 11/15.
Pragmatics Profile of Clinical Evaluation of Language Fundamentals	88 Criterion Score	Below criterion. 142 or greater indicates no concern.
Social Competence Scale	T Score of 50	Average. Scores between 30 and 60 are average.

Part 3 of the IEP: Transition. Starting at age 16, and earlier if the team determines necessary, the IEP will state what services a student needs to live independently, go to college, go to a trade or training program, or otherwise participate in their postsecondary outcomes. This part also is critical because it identifies which agencies may support the child as an adult, and links the child and parent with multiple community supports. Figure 14 shows the various transition services included in this part of the IEP.

Part 4 of the IEP: Outcome, assessment, and curriculum. For most students, the regular or general curriculum will be used, even if the child's behaviors affect learning. For most children, the goal at the end of high school will be a diploma. Some states have various forms of

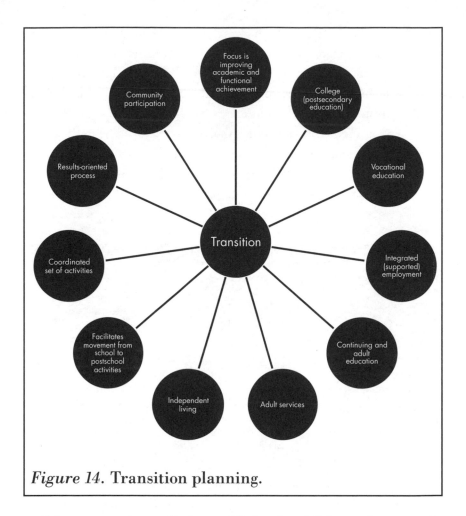

Figure 14. Transition planning.

a diploma, sometimes called a modified or tiered diploma. A very small number of students will need an alternate, functional life skills curriculum, and will be removed from the requirement to take standardized state tests. Some states have different curricula and requirements for teaching children who are highly gifted. It is critical that the right and appropriate curriculum is selected. The cornerstone of the child's plan will be instruction, and curriculum is required for effective instruction. This section of the IEP, therefore, can include consideration of the appropriate instruction for behavioral or social skills.

Part 5 of the IEP: Annual goals. Annual goals are required for every area that affects a child in which he needs specialized instruction. Specialized teaching that is adapted to meet a child's unique needs can be needed in any area, not only academics. Goals for instruction should be: **g**ood for the child, **o**bservable, **a**ttainable, **l**ogical, and **s**cientifically sound. Also, goals should include four components (called CBET): a condition statement, behavior, evaluation methods, and timeframe. Here's an example of a good CBET goal:

Condition: Given social skills instruction in an evidence-based curriculum and role play,
Behavior: Joseph will make comments that contribute to group discussion.
Evaluation Methods: As evidenced by a positive tone of voice, language, and volume, Joseph should give feedback or make requests each class period. Mastery is 9 of 10 periods with no prompting, based on the teacher and student rating per day, or 90% of checklist completed for each time he makes a comment, with interval recording two times a week.
Timeline: By the end of the semester.

Reading this goal, it is clear that the student is working on making comments to others. It also is clear that the mastery of the goal can occur after role-play and practice. This, the condition statement, can be used to drive an intervention. The mastery criteria include a checklist, with interval recording of data per week. Or, the mastery criteria can include the use of a tracking system for the targeted behavior.

Condition: Given a separate space in an adjoining classroom, cool-down time of up to 20 minutes, and verbal problem-solving with staff,
Behavior: Jillian will select and follow steps from graphic organizer for one solution to the problem.

Evaluation Methods: Within 10 minutes of returning to classroom, Jillian will follow all steps 4 out of 5 times, as indicated on a checklist that matches the graphic organizer. *Timeline:* By the end of the month.

It is clear from this goal that Jillian needs to work on taking a break before reacting, and that to meet the goal, she will follow through on steps after problem solving with a favorite staff member. The goal also makes it clear that teachers should use a graphic organizer and checklist as visual cues. Graphic organizers and checklists can be used to measure progress over time, help the child visualize expectations, communicate with parents, and provide a multisensory way of problem solving. The goals can inform the teaching of the skill, including the activities that will be used to measure progress. Most of all, however, the goals tell the parents and staff what behaviors to expect, and what data sources will used to monitor and evaluate progress.

Part 6: Accommodation, modification, supplementary aides, and services. What is good teaching to some is considered accommodation for others. In some classrooms and schools, all students receive extended time and ability to retake tests, while in other schools, extra time or ability to retake tests may be a testing accommodation. In the tools at the end of the chapter, the reader will find a reproducible resource that is designed to guide the selection of accommodation for both the classroom and for tests. Accommodations that are used in testing also should be used in the classroom. While considering accommodations in the context of the IEP, the reader also should consider that the same type and amount of accommodation can be recommended through the 504 Plan, discussed later in this chapter, or other plans developed by the school district. Tool 9.3 includes some ideas for accommodations in the classroom.

There are substantial differences between accommodation and modification. Accommodations do not change the curriculum, while modifications do change the amount, type, or nature of the curriculum. Accommodations should not necessarily change how a child is graded, but a modification may change the way a child is graded. When a child with EBD requires a different social or emotional curriculum such as instruction in social skills, this may be considered a modification to supplement the typical curriculum, or this may be considered an additional service, for example.

Accommodations include:

- variations on ways to present the curriculum;
- variations in how students respond;
- adaptation of the environment;
- adjustment of the timing of instruction or testing; and
- testing accommodations that do not change the content being tested, but support students in showing their knowledge of the content.

Modifications include:

- reduction or addition to the curriculum;
- identification of different grading practices to address the change of content;
- delivery of a different, reformatted, or adjusted demand for content; and
- a change in what the child is learning, or how she is assessed in the adjusted curriculum.

The definition of supplementary aides and services is broad and varies from child to child. IDEA notes that supplementary aides should be provided in regular education classes and in both extracurricular and nonacademic settings. Examples of supplementary aides and services include:

- dedicated adult aide;
- data collection on a daily basis;
- behavior supports;
- social skills instruction;
- assistive technology services;

- services needed for the child to progress in the curriculum, such as tutoring; and
- services that are different from related services as described in the next section.

There is an almost infinite list of supplementary aides and services needed by a child with a disability to meaningfully access the curriculum and make substantial progress.

Part 7 of the IEP: Related services. Related services are services a child needs to benefit from her special education program, including specially designed instruction to meet her unique needs. On the left side of Table 5, the named related service is listed. Some of these services use paraprofessionals or assistants. The IEP, through the decisions of the MDT, can specify the title and professional qualifications needed for the child to have FAPE.

On the right side of Table 5, general purposes of the related service providers are listed. Before agreeing to provide related services, the MDT will conduct an evaluation and recommend the service, usually after developing appropriate goals. When there is a professional organization that has different licensing criteria, the website is listed under the name of the service.

This list is not meant to be exhaustive; it is based on the listing of related services in IDEA. The listed services must be specified and provided as specified in the IEP.

Part 8 of the IEP: Consideration of special factors, including the BIP. The considerations of special factors part of the IEP must consider a child's need for Braille, communication needs, assistive technology devices and services, and the child's native language. Relevant to challenging behavior, this section requires the MDT to develop a BIP, and consider the need for FBA. In the tools section of this chapter, a number of accommodations, which also may be put into the BIP, are listed, and can be used by parents, students, and educators. A BIP should provide for "positive behavior supports and strategies" (IDEA,

Table 5

Related Services and Their Purposes

Related Service	General Purposes
Speech or language pathology (See http://www.asha.org)	For identification, diagnosis, or appraisal of communication disorders. For treatment or counseling for communication disorders. For pragmatic, or social, language disorders. For listening, following directions, or expressing oneself. For prevention of communication disorders.
Transportation	For travel to and from school, usually door to door.
Audiology services (http://www.asha.org)	For hearing loss or deafness.
Interpreting services	For transcription, signing for children who are deaf or hard of hearing, technological transcription, and special transcription for children who are deaf and blind.
Psychological services	For development of positive behavior supports and strategies, counseling, consultation, assessment, and training.
Physical therapy (http://www.apta.org)	For gross motor and other motor problems. For physical movement and activity.
Occupational therapy (http://www.aota.org)	For functional independence, through skills provided by a qualified occupational therapist. For preventing or limiting impairment of functional activities.
Transition services	For a coordinated set of activities to develop achievement and functional performance, to allow the child movement from school to postschool activities.
Travel training	For students with cognitive disabilities, who need instruction in awareness of the environment and how to get from place to place in the school or community.
Recreation; therapeutic recreation	For leisure skills assessment, leisure education, therapeutic recreation services, or recreation programs and services.
Early identification and assessment	For assurance that a plan to identify a child's disability is found and addressed as early as possible.
Social work services (http://www.socialworkers.org)	For counseling or other mental health direct or indirect services. Services provided by a licensed or otherwise qualified social worker.
School health services	For medication at school, collaboration with prescribing doctor, medical monitoring, or monitoring of medication effect in classroom, when nurse or other health professional is a required member of an MDT. Can be delivered by a nurse or other qualified personnel.
Counseling services	For guidance counseling, social skills counseling, or other counseling. Provided by social workers, guidance counselors, psychologists, or otherwise qualified professionals.

Table 5, continued

Related Service	General Purposes
Rehabilitation counseling	For restoring, remediating, or rehabilitating a skill lost by a disability, event, or condition.
Parent counseling and training	For helping parents understand the child's special needs, for instruction for parents about developmental (what is normal?) skills, and for skills the parents need to support the implementation of the IEP.
Orientation and mobility services	For students who are usually blind or visually impaired who need a special service to be oriented in the school or community, or help getting around the school, community, or job settings.
Medical services (http://www.ama-assn.org)	For evaluation of medical needs. Inserting, mapping, repairing, or managing a surgically implanted device is not included. Must be done by a medical professional, who is part of the MDT.
Vision services	For low vision, visual impairments, vision conditions, and blindness.

2004, p. 46683), and overall, IDEA calls for research-based, quality, peer-reviewed interventions and methods.

Behavioral intervention plan (BIP). The BIP must be based on a sound FBA. If the whole team, including the parent, has not engaged in the problem-solving process involved in the FBA as described in Chapter 7, a BIP should not be developed. A good BIP will answer the 5 W questions—who, what, when, where, why—and the 2 H questions—how, and how long, as summarized below:

- *Who?*: Persons responsible for actions by title and name.
- *What?*: What specific scientifically sound interventions will be provided?
- *When and by when?*: What days of the week, dates, or time periods will the "what" occur?
- *Where?*: Will the child be removed from the classroom to receive the service, and if so, to where?
- *Why?*: Which goals are being addressed by the intervention? Why is the intervention being considered?
- *How?*: How will the intervention be delivered? What are

the components of the intervention and how is instruction delivered?

- *How long?*: How long will the sessions last, for what duration? What date will the interventions be reviewed? What date will the interventions end, and how will we know their effect?

For whom should the BIP be developed? A BIP should be considered by the MDT any time a behavior interferes with a child's learning or his peers' learning. At any of the nine stages of the special education process, whether a child is eligible for special education or whether there are milder concerns from the classroom teacher, a BIP can be developed.

IDEA does not require a BIP, unless a child is being repeatedly suspended from school or removed from the classroom because of behavior. IDEA does, however, require that the child's behavior needs are met by interventions and strategies, when the behaviors are interfering with a child's learning or his peers' learning. It would be a mistake to conclude that the BIP (developed as a result of an FBA) is not required by IDEA in situations where discipline is not a concern. The law specifically mentions the BIP and FBA in its discipline sections, but FBA and analysis of a child's response to a BIP can and should be part of the whole evaluation process. The FBA and BIP can be useful tools for evaluation of a child in all areas of suspected disability, and to fully understand the nature of a child's needs (Von Ravensburg, 2006–2008). Nonetheless, Congress says that it makes "good sense" for an FBA and BIP to be developed for a child who needs it to receive a FAPE (IDEA, 2004, p. 46683).

A BIP should be written in a form and mode that the parent can understand, and should become a part of the child's existing IEP or 504 Plan, if one exists. A BIP also can stand alone, however, if the school chooses to use it with a child who is not yet eligible for the IEP or 504 Plan.

What does the BIP contain? Although there is no mandated format for the plan, there are widely understood best practices that should be followed when developing a BIP. A BIP should describe the following (IDEA, 2004):

- What the intervention will look like (i.e., its steps or procedures).
- What materials and/or resources are needed and whether these are available within existing resources.
- Roles and responsibilities with respect to intervention implementation (i.e., who will be responsible for running the intervention, preparing materials, etc.).
- The intervention schedule (i.e., how often, for how long, and at what times in the day?) and context (i.e., where, and with whom?).
- How the intervention and its outcomes will be monitored (i.e., what measures, by whom, and on what schedule?) and analyzed (i.e., compared to what criterion?).

Part 9 of the IEP: Extended school year and extended school day services. In times that schools are not in session, students with disabilities may need extended school year (ESY) services, so that a break in school does not cause the student to regress, or prevent the child from retaining skills or acquiring skills in the future. States have different requirements for the criteria for eligibility for ESY services, but the state requirements cannot limit the services globally defined by IDEA. There have been many legal actions related to ESY (Kraft, 2000). Some of the earliest cases involve students with emotional disturbance, where parents have successfully advocated that the standard (180 day) school year is not enough to adequately address a child's needs. In fact, in many states, one factor that makes a child eligible for ESY services is the child's interfering behaviors. Other factors include the nature and severity of the child's disability, regression risk with a break from school, emerging skills that must be continued or will be lost, whether the IEP goals relate to critical life skills, or general special circumstances. Table 6 shows the IDEA requirements for ESY services (Florida State Department of Education, 2002; IDEA, 2004).

Table 6

IDEA Requirements for ESY Services

ESY Services Should Be:	ESY Services Should Not Be:
Individually determined	The same for all students
Determined by the MDT to provide FAPE	Limiting to any disability category
Provided in the least restrictive environment (LRE)	Only in the summertime

Part 10 of the IEP: Placement in the least restrictive setting. In an ideal world, all students with learning or behavioral differences would be with their peers in neighborhood schools. In this ideal world every student would be able to have an individualized education and schools would be flexible enough to create a personalized learning environment for all. Unfortunately, most schools create programs for the general population—for the majority of students who are assumed to learn well in a large-group setting. Not all students benefit from this group-oriented process. Some students will only progress if their individual needs are considered and very intensive services are provided in a very intensive setting. For example, a student who becomes highly distracted or anxious in large groups might need a smaller environment with reduced distraction to be able to concentrate. Similarly, a student who has frequent outbursts or has trouble utilizing language to communicate his or her needs might need more frequent decoding by an adult or positive interaction with a teacher.

The majority of children and youth with emotional and behavioral difficulties are educated in their neighborhood schools (Newman, Wagner, Cameto, & Knokey, 2009). Greater than 80% of students with EBD are served in general education classes with a mix of specialized instruction and related services like counseling, psychological services, speech and language therapy, and crisis intervention services. Students whose behavior becomes unmanageable in the comprehensive school are removed to alternative settings, private therapeutic day programs, and in rare instances (less than 5% of students with EBD), residential treatment centers.

Students with emotional or behavioral challenges may need accommodation in the general education environment in order to make progress academically and socially. Or, students with EBD may require a placement in a setting that is removed from the general classroom. Services delivered through a continuum of services are not only required by IDEA (see Section 300.115 of the legislation), but they are necessary to serve kids with challenging behaviors in the neighborhood school. Figure 15 shows a continuum of placements that may be considered by schools. Unfortunately, most districts are set up so that a child who needs a smaller setting must be placed in another school to meet his unique needs. Although different options for placement may have benefits, the MDT is required to consider potential harmful effects of a placement. The following sections discuss the various placement options for students with EBD and also detail the promises and the potential pitfalls of each option.

The standard for removing a child from the general education setting to the special education setting, where all students have educational disabilities, is unique to each child. A child whose needs cannot be met through services and accommodation may be removed from the general classroom; some students may require a special school placement. Some students absolutely require removal from the general education setting to special education or a residential setting. Many of the special education settings in the school systems do not serve the needs of all students with behavior or conduct problems, so decisions must be made per individual child, with understanding of the resources, methods, philosophies, and procedures of the school district.

General education environments. In recent years, parents, professionals, and policy makers have attempted to better include students with all learning, cognitive, physical, and behavioral differences in their neighborhood schools and in typical classrooms. The law mandates that students be educated in the least restrictive environment (LRE) available and many states have quickly moved to eliminate

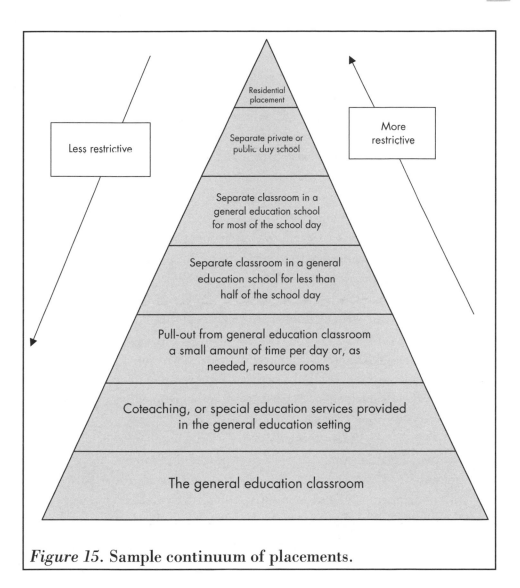

Figure 15. Sample continuum of placements.

separate classrooms for students with disabilities. For example, some school districts have declared themselves an all-inclusive school district and plan to individualize for students with disabilities and differences within each general education school building. Additionally, with the advent of movements such as Response to Intervention (RtI), interventions should be tried and recorded in general education as soon as a need is detected.

Promises. Including all students in one system has many benefits. First and foremost, one public system for all helps ensure the civil rights of people with differences. In other words, students with disabilities are exposed to the same learning options and opportunities as other students and are not relegated to trailers, basements, or a second-class parallel system. In general education, all students are exposed to the county's curriculum and have the opportunity to excel. Inclusive environments also help students with differences make friends and feel like typical members of society.

Responsible inclusion demands that school systems prepare staff to accommodate and modify instruction to meet the needs of students with differences and use data to track the progress of students who are learning in a larger group setting. Programs that successfully include students with disabilities in general education have excellent coteaching between a general education teacher and a special education teacher, have a data collection and evaluation system that can help track the progress of students so that all know when more intensive instruction or intervention is needed, and provide intensive remediation services when needed.

Potential pitfalls. Although the concept of inclusion is a correct one, the practice of inclusion has a series of potential pitfalls. When staff are untrained to meet the needs of diverse learners and are expected to still maintain large classrooms, students with challenges often have their needs unmet. Students with behavioral challenges spend a great deal of time in isolation or away from the general education class. In these circumstances they are away from the general education environment and are with assistants or administrators who may or may not be trained in education or in special education. Untrained personnel tend to rely on punishment and exclusion rather than develop individual plans. Students with behavioral challenges rarely have friends and often are marginalized socially without purposeful intervention by teachers and administrators. Just being exposed to their general education peers is not enough. In fact, at the high school level more students with behavioral challenges are dropping out (Newman et al., 2009).

Special programs or self-contained classrooms. Students receiving intensive special education and related services were historically taught in self-contained classes in which only students with disabilities were served. These children traveled together as a group to lunch and to their elective classes. This type of programming exists today only for students with the most severe disabilities. The majority of children with disabilities who are served in public schools spend some percentage of their school day with nondisabled students. Some students require the consistency, routine, and managed sensory environment of small classrooms to be successful. Students who require a full day of special education and related service are placed in separate wings or stand-alone buildings. A child may receive 100% of his education with other children with disabilities or may receive part of his daily education in the special education setting.

Promises. Perhaps the biggest benefit for special classes is the amount of staff attention and support given to each individual student. Because of the small class size, teachers and school staff can be more flexible in meeting academic and social goals and can modify instruction more easily. In addition, special classes also can allow a break from a more traditional approach to learning in order to meet the unique mental health needs of students.

Potential pitfalls. Unfortunately, special classes that only serve students with disabilities also have some potential problems. In a specialized school or a self-contained classroom, the staff often are not focused first on academics and can oversimplify lessons and "water" down the general education content. Sometimes students with disabilities are not receiving the same exposure to grade-level content as other students. Although this is not true of all specialized settings, many school systems are trying to downsize self-contained classrooms.

Residential treatment centers or therapeutic boarding schools. Approximately 3%–5% of children with EBD are placed in residential treatment centers. A residential treatment center is a facility that provides 24-hour care for children. They may be locked or unlocked. Students are placed in these facilities in one of four ways:

- The local school system, through an IEP team process, determines that the child requires 24-hour instruction in order to make progress on the IEP.
- The local school system may partner with another agency to provide residential placement. Agencies such as the Department of Social Services, Department of Juvenile Justice, or the local mental health department agrees to pay for the residential component of the program.
- The child is court-ordered into residential treatment. In this case, the local department of juvenile justice is usually responsible for funding and managing the child's placement.
- Parents/guardians may elect to privately place their children in a residential treatment center.

Residential treatment centers are departmentalized institutions of care that provide intensive, structured programming 24 hours per day, 7 days per week, and 365 days per year. The quality of these programs varies widely. Within 24 hours of admission, an Individualized Treatment Plan (ITP) may be developed. Children are assigned to treatment teams consisting of a psychiatrist, licensed social worker, and nursing, residential, and education staff. The constellation of staffing will vary from facility to facility. This team monitors the student's progress on a frequent basis. Staff to student ratio rarely exceeds four students to one staff member. Two staff are assigned to each classroom. Programs are therapy-integrated, which means that individual and group therapy occur during the school day and all staff is trained regarding the use of therapeutic language, positive behavior supports, and behavior management techniques, including the judicious use of passive physical and chemical restraint, if necessary.

Promises. Programs that serve children with EBD can be therapeutic for students and their families. Healing takes time and is invisible. Creative programming and opportunities to participate in the community are important features of any program that works with children with EBD. Staff who are prepared to work specifically with students with behavioral challenges can look beyond the behavior to the child underneath. Through relationship and consistency, residential treatment centers can reach the most troubled children through an all-encompassing intervention approach. Some programs offer therapeutic horseback riding, outdoor adventure programming, therapeutic recreation, and community service experiences in addition to excellent teaching. Residential treatment centers also use positive behavior supports and sophisticated clinical interventions to give students opportunities to be normal and escape from patterns of problem solving that have not been productive.

Potential pitfalls. The residential treatment center industry has been highly scrutinized over the past 15 years. Parents agree to have their children placed in these facilities during times of great stress; they are relieved to have their children in a contained environment and to take a break from the daily stress and conflict that accompany children and families who are in crisis. Nationally, there have been many problems associated with residential treatment center care. Serious student and staff injuries, poorly managed medication administration, and poor quality custodial care are some of the issues plaguing the industry. In order for a residential treatment center to receive federal funding, it must be approved by the Joint Commission (formerly known as the Joint Commission for the Accreditation of Healthcare Organizations or JCAHO). School programs affiliated with residential treatment centers are approved by the state department of education within the state that they are located. These entities require intense compliance regarding a multitude of regulations. They do not provide quality assurance monitoring. Each entity has rigorous compliance standards. Complaints and findings of investigations are available to the public under the Freedom of Information Act.

The 504 Plan

Section 504 is so named because it relates to the 504th Section of the Rehabilitation Act of 1973. Both a 504 Plan and an IEP should assure that a child is receiving a free appropriate public education. There can be many other similarities between IEPs and 504 Plans (see Figure 16). This is because there are no set requirements for what the 504 Plan should contain. The 504 Plan can contain any of the above-described parts of the IEP. The tools at the end of this chapter on possible accommodations can be used for ideas when developing the 504 Plan. What goes into the 504 Plan is up to the MDT. The scope of evidence-based methods or accommodations possible in the 504 Plan includes:

- regular education,
- special education,
- related services,
- necessary accommodations,
- modifications, and
- supplementary aides and services.

An individual student plan can take the form of an Individualized Education Plan, 504 Plan, or informal plan created by the school. A Behavior Intervention Plan should accompany these, as we have discussed in this chapter. In the upcoming chapters, we discuss how all aspects of the individual child must be considered, including biological and neurological factors. In the development of an effective plan for school success, the MDT should consider the factors explored in the next three chapters—brain factors, biological factors, and medical factors—so the child is seen as a whole person and all of his needs are met for school success.

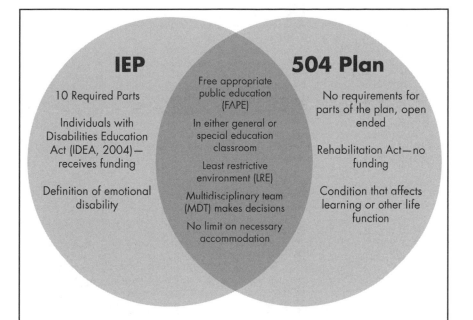

IEP

10 Required Parts

Individuals with
Disabilities Education
Act (IDEA, 2004)—
receives funding

Definition of emotional
disability

Free appropriate
public education
(FAPE)

In either general or
special education
classroom

Least restrictive
environment (LRE)

Multidisciplinary team
(MDT) makes decisions

No limit on necessary
accommodation

504 Plan

No requirements for
parts of the plan, open
ended

Rehabilitation Act—no
funding

Condition that affects
learning or other life
function

Figure 16. Comparing the IEP and 504 Plan.

Tool 9.1
Individual Plan Worksheet

Parents and educators work together toward common goals when components of student plans are well defined and documented. This worksheet can be used before, during, or after MDT meetings to structure questions, discussion, and sharing of information. The first column lists the elements required in an individual student plan. The middle column should be used to document those aspects of the student's plan, and the last column is used to keep track of things to do before, during, and after the MDT meeting.

Individual Plans Should:	Documentation:	To-Do:
Be based on proper evaluation of behavior, including FBA	List date of evaluations used, and description:	To-do list and who is responsible:
Include scientifically based, or at least evidence-based, positive behavior supports, methods, and interventions	List evidence basis or scientifically based research, including name of intervention and description: List strategies, and under what conditions strategies are effective: List methods and instructional methods:	Follow up and to-do list, including persons responsible:
Be multimodal, both proactive and reactive	Proactive interventions and strategies: Reactive interventions and strategies:	To-do and who:

Individual Plans Should:	Documentation:	To-Do:
Include specific present levels of performance	Strengths: Needs:	To-do list and follow up:
Assure instruction for emotional and behavioral skills or social skills is based on a curriculum	Name the curricula here, including websites to the curricula, usually available at the state or district websites: Include social skills curricula or emotional and behavioral skills curricula:	To-do or notes:
Define goals, along with or in conjunction with the IEP goals, if any	Refer to IEP goals: If no IEP, write goals:	Draft goals here:
Be individualized Involve parents	Parent involvement? Best way to communicate?	Notes:

Individual Plans Should:	Documentation:	To-Do:
Incorporate how progress will be monitored, and include data collection tools	See Chapter 6 for a list of formal and informal evaluation tools.	Notes or to-do:
Include meaningful accommodations	See Tool 9.3 for suggestions and ideas.	List accommodations or refer to 504 Plan or IEP:
Consider necessary related or supplementary services, including assistive technology	Related services: Supplementary aides and services, if any: Assistive technology, if any:	Notes and to-do:
Be meaningful to the child and include parents	List how the child will be involved in the development and implementation of the plan: If appropriate, list child's future goals, after school:	Notes:

Tool 9.2
Checklist for Parents

Place a check mark next to the items you as a parent have considered, and circle those to discuss with a school-based professional or other expert:

❏   Am I asking for services first, without understanding the process that drives the agreement for services, or without the team first recognizing the need in that area?

❏   Am I aware of my rights for consent, that my input does not automatically "trump" the other members of the MDT?

❏   Am I assuming that the recommendations from evaluation reports, especially reports that I paid for, will be incorporated into the program?

❏   Do I understand the information in evaluations prior to meeting with the school team, or am I expecting services before evaluations are complete?

❏   Am I reading and understanding the paperwork that is used in the school meetings and afterschool meetings?

❏   Am I continually interacting with teachers and all staff and involved with my child's school and classroom? Am I avoiding meeting with the team only once per year?

❏   Have I requested data, and do I understand how data will be collected? Am I keeping a portfolio or running record of my concerns?

❏   Do I avoid being either being "best friends" or "worst enemies" with the MDT members (making it personal)?

❏   Do I need help understanding the process for developing a plan? Are there people with special knowledge of my child who I can bring to the meetings where plans are developed? Can I arrange for the private therapist or doctor to participate in the school meetings and document recommendations in written reports?

❏   Have I put my concerns in writing before and after the school team meetings?

Tool 9.3
Possible Accommodations for Kids With Challenging Behavior

Timing

- Extend time
- Allow completion over several days
- Adjust the order of tasks or tests

Presentation

- Read aloud; indicate full text or partial text. Include use of technology that reads aloud
- Enlarge print or clear print for reading material
- Teach underlining and highlighting skills
- Pair oral with visual cues
- Give one direction at a time and check understanding
- Simplify language used in directions
- Shorten directions
- Break down directions in bullet form
- Repeat directions
- Ask student to paraphrase or repeat direction

Environment

- Limit or structure visuals posted on walls
- Label materials clearly in organized fashion
- Limit group noise
- Be aware of lighting changes
- Provide visually clear worksheets
- Small-group testing

- Test individually
- Specify reduced ratio staff to student
- Give preferential seating: front, near teacher, away from noisy machines, away from distracting peers, near study buddy
- Increase distance between desks

Product

- Shorten assignment expectation
- Adjust workload: fewer problems, more practice problems, more enrichment, eliminate or reduce homework, specify time to work on homework
- Break long-term or multistep tasks into component parts
- Allow alternate product such as oral presentation of an essay, PowerPoint presentation, web-based product, illustrations
- Adapt assignment to minimize writing (e.g., circle, cross out, write above line)
- Allow student to orally dictate, with human scribe, recorder, or technology

Process

- Establish routines and subroutines for structure and consistency
- Provide visual schedule or written routines
- Prepare child for changes in routine by practice, modeling, and discussion
- Put student first in line
- Give student a job between transitions
- Provide closer supervision during transitions
- Establish, teach, model, and post expectations
- Provide movement breaks after or during seated work periods
- Limit or remove distractions from tabletop and desktop
- Shorten work periods

Content and Study Skills

- Provide outline, syllabus, and study guides in advance of tests
- Allow open-notes or open-book tests
- Test one skill at a time
- Adjusted notetaking, use alternate forms for notes (e.g., fill in the blank, circle)
- Give student peer copy of notes
- Give student teacher copy of notes
- Limit copying from board or texts

Organization

- Spend time with student each period organizing materials
- Check homework and review mistakes individually
- Allow assignments to be e-mailed

Giftedness and Strengths

- Use adjusted questioning techniques
- Use areas of interest and strength to relate to task or curriculum
- Give child chances for leadership

Grading

- Do not downgrade for handwriting or spelling
- Permit extra credit assignments
- Permit re-revision after feedback
- Specify if effort is graded; whether student graded compared with himself, peers, or both; and how a parent should understand the grading

chapter 10

The Brain and Behavior

I N this chapter we will address a simple question: What does the brain have to do with behavior? The answer is simple as well: The brain has everything to do with behavior! That is, all behavior is controlled or mediated by the brain. The brain, in turn, is shaped by genetics and the environment. To make the matter more complex, we also must consider a child's motivation, desire, and will.

Educational recognition of the role of the brain on behavior, what we will call neurobiology, has not always been the case. For much of the latter 20th century our school-based interventions were too often been based upon a simple behavioral model of antecedent-behavior-consequence (ABC Model). Unfortunately, this model remains a primary tool used in schools. Any analysis of behavior, as we discussed in Chapter 7, should include a full analysis that includes neurobiological factors.

Myth	Truth
Early brain injuries or prematurity are of little concern by the time a child reaches school-age years.	Such conditions are likely to ripple through a child's development and may have a substantial impact on learning skills, emotional regulation, and psychological functions.
Psychological trauma by abuse or neglect early in life does not affect the structure or physiology of the brain.	Recent studies suggest that exposure to such trauma may alter the chemical and structural development of the brain, increasing the risk for behavioral and emotional difficulties.
The brain has reached its physical maturity around the age of 16.	The brain's physical development continues well into our mid-20s.
Sleep for teenagers is a relative factor with little relation to academic performance.	Teens who get the least amount of sleep get lower grades than teens who get more sleep.
Students with emotional and behavioral disorders can be accurately diagnosed using new neuroimaging techniques.	Not yet! Although these tools have been remarkably useful in studying the brain and unlocking important relationships, they have not reached a level of reliability and validity to be used as a diagnostic tool on an individual student.
The wiring of the brain is generally complete at birth and remains fixed throughout our lives. You get what you got!	Cells that fire together wire together. The brain is the only organ incomplete at birth. It is dependent on input from the environment to complete its development. The brain learns what it does. This has positive and negative implications for children. For example, repeated practicing of a skill will substantially strengthen the neural network supporting that skill. Failure to practice a skill or engage in a particular activity will weaken networks that support that activity. This seems fairly obvious but merits important consideration with regard to emotional factors. If a child is permitted to remain anxious for extended periods of time, will the brain wire itself for greater anxiety? Will a student who practices evidence-based self-calming or anxiety management strategies become increasingly more effective at managing anxiety? The brain reaps what it sows.

Myth	Truth
Depression and anxiety are emotional problems, not cognitive problems, and, therefore, do not merit the same academic services or accommodations as those employed with students identified with learning or attention disorders.	Although depression and anxiety are certainly classified as emotional disorders, the neurobiology of depression and anxiety directly impact multiple areas of cognitive functioning. All symptom descriptions of depression and anxiety include features such as diminished attention, diminished concentration, diminished working memory, lack of initiation, or slowed processing speed.
Nonpharmacological interventions do not impact the biology and structure of the brain.	Interventions such as placement in a therapeutic educational environment, counseling, research-based academic instruction, and physical movement all have the capacity to change the neural architecture and function of the brain. The biological immaturity of the adolescent brain is as much of an advantage as it is a disadvantage.

This chapter will address the following questions:
- What basic assumptions regarding brain and behavior can be derived from recent research?
- What is the structure of the brain, and what parts are responsible for behavior?
- What do neuroimaging studies tell us?
- What is neurofeedback, and what are neurofeedback interventions?
- What is the role of diet, exercise, and sleep in regulating behavior?
- How can parents and family members contribute to school success for children with EBD?

A distinction between physical and mental disorders can become clear by the example of two 14-year-old girls attending the same local high school.

Kelly has been diagnosed with Acute Lymphocytic Leukemia. Her physical disorder, a blood cancer, resulted in the need for complex treatment regimens, including chemotherapy and radiation therapy, which impacted cognition; periods of time away from school in order to provide both treatment and control of secondary symptoms; and difficulty learning new material because of both the disease's process and the negative side effects of treatment. The high school's response to this young lady was quite remarkable. She was routinely assisted by her classmates in making sure that she received all appropriate notes, materials, and due dates. The faculty was generous in allowing her to make up missed work and provided a number of formal accommodations, including extended time on tests and tutorial support. Finally, the school, as a community, held a fundraiser for the young woman in their school's gymnasium, which included the opportunity for individuals to make donations to the family and The Leukemia & Lymphoma Society. Students organizing the bake sale even wore her picture on their T-shirts!

Contrast this with Lindsay's situation. She too had missed many days of school in order to manage her illness in an inpatient setting. She too required a complex medication regimen that often resulted in difficulties with sustained attention, alertness, and memory. This same school's response to this young woman, however, was markedly different. She received no accommodations or modifications in her class work. Classmates were reluctant to help her and often treated her as a pariah. She was, in many ways, made peripheral to her community and left to the margin. This young woman had been diagnosed with a bipolar disorder, which included suicidal behavior, multiple hospitalizations, missed school, and a complex psychopharmacological treatment regimen.

Disparate responses of two young women with well-known, biologically mediated disease processes that impacted their physiology, cognition, learning, and overall health status show that stigmas are still attached to people with emotional and behavioral disorders.

Basic Assumptions

When it comes to emotional disorders, oppositional behavior, or challenging behaviors, many look toward deficits in will or motivation as driving causes. Such assumptions may yield moral judgments about a student's behavior, limited empathy, and frustration among educators, parents, and caregivers. Sometimes our reactions to challenging behavior are based upon incomplete or misguided assumptions and may leave youngsters feeling diminished, misunderstood, or helpless.

Educators seem to be increasingly aware of brain-behavior relationships and are becoming more effective in applying such research to problems such as learning disorders, Attention Deficit/Hyperactivity Disorder (ADHD), and chronic illnesses. But educators want effective interventions that are easy to use. Educators, program development specialists, and administrators seem less sure of how to make use of expanding neuroscience knowledge for youngsters with challenging behaviors. There still exists a research gap between research and practice. Some basic assumptions of brain-behavior relations have been uncovered or clarified by recent neuroscience research, as shown in Figure 17.

Brain Structures

Although an in-depth discussion of brain anatomy is beyond the scope of this book, it is important to consider structures key to the regulation of behavior and emotions.

The Cerebrum

The cerebrum is the largest portion of the brain and consists of two hemispheres connected together by the corpus callosum, the brain's largest white matter tract. The cerebrum often is divided into four lobes: frontal, temporal, parietal, and occipital. Each lobe or area is connected to other structures but maintains a degree of regional specificity or responsibility for more specific functions. The cerebrum's surface, the neocortex, is convoluted into hundreds of folds, called sulci and gyri, which help to maximize surface area. The neocortex is where higher brain functions take place.

- *Neuroimaging and Research*: Recent technological advances in neuroimaging have been critical in unlocking the relationship between brain and behavior.

- *Brain Changes and Matures*: Neurodevelopmental maturation proceeds in an orderly manner and underlies and drives changes in behavior, cognition, and emotions.

- *Early Intervention*: Early life's stressful experiences may permanently impair regions of the brain responsible for emotional and behavioral control, predisposing the student to later-life neurobehavioral deficits.

- *Stress*: Severe early stress induced by deprivation and abuse is not only environmentally, but biologically, related to later emotional and behavioral difficulties.

- *Executive Functioning*: Skills such as moral reasoning, impulse control, judgment, and motivation are directly subject to the biological maturation of the prefrontal cortex or the brain's executive control center.

- *Adolescents*: The adolescent brain is not structurally or functionally comparable to the competent adult brain.

- *Plasticity*: The brain maintains tremendous plasticity throughout its course of development. Plasticity is the brain's capacity to change and compensate based on input or intervention from the environment. Plasticity remains robust well into the third decade of life.

Figure 17. **Basic assumptions about the brain.**

The Frontal Lobes and Prefrontal Cortex

The frontal region is typically associated with executive functions. Executive functions are a set of cognitive processes supporting self-control, inhibitory skills, planning, and organization. The prefrontal cortex is involved with reasoning, judgment, self-control, complex learning, aspects of motor function, and mood regulation. The frontal lobes and more specifically, the prefrontal cortex, are regarded as critical structures in one's capacity to guide and direct behavior, regulate the expression of emotion, set goals, and execute plans.

Humans have exceptionally large frontal lobes compared to other

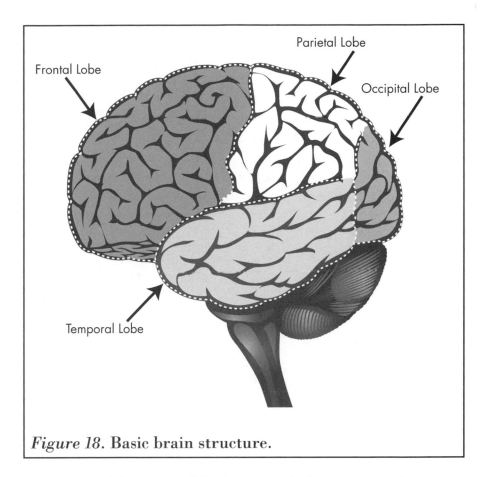

Figure 18. Basic brain structure.

organisms. This region of the brain was the latest to arrive from an evolutionary standpoint, last to develop from an individual standpoint, and vulnerable to many environmental risks. Neurodevelopmental disorders and injuries to the prefrontal cortex or frontal lobes may result in significant cognitive and mental changes. In many cases, early damage to these structures may not be evident until adolescence, when such structures are called into action. The frontal lobes are considered the seat of our personality and overall social, emotional, and cognitive navigational system. Figure 18 shows the various lobes of the brain.

The Limbic System

Emotions are an extremely complex brain function. The emotional core of the brain is the limbic system. This region has direct connections with memory structures, the olfactory bulb, the hypothalamus, and the prefrontal cortex. Mood and personality characteristics are mediated through the prefrontal cortex and the limbic system. This brain system is comprised of several key structures including the hippocampus, amygdala, thalamic nuclei, and fornix. The limbic system has direct connections to the endocrine system and the autonomic nervous system.

Motor Cortex

The motor portion of the cerebrum can be divided into the premotor cortex and the primary motor area. Both are located in the frontal region. The premotor cortex is responsible for repetitive motions of learned motor skills, while the primary motor area is responsible for control of skeletal muscles. Different areas of the brain are associated with the movement of different parts of the body. Injury to the motor cortex can result in motor disturbance in the associated part of the body.

Neuroimaging

Neuroimaging is a term used to describe a number of techniques used to study the anatomy and function of the brain.

CT Scan

Prior to the development of the computed tomography (CT scan) in 1972, our techniques for brain study were somewhat crude and less sophisticated. We learned from dissection, missile injuries (often related to war), autopsy, and by studying people who had suffered strokes or some other brain-related malady.

The CT scan allowed researchers to view the brain without surgery. With the advent of the CT scan, scientists and researchers were able to correlate a damaged area with a human behavior. Since the advent of the CT scan, there has been a rapid development of many other imaging techniques. These techniques are unlocking answers to questions regarding behavior, cognition, and emotion. These techniques also are raising important new questions regarding self-control, responsibility, and culpability.

Other Tools

Functional neuroimaging remains an investigative tool and has been integral in investigating and understanding the relationship between brain, brain structure, brain function, and mood and behavioral health disorders. Science proceeds in an uneven course marked by rapid advances and periods of slow progress. Technological innovations often drive periods of steep progress. The development and refinement of neuroimaging tools has fueled our current boom in understanding the relationship of brain to behavior. It is our hope that this knowledge will create a shift in our understanding and education of students with challenging behaviors.

At present, functional neuroimaging is not endorsed as a technique for individual diagnosis or treatment planning.

Neuroimaging Studies and Aggression

Several studies have indicated decreased prefrontal glucose metabolism on PET scans in persons with impulsive aggression related to control subjects. Raine and colleagues described brain metabolism of a group of 41 violent criminals in 1997. The violent criminals had decreased activity in the prefrontal lobes and increased activation in the right amygdala compared to their controls. Murderers who had committed impulsive, affectively driven crimes showed the greatest reduction of prefrontal metabolism whereas predatory murderers with proactive, planned aggression did not.

In cases of juvenile delinquency, Ishikawa and Raine (2002) have indicated that autonomic underarousal and antisocial behaviors have been linked to deficits in the orbital frontal cortex in several areas of the prefrontal cortex, anterior cingulate, hypothalamus, and amygdala. This underarousal may be an uncomfortable psychophysiological state that predisposes one to antisocial behavior by encouraging the individual to seek out stimulation in an effort to boost the psychophysiological arousal (Raine et al., 1997).

Researchers also found that dysfunction in this prefrontal cortex may interfere with the ability to use emotional memory to guide current behavior based on the anticipation of future consequences (Damasio, 1994). Such impairment could result in chronic antisocial behavior or repetitive violence by impeding the development of a social conscience.

The Brain and Behavior

What causes behavior and what brain factors are most important? To what extent should children and adolescents be responsible for such behavior? Is a child of any age responsible for her behavior? The following sections look at the confluence of brain and behavior.

Behavioral Disorders and Aggression

Neurobiology plays an important role in all emotional and behavioral disorders. Of particular interest, however, is aggressive behavior because it affects the rights and safety of others (Pliszka, 2003). There is likely not to be found a single gene or biological cause for antisocial behavior. However, there is a growing body of research indicating that neurobiological factors play an important role in the development of both aggression and antisocial behavior. Antisocial behavior may be diagnosed as Conduct Disorder or antisocial personality disorder in early adult life (see the next chapter for a discussion on diagnoses). This disorder is characterized by behavior that violates the rights of others such as stealing, property destruction, physical aggression, lying, and sexual offenses, and also may include criminal activity.

ADHD With Conduct Disorder

Several studies have indicated that ADHD, when combined with familial stressors and learning differences, is highly predictive of delinquent behavior during the teenage years (Loeber, Burke, Lahey, Winters, & Zera, 2000). In youngsters with ADHD without Conduct Disorder, only 3.4% were classified as "multiple offenders" while 20.7% of adolescents with Conduct Disorder, but no history of ADHD, were multiple offenders. In the comorbid group of ADHD/Conduct Disorder youngsters, nearly ⅓ (30.8%) had committed multiple crimes. A number of neurobiological factors have been implicated in the study of impulsive and aggressive behavior. Studies have examined the role of serotonin, an excitatory neurotransmitter, and suggest that there may be a developmental aspect of serotonin's role in aggressive behavior.

In 2007, Shaw and colleagues at National Institute of Mental Health compared the scans of 446 children with and without ADHD. The brains of the children with ADHD developed normally, but lagged behind their typically developing peers by about 3 years. This cortical immaturity may be reflected in the behavior of such youngsters. Many parents describe their ADHD adolescents as less mature than their non-ADHD peers and less effective in executing control of their emotions and behaviors. Such youngsters are at increased risk for EBD as a consequence.

Family Environment, Brain, and Behavior

With regard to developmental models, the interaction of early family environmental risk factors disrupts both the socialization process and the maturation of frontal gray and white matter. This disruption may contribute to the child's failure to learn to inhibit impulses and/or decreased responsiveness to discipline. The failure to internalize and act according to social norms may lead to peer rejection, foster the development with delinquent peer groups, adversely affect school performance, and result in disregard for authority and socially normative behavior (Ishikawa & Raine, 2003). Repetitive engagement of antisocial behavior with little consequence during the postadolescent decrease in gray matter and increase in white matter may actually facilitate or wire the persistence of antisocial behavior into adulthood by strengthening the neural connections subserving such behavior.

Early Intervention

Birth Through Preschool Years—"The Magic Years"

Much has been written of the magic of the first 3 years of life in recent times. Magazine covers parade each new study calling for classical music, math, foreign languages, and exquisite mobiles for our cribs. Surely, there is some truth to these pronouncements, but the real take-home points may be found in the less sensational findings. Here's what we know:

1. early mother/caregiver interactions are important in developing self-calming skills;
2. a rich sensory environment favors more positive development; and
3. alcohol, stress, and instability are not good for the brain.

We are born with more cellular connections or synapses in the brain than we need. Early development of the brain is a process of pruning unused connections and strengthening those that are used. There are cortical windows of time in which youngsters are especially sensitive to select experiences. These windows of opportunity are more tightly defined for basic processing such as vision or sensation. Language has a broader window and executive functions mature throughout the first two decades of our lives.

Common Early Risk Factors for EBD

Self-calming and attachment. Self-calming has a cortical window that can be markedly disrupted by early deprivation, neglect, or abuse. Infants begin to develop self-calming skills shortly after birth while in the arms of their mothers. Caregivers use voice, movement, scent, and song to sooth. These actions help shape and carve neural networks for future use. Children with environmental deprivation often are exposed to less sights, sounds, color, language, touch, or exploration than normal youngsters. Their brains may be anatomically smaller than typically developing children.

Violence and abuse. Infants exposed to violence and abuse may show physical symptoms of fear in response to subsequent stressors. Such youngsters often demonstrate a different physiology marked by higher resting heart rates, higher cortisol levels, and problematic sleep patterns, suggesting underlying neurodevelopmental anomalies.

Intrauterine alcohol exposure. Intrauterine substance exposure is a well-documented risk factor for infants and is related to subsequent neurodevelopmental disorders. At present, there is no known safe amount of alcohol to drink while pregnant, so there doesn't appear to be a safe time to drink during pregnancy. Fetal Alcohol Spectrum Disorders (FASD) are a range of disorders that can be caused by prenatal exposure to alcohol or the mother's consumption of alcohol during pregnancy. The most severe of these disorders is Fetal Alcohol Syndrome (FAS). Fetal Alcohol Syndrome is the leading known preventable cause of birth defects, intellectual limitations, and behavioral disorders. The Centers for Disease Control and Prevention (CDC) studies estimated that Fetal Alcohol Syndrome prevalence rates range from 0.2 to 1.5 per 1,000 live births and Fetal Alcohol Spectrum Disorders are thought to occur three times as often as FAS (Sampson et al., 1997). Children with known FASD should be considered at significant risk for subsequent emotional and behavioral disorders. Figure 19 summarizes some of the common symptoms and difficulties associated with this problem.

Prematurity. Premature birth has become a much recognized and studied risk factor for children. The survival of very preterm (VPT) and very low birth weight (VLBW) infants has greatly increased in recent decades (Hack & Faranoff, 1999). Infants born very preterm are at an

- Small stature

- Facial abnormalities

- Coordination difficulties

- Hyperactivity

- Learning disabilities

- Cognitive limitations

- Developmental delays

- Sleep disturbance

- Poor impulse control or judgment

Figure 19. **Common symptoms and difficulties associated with Fetal Alcohol Syndrome.**

increased risk for perinatal brain injury and long-term behavioral and cognitive difficulties. A number of studies have examined lingering academic and executive function deficits in children born very preterm. These deficits persist well into the third decade of life. Executive functions appear to be particularly vulnerable to prematurity. As discussed in earlier chapters, executive functions often mitigate or aggravate the expression of an EBD. Hence, it is quite common to find deficits in executive functioning in many youngsters identified with behavioral disorders.

Children born prematurely were four times more likely to have emotional or behavioral problems in one study (Johnson et al., 2009). Thirty-one percent of preterm children were described as hyperactive compared to 9% in the full-term group. Thirty-three percent displayed problems with attention compared to 7% in the full-term group. Boys were more likely to evidence behavioral problems while girls experienced more internalizing emotional difficulties such as anxiety and depression.

Risk Factors in Childhood

Postnatal brain injury and traumatic brain injury. Postnatal brain injury is an injury to the brain that occurs after birth. Such injuries may occur as a result of falls, striking the head on an object, or the head being struck by an object. Most injuries are referred as a traumatic brain injury (TBI) and are characterized by some disturbance in consciousness and a predictable set of physical, emotional, and cognitive effects. Most children who sustain a simple concussion experience a strong recovery. It should be noted that multiple minor head injuries or concussions also may result in a similar pattern of behaviors and moods negatively impacting both learning and interpersonal relationships.

However, children who experience more serious head injuries resulting in a loss of consciousness, hospitalization, or secondary effects such as a bleed in the brain, neurologic deficit, and the need for surgical intervention may experience long-term residual effects. Even brain injuries that initially heal quickly can have lasting effects. If structures in the brain responsible for aspects of emotional control and self-regulation are damaged at an early age, this damage may not be apparent until those areas are called into action. Early brain damage may emerge in adolescence through temper control problems, impulsivity, mood instability, and social or academic difficulties. Damage to executive control centers such as the prefrontal cortex may not be apparent until the youngster reaches early adolescence and is required to execute a much more complex set of self-regulatory skills. Early brain injuries may ripple through a child's development, causing disruption many years down the road. Any assessment of a student for eligibility as a youngster with an EBD should include a thorough review of past history to rule out such injuries.

Abuse, neglect, and deprivation. Childhood abuse (physical, emotional, or sexual), deprivation, and neglect are obviously traumatic for a youngster. We often consider this trauma to be psychological in nature. However, recent studies suggest that such trauma also may have a direct impact on the chemical and structural environment of the developing brain. Early stressful experiences may alter a number of brain functions that increase the risk of emotional and behavioral disorders.

Severe abuse in childhood can result in the hypersecretion of Corticotropin-Releasing Factor (CRF; Heim et al., 2000). This high level of CRF is thought to be a mechanism underlying the psychopathology that often follows abuse. Abuse often leads to a state of chronic hyperarousal and specific neurochemical changes that, again, may be associated with subsequent problems in the regulation of emotional behavior (Kendall-Tackett, 2000). The dissociative amnesia or memory loss that often is induced by psychological stress of abuse may be the result of the toxic action of high, prolonged levels of glucosteroids on the hippocampus, the brain's center for working memory (Joseph, 1999).

Dr. Allan Shore (2001) has proposed that early mother-infant interactions may be particularly important for the development of the frontal structures necessary for regulation of mood and behavior. By contrast, stressful experiences early in life may permanently damage or alter these frontal structures, predisposing an individual to psychiatric diseases later in life.

Adoptees. One group of youngsters that has received considerable attention includes Russian and Romanian émigrés. A number of studies have found such youngsters to be at high risk for developmental delays, and many have problems forming secure emotional attachments (Chugani et al, 2001; O'Connor et al., 2000; Rutter & the ERA Research Team, 1998). An unexpected number of such adoptees have clinically significant emotional and behavioral difficulties. Some researchers have suspected that even benign neglect or lack of stimulation may predispose such youngsters to difficulty in regulation of mood, frustration tolerance, and self-calming.

Adolescence. Much has been written about the teen brain during the past decade. Neuroimaging studies have raised questions regarding many long-held assumptions about teenagers, brain development, and maturation (Giedd et al, 1999). The brain reaches about 95% of its adult volume by the age of 6 and continued development includes the process of pruning those unused connections, while strengthening those synapses used frequently.

Myelination also continues through our early adult lives improving speed of processing. In general, girls' brains mature somewhat earlier than boys' brains. More advanced functions, such as those responsible for integrating information for the senses, reasoning, and other executive functions mature last (Giedd et al., 1999). During teenage years, hormonal surges play an important role in both brain development and function.

Studies have found that adolescent brains are actually quite different from the mature adult brain. A study compared the MRI scans of young adults (ages 23 to 30) with those of teens (ages 12 to 14). The study found that the areas of the frontal lobes showed the greatest difference between young adults and teens (National Institute of Mental Health, 2001). Parietal and temporal areas appeared largely mature in the teen brain. The increased myelination in the adult frontal cortex seemed to relate to maturation of cognitive processing and other executive functions. Overall, the brains of teenagers seemed more structurally similar to younger children than to young adults.

Adolescent brains seek risk. A number of researchers have examined the role of puberty and brain development in teenagers. The relationship between hormone and brain contributes to an appetite for thrills, strong sensations, and excitement, which serve to promote exploration and independence (Dahl & Spear, 2004). We also know that the parts of the brain responsible for sensation seeking are just getting turned on at the onset of puberty while the centers for exercising judgment are still maturing throughout adolescence. This time gap between the impulse toward risk taking and the brain's ability to appropriately analyze potential consequences may result in a "look before you leap" approach. Dahl and Spear (2004) offered the analogy of teens as unskilled drivers trying to maneuver a car turbo-charged by puberty.

Adolescent brains may misperceive emotions. Deborah Yurgelun-Todd (as cited in Bradley, 2003) of Harvard University studied the manner in which adolescents process emotions. She examined teenagers, ages 11 through 17, via neuroimaging while identifying emotions on pictures of faces. She found that teens often misread facial expressions, seeing sadness, anger, and confusion instead of fear. She observed that the adolescents tend to use the amygdala when responding to emotions rather than the prefrontal cortex, which often is used by adults. The latter may allow a more reasoned assessment of the emotions of others. She felt that this adolescent manner of analyzing emotions with the amygdala may result in a more reactionary, less reasoned perception of situations that that evidenced by adults.

Teen impulsivity and inhibition. In all, Yurgelun-Todd (2007) indicated that teenagers respond more strongly with a gut response than they do with evaluating the consequences of what they were doing. As a consequence of this gut-oriented response, in terms of behavior, they are more spontaneous and less inhibited. An adolescent male may look mature, when he is not. These startling findings regarding adolescent brain development have important implications for a number of areas of public policy including laws regulating driving and issues related to juvenile justice.

Sleep and hormones. Recognition of teen brain development also has led to reconsideration of sleep. Interestingly, teens need more sleep than younger children. Researchers have recognized that sleep is regulated by the production of melatonin that sets that natural bed and rise times for teenagers. Teenagers have melatonin levels that remain elevated in the school day. This means that the brain is telling teenagers that it's still time to be in bed while we are telling them that it's time to go to school. Hormones responsible for sexual maturation and growth are released while sleeping. The average teen is actually not ready to wake up until 8 or 9 o'clock. The average high school teen sleeps about 7 hours a night. Researchers have found that teens who get the least amount of sleep earn C's and D's whereas those who receive more sleep earn A's and B's. Many states such as Virginia, Washington, Maryland, and Washington, DC, have looked at pushing back high school start times. Parents also should encourage teens to go to sleep at a reasonable time and to minimize lighting at night and open curtains in the morning. Light absorbed through the eyes can reset the biological clock.

Alcohol and substance abuse. Finally, it may be important to consider the role of substances and substance abuse in teenagers. Teenagers with EBD are at high risk for substance experimentation and substance abuse. Teenagers who abuse substances are at greater risk for behavioral disorders, mood disorders, and rule-breaking behavior. It is important to note that substances such as marijuana impact memory, learning, judgment, and reaction time.

Alcohol remains, by far, the most dangerous drug for teenagers. Teenagers stand a much higher chance of dying from alcohol than from marijuana, heroin, cocaine, and hallucinogens combined (Bradley, 2003). Bradley (2003) has suggested that we are simply reluctant to admit that alcohol is really a drug, let alone an extremely dangerous drug, particularly to teenagers. More than 10,000 teenagers are buried every year as a result of drinking and driving (Bradley, 2003), which paints the picture of a serious, universal problem.

School Success and Interventions

Teacher Training

One of the most basic and self-evident strategies to support the success of students with EBD is an understanding of those factors that drive and impact behavior. It is important that our teachers are kept abreast of emerging neuroscientific findings regarding the impact of early development, genetics, and normal brain development. These subjects may be inconsistently addressed in the curriculum by which teachers are educated or may be relegated to continuing education. It may be time to ensure that neuroscience has a predictable and consistent place in the training of our teachers. Through a timely, consistent, and uniform understanding of neurobiological factors governing behavior, teachers may ultimately be more effective in the design, implementation, and evaluation of programs serving youngsters with EBD.

Neurofeedback

Neurofeedback training is a term used to refer to those strategies that promote the direct training of brain function with the ultimate goal of greater cognitive efficiency. Neurofeedback is sometimes called EEG biofeedback because it's based on electrical brain activity—electroencephalogram, or EEG. Simply, neurofeedback is biofeedback applied to the brain directly. It is training to improve self-regulation, a necessary aspect of brain function. Neurofeedback has been used to address a number of problems related to brain dysregulation, including anxiety and depression, attention deficits, behavioral difficulties, sleep disorders, emotional disturbances, and physical symptoms such as headaches.

Most neurofeedback approaches involve the application of electrodes to the scalp in order to listen in or assess brain wave activity. This signals a process by a computer that extracts important information reflecting brain activity. Neurofeedback strategies are designed to change or enhance certain frequencies and diminish others. Neurofeedback typically is provided by a behavioral health specialist such as a psychologist or counselor. Training is typically done on a one-to-one basis in an office setting and is not thought to be a curative agent, but rather an intervention to promote more effective brain functioning.

Cogmed and Play Attention. One of the more popular neurofeedback programs available today is entitled Cogmed Working Memory Training (Klinberg, Forsberg, Westerberg, & Hirviloski, 2002). Cogmed is a training program for working memory that was created for children with attention problems. This program is comprehensive and home-based, although each participant has a personal coach at a Cogmed-qualified practice who leads the training, provides weekly feedback, and analyzes treatment results. Cogmed is only available through licensed psychologists and medical doctors.

Play Attention™, developed by Peter Freer, is a feedback learning system that can be used from home under the supervision of a licensed provider, or in a provider's office. This program is designed to enhance attention and teach skills necessary for success in the classroom. It is designed to improve focus, behavior, academics, and social interaction skills. One does not have to be a psychologist or a health care provider to administer the program. There is both a home version and a professional version. Again, such strategies have supportive evidence but remain experimental in the view of many professional organizations.

Mindfulness and Meditation

Mindfulness and meditation are forms of well-directed mental exercise that has been applied to improve attention and emotional self-regulation. Mindfulness is an awareness of one's body, feelings, and consciousness. According to Dr. Jon Kabat-Zinn (2005), mindfulness meditation is about learning to experience life fully, moment by moment. Through the practice of mindfulness, one can learn to develop greater calmness, clarity, and insight. Kabat-Zinn stressed that mindfulness helps one transform his relationship with his problems, fears, and stressors, promoting greater control over self-destructive behaviors and negative feelings. Mindfulness meditation is a type of meditation technique thought to enhance emotional awareness and psychological flexibility (Davidson et al., 2003).

Mindful Kids/Peaceful Schools. At Toluca Lake Elementary School in Los Angeles, Daniel Murphy's second-grade class files into the auditorium carrying round blue pillows decorated with white stars. They sit in a circle, eyes closed, quiet and concentrating. Two teachers give the children instructions on how to pay attention to breathing, telling them to notice the rise and fall of their bellies and chests and the passage of air in and out of their noses.

Toluca Lake is one of the growing numbers of schools using mindfulness training in an effort to combat increasing levels of anxiety, social conflict, and attention disorder among children. Once a week for 10–12 weeks the students at Toluca take time out from their normal curriculum to learn techniques that draw on the meditative practice of mindfulness, which is meant to promote greater awareness of one's self and one's environment. Bringing this practice to schools is about teaching kids how to be in a state of attention where they can perceive thoughts, physical sensations, and emotions without judgment and with curiosity and an open state of mind. This program is one of several mindfulness education programs that have sprouted up around the country. Others include the Impact Foundation of Colorado and the Lineage Project in New York City, which teaches mindfulness to at-risk and incarcerated teenagers.

Diet and Exercise

One's diet is clearly related to behavioral and mental health, largely because it is responsible for our physical health. Omega-3 fatty acids or dietary essentials are considered to be critical to brain development and functioning. A number of studies have indicated that a lack of Omega-3 may contribute to a number of psychiatric and neurodevelopmental disorders (Richardson, 2006). Omega-3 fatty acids cannot be manufactured by the body and, hence, must be obtained from food. Omega-3 fatty acids can be found in fish such as salmon, tuna, and halibut, and other marine life such as algae and krill. Certain plants or nuts also contain Omega-3 fatty acids.

Movement and exercise. Recent studies have shown a benefit to achievement and behavior when movement and multisensory kinesthetic activity is incorporated into the class period (Cooper-Kahn & Dietzel, 2009; Ratey & Hagerman, 2009). Movement can relieve stress, which can have a deteriorating effect on the brain. A constant state of stress is bad for the brain, and bad for effective learning. All people experience physical effects of stress, which can be relieved by exercise's chemical and physical benefits.

Role of the Parent

Parents, caregivers, and family members play a number of important roles in the relationship between emerging neuroscience and the education of their children. At a biological level, understanding the nature of genetics and hereditability of certain conditions may be quite useful in appreciating risks for children. Parents whose histories are remarkable for mood disorders are more likely to have children at greater risk for mood disorders. Recognizing family patterns may permit a more proactive and preventative approach for children. Early recognition of signs or symptoms, which may present initially in the classroom, should drive early intervention. Cultural concerns regarding the expression of distress also merit consideration. Sometimes cultural norms may frown upon the overt expression of depression, anxiety, or other psychological symptoms interfering with school progress. In such cases symptoms may go unrecognized or untreated for unreasonable lengths of time. Consultation with a family physician or pediatrician may be helpful in recognizing potential risk factors for children.

Parents and family members play a more direct role through the impact of one's home environment upon neurodevelopment (see Tool 10.1 for some suggestions for parents). Stress within the home may have a direct impact upon brain centers responsible for emotional regulation, alertness, and self-regulation. We'd like to think that what happens at home stays at home, but, in fact, it doesn't. Stressors within the family may become evident in a child's relationships with peers and teachers or through the quality of his or her academic performance.

This chapter has shown how important neurobiological factors are when assisting a child with her challenging behavior or emotional behavioral disorder. Medical and psychological professionals such as psychiatrists, neurologists, neuropsychologists, or psychologists use a common system to make diagnoses of Conduct, Oppositional Defiant, personality, or social disorders. Therefore, with this neurobiological information, the next chapter will inform how diagnoses are made and used to support a child with challenging behavior.

Tool 10.1

Tips for Parents to Understand the Connection Between Brain and Behavior

- Seek information regarding to role of genetics in emotional and learning disorders.

- Learn early signs of emerging behavioral or emotional differences.

- Recognize that emotional and behavioral disorders are not directly related to intelligence.

- Understand that conditions such as anxiety or depression, regardless of the etiology, may negatively impact cognition and learning.

- Appreciate the role of family stress, not in only the psychological status of your child, but in his or her neurodevelopmental status as well. Find ways to lessen or reduce family stress.

- Seek advocacy and consultation on how to share private psychiatric information with appropriate school officials.

chapter **11**	# Diagnoses
	What Do They Mean?

IN   Chapter 10, we reviewed a number of brain-based issues relevant to students with emotional differences and challenging behaviors. We discussed the role of early brain development and risk factors associated with subsequent emotional problems. We examined neuroimaging research and a number of interventions and practices that support self-regulation, mood stability, and behavior.

This chapter highlights how the spectrum of challenging behaviors is diagnosed, stressing common diagnoses such as Oppositional Defiant Disorder (ODD) and Conduct Disorder (CD). Challenging behaviors are commonly discussed in two general categories: internalizing behaviors and externalizing behaviors. Internalizing behaviors often are described as passive noncompliance, refusal to complete tasks or work, shut-down behaviors, or avoidant behaviors. Externalizing behaviors

Myth	Truth
Labels such as Oppositional Defiant Disorder or Conduct Disorder are just excuses for describing undisciplined or poorly behaved children.	Oppositional Defiant Disorder and Conduct Disorder are well recognized and researched behavioral health disorders marked by difficulties in both regulating one's behavior and adhering to the rules and expectations of various environments. These diagnostic descriptors are used when behavior is no longer within the realm of normal expectations given age and development.
Any child can be described as oppositional or defiant; that's the way kids behave.	Although most children may meet one or more of the symptom criteria for ODD or CD at some time or in some way, it is the pattern, intensity, and persistence of such symptoms that drive a diagnostic label.
It really doesn't matter what co-occurring or comorbid conditions are apparent, as long as you know the main problem.	Failure to recognize or understand co-occurring or comorbid conditions may result in the failure of an educational, therapeutic, or pharmacological intervention.
It is almost impossible to predict which conditions will occur together.	In fact, studies have identified a number of conditions that are likely to occur together. For example, depression and anxiety often occur together. Bipolar disorder and attention disorders often co-occur, and learning and attention disorders frequently occur together. These co-occurrences are related to shared neurologically mediated or brain-based mechanisms.
The fact that a child may be gifted is not really important when there is a significant emotional disorder.	Giftedness, or strong cognitive ability, is an important factor in all children, particularly those with emotional differences. Giftedness may be an asset in helping a youngster understand his own emotional difference and support the choice of particular interventions or educational options.

may include aggressive behavior, property destruction, bullying or teasing, or conduct problems such as stealing, setting fires, and behaviors that violate the rights of others. Children with emotional differences may demonstrate a combination of internalizing and externalizing behaviors.

This chapter will address the following questions:

- How much variability in behavior is normal?
- What is the text revision of the *Diagnostic and Statistical Manual*, fourth edition (*DSM-IV-TR*)?
- What are the symptoms of an Oppositional Defiant Disorder?
- What are the symptoms of a Conduct Disorder?
- How frequently do behavioral disorders and ADHD or autism spectrum disorders co-occur?
- Are there brain-based functions or dysfunctions that are consistent among co-occurring conditions?
- What are the benefits of recognizing co-occurring disorders versus the risks of failing to identify such conditions?

The Laundry List

A couple of years ago, a young man named Dylan was referred for neuropsychological assessment. Dylan was a freshman at a local high school who had a rough time, both behaviorally and academically, throughout middle school. He was described as increasingly disrespectful of his teachers, at times noncompliant, and at others, outright defiant. He had gotten into a number of verbal altercations, resulting in disciplinary reports, and was even suspended on one occasion. Dylan's mother reported that his grades had dropped rapidly through middle school and that relationships with his friends had deteriorated. He was ultimately found eligible for special education services as a student with an emotional disability.

Dylan's parents brought him for a neuropsychological evaluation.

Results of the neuropsychological assessment revealed a number of interesting findings. First, Dylan was born prematurely at 32 weeks. Second, his early development was remarkable for significant restlessness, impulsivity, and inattention. He had always had a difficult time completing work in a timely manner and required considerable supervision through elementary school. One teacher had actually suggested that he might have an attention disorder, but he responded well to some simple accommodations in the classroom. Dylan also had reading difficulties. On measures of reading, his decoding, comprehension, and fluency skills were more than two grade levels below his current placement. His intelligence scores, however, were quite high.

When the assessment was completed, a number of diagnoses were indicated, including an anxiety disorder, ADHD, Oppositional Defiant Disorder (ODD), and a reading disorder (dyslexia). His mother looked at the *DSM-IV* diagnoses and said, "My gosh, what a laundry list! What doesn't he have?" In the conversation that followed, the parent and the clinician, one of this book's authors, discussed that it is not uncommon for youngsters to demonstrate symptoms of several conditions simultaneously and that research has shown that many youngsters evidence co-occurring conditions. There often are brain-based mechanisms that actually predict the co-occurrence of ADHD and anxiety, or anxiety and depression, or ADHD and Oppositional Defiant Disorder.

In trying to understand how Dylan reached the point where his behavior had become so difficult to manage, we discussed the role of prematurity and its relationship with neurodevelopmental differences and his biological predisposition toward impulsivity and difficulty with aspects of executive functioning that are increasingly required of students as they progress through middle school to high school. We discussed the gap between his current reading skills and classroom demands despite above-average intelligence. We examined a history of anxiety and low-frustration tolerance and the emergence of increasingly oppositional and defiant behavior. We recognized that his tendency to become both impulsive and defiant had created a number of difficulties with teachers and friends. Finally, Dylan's teachers recognized that he was actually a very bright student who performed poorly in school. He was not, however, an unmotivated or reluctant student.

With a more thorough and accurate understanding of Dylan's profile, we were able to address each area of need within the context of his IEP, providing science-based intervention, appropriate accommodations and modifications, private psychiatric services, and school-based psychological services to support his progress. The laundry list of diagnoses can be overwhelming. However, understanding a child diagnostically can help develop an intervention plan that can ultimately support a child's success.

A Problem Becomes a Disorder

Behavior, emotions, and social skills occur on a continuum. Some misbehavior is normal. A parent or educator must understand what is typical before understanding what behavior is atypical, or at "disorder" level. Children with EBD often are described as immature, exhibiting behavior more common of younger children. Or, milestones are met, but the child demonstrates an unusual number, amount, duration, or severity of behavior. But what is unusual? By looking at typical development in children, a child's behavioral challenges are better understood.

Preschoolers

Preschoolers may face a number of developmental challenges impacting basic motor function, language function, and self-regulation. From an emotional standpoint, some preschoolers may demonstrate significant separation anxiety, defiance, aggression, or hyperactivity, which brings them to the attention of parents and teachers. Separation anxiety may represent a transient or short-term problem responsive to a simple behavioral plan. Other children, however, may demonstrate a degree of anxiety that goes far beyond that anticipated as this age level. Such youngsters may be difficult to settle, evidence repetitive behaviors such as tics, harbor multiple fears, and become easily upset or provoked in the classroom.

Preschoolers with more severe levels of anxiety will require thorough assessment and a more proactive and multimodal intervention plan. It is important to rule out underlying weaknesses in language or adaptive skills that may contribute to or exacerbate anxiety.

From a neurobiological standpoint, one of the primary goals for preschoolers is to develop the capacity for self-calming, sensory tolerances, and comfort when away from parents or caregivers for progressively longer periods of time. In the classroom, preschoolers with such difficulties may require a formal special education program and both special education and related services.

Elementary School

Early elementary school is the time for rapid academic skill development. The brain is primed for skills such as rhyme sensitivity, phonemic awareness, language, sequencing, and enhanced fine motor skills. Emotionally, youngsters are required to spend much longer amounts of time away from home, in larger classes, with a variety of students. One of the most frequent behavioral concerns of elementary school students involves self-control and control of one's impulses. Boys often come to the attention of educators for negative behaviors at this time. There are important gender differences at this age that will be discussed in later chapters. Suffice it to say, however, that boys are more active, less verbal, and may require a more organized and predictable level of structure than elementary school girls of the same age.

When elementary school students come to the attention of parents and teachers for concerns regarding their emotional status or behavior, it is important to consider the antecedents and consequences of behavior and a particular child's need for sensory regulation, structure, and movement. Teachers often implement a variety of informal interventions such as preferential seating, a behavioral chart, a buddy system, or proximity controls. Consideration of these issues may help mitigate or lessen the impact of restlessness, impulsivity, or defiance in the classroom. These informal interventions should be documented in order to monitor response and consider the need for a more formal, data-driven plan.

Toward the end of elementary school, students are required to navigate an increasingly complex social structure. They must interpret language that is more inferential and nonliteral, respond to nonverbal as well as verbal communication, and allow important school relationships to transcend to their homes or communities. We are social beings, and the formation of social hierarchies is an important aspect of our neurobiology. Some children may be bullied while others may be marginalized or ostracized from their peers. Students with depression or anxiety may be less attentive to social cues or less motivated to remain socially engaged. Students with temper control problems may behave in a more volatile or less predictable manner, resulting in a decreased number of opportunities for positive social interaction. Again, the opportunity cost of emotional and behavioral difficulties can be quite substantial and may rapidly diminish the chance to learn important academic and social skills. It is important to weigh the opportunity cost of an emotional or behavioral difference with the risk of various treatment options.

In elementary school students, the most common co-occurring conditions include attention, language, and learning disorders. Before attributing a grade-schooler's defiant behavior to emotional issues one should effectively rule out problems of impulsivity, receptive and expressive language skills, and emerging literacy skills.

Middle School

Middle school places a substantial demand on a student's capacity for executive functioning. Executive functions refer to a set of operations, typically associated with the prefrontal cortex and its subcortical connections, responsible for self-control, initiation, sustained attention, working memory, organizational skills, and self-monitoring. Executive functions also are critical for regulation of one's behavior and emotional responses. A number of authors have provided helpful descriptions of executive functions, including Cooper-Kahn and Dietzel (2009).

It is normal for typical middle school students to have some difficulty acclimating to remembering a locker combination, changing classes from one room to another, maintaining a planner or schedule, and applying the skills of reading, math, and writing to literary analysis, quantitative reasoning, and written responses. Students with emotional considerations often have a number of additional challenges, particularly in the social realm. Some find middle school lonely, alienating, or agitating. Youngsters with more severe EBD may be increasingly separated from the general education environment, placed with other youngsters exhibiting similar difficulties in smaller classrooms, may use a wider range of psychotropic medications designed to influence emotions or behavior, and, in some cases, be subjected to legal contingencies as a result of misbehavior. From a brain standpoint, hormonal changes will begin to interact with aspects of temperament, self-control, and mood, which may escalate difficulties in the classroom.

High School

Ninth grade is arguably one of the most difficult years of a student's life. Puberty is typically in full swing, the brain has yet to develop appropriate mechanisms for reasoning and self-control, and students are expected to be more autonomous and self-reliant. The core developmental tasks of gender identity, self-identity, and socialization are apparent for all youngsters at this age.

The interaction of genetic predispositions and hormonal changes may result in previously unidentified adolescents to come to the attention of teachers and administrators. The appearance of more serious psychiatric and personality disorders may become increasingly apparent and disabling. From a neurobiological standpoint, adolescence is truly an interesting time in that nature has created a hormonally charged, risk-ready, thrill-seeking teenager without the advantage of reasoning, good judgment, and anticipation of consequences. Challenges of sexuality, substance use, and driving create real risk factors for all adolescents. The normal challenges of adolescence may be greatly exaggerated in children and adolescents with EBD.

The potential consequences of mood and behavioral disorders throughout adolescence may include greater separation from typically developing peers; consideration of more restrictive placements such as private and separate day schools, psychiatric hospitals, and residential treatment centers; and increased interactions with the mental health and juvenile justice systems. Students with EBD may be placed on a cocktail of medicines and provided with intensive psychotherapeutic supports. For adolescents with serious emotional disorders, a risk management paradigm may make the most sense. Minimizing the risk of physical harm, addiction, and legal and psychiatric complications should be a priority and may actually supersede basic academic considerations. It often is necessary to develop IEPs that reflect this complexity and risk-management approach.

What Is the *DSM-IV-TR*?

The text revision of the fourth edition of the *Diagnostic and Statistical Manual of Mental Disorders* (*DSM-IV-TR*) was published in 2000 by the American Psychiatric Association for use by mental health professionals in making diagnoses. The *DSM-V* is scheduled for publication in 2012. The purpose of the *DSM-IV-TR* is to provide diagnostic criteria for mental disorders offered as guidelines for making diagnoses. Such criteria enhance agreement among clinicians and researchers treating individuals with emotional and behavioral disorders. In order to appropriately use the *DSM-IV-TR*, one requires specialized clinical training that provides a body of knowledge and clinical skills. The diagnostic criteria set forth in the *DSM-IV-TR* reflect a consensus of current formulations of evolving knowledge in mental health and behavioral health fields. The purpose of the *DSM-IV-TR* is to provide clear descriptions of diagnostic categories in order to enable clinicians to diagnose, communicate about, study, and treat people with various mental disorders. The *DSM-IV-TR* is behavioral in its descriptions and does not specify etiologies for various conditions.

The *DSM* undergoes revision periodically in order to stay abreast with emerging research, clinical practices, and advances in our understanding of behavioral health disorders. The fifth revision is well under way and will include a number of welcome changes in sections addressing neurodevelopmental and behavioral disorders in children and adolescents. Many of the proposed changes have yet to undergo field testing. The American Psychiatric Association offers links through its website to both draft criteria and workgroups addressing diagnosis relevant to children with challenging behaviors.

What Is Oppositional Defiant Disorder?

Oppositional Defiant Disorder (ODD), as defined by the *DSM-IV-TR*, is marked by a recurrent pattern of

> negativistic, defiant, disobedient, and hostile behavior toward authority figures that persists for at least 6 months . . . and is characterized by the frequent occurrence for the following behaviors: losing temper, . . . arguing with adults, . . . actively defying or refusing to comply with requests or rules of adults, . . . deliberately doing things that will annoy other people, blaming others for his or her own mistakes or behavior, . . . being touched or easily annoyed by others, . . . being angry and resentful, or being spiteful and vindictive. (APA, 2000, p. 100)

Real-life behaviors that may signal ODD include:
- arguing over the smallest requests,
- agitating behavior toward siblings,
- frequent willingness to challenge rules,

- "under the radar" misbehavior in the classroom,
- frequent pleadings regarding what is or isn't fair, or
- vindictiveness toward peers or siblings.

The behaviors must occur more frequently than that typically observed in children of the same age and developmental level. And to be at disorder level, the behavior must lead to significant impairment in "social, academic, or occupational functioning" (APA, 2000, p. 100).

The requirement that the behaviors must occur more frequently than is typically observed suggests a consideration of what is normal for a particular age. In other words, the range of normal behavior with regard to defiance in a 4-year-old is quite different than the range of normal behavior for an 11-year-old. The second criteria— namely, that the behavior must lead to significant impairment in social, academic, or occupational functioning—indicates that the behavior must be severe enough to interfere with one's day-to-day functioning.

The most common developmental disorder associated with ODD is ADHD. Some children may also evidence learning or communication disorders. The *DSM-IV-TR* indicates that rates of ODD range from 2% to 16%, depending on sampling methods and populations.

What Is a Conduct Disorder?

According to the *DSM-IV-TR*, a Conduct Disorder is characterized by:

a repetitive, persistent pattern of behavior in which the basic rights of others or major age-appropriate societal norms or rules are violated. . . . These behaviors fall into four main groupings: aggressive conduct that causes or threatens physical harm to other people or animals, . . . nonaggressive conduct that causes property loss or damage, . . . deceitfulness or theft, . . . and serious violations of rules. (APA, 2000, pp. 93–94)

In order to meet criteria for the diagnosis of Conduct Disorder, these behaviors "must have been present during the past 12 months with at least one behavior present in the past 6 months" (APA, 2000, p. 94). Again, the disturbance must cause significant impairment in social, academic, or occupational functioning, similar to ODD. Conduct disorders in the *DSM-IV-TR* are subtyped into Childhood-Onset Type, which is defined by the onset of at least one criterion characteristic prior to the age of 10, and Adolescent-Onset Type in which there was an absence of any criteria characteristic of conduct disorder prior to the age of 10.

The *DSM-IV-TR* also provides for severity specifiers, which include mild, moderate, and severe. There are a number of associated features evident with Conduct Disorder, including deficits in academic achievement, particularly reading or verbal skills, learning or communication disorders, ADHD, and anxiety, mood, or substance-related disorders. Finally, although not indicated in the *DSM-IV-TR*, there may be important gender differences in the expression of conduct problems. Boys may be more likely to garner attention for aggressiveness, destructiveness, and refusal to follow rules. Girls may be more subtle and secretive regarding rule-breaking behavior. Conduct problems in girls may be more likely to present in the context and quality of their peer relationships.

Common Co-Occurring Conditions

Co-occurring conditions are a set of symptoms or diagnoses that tend to occur together. Many co-occurring conditions may share common neurological substrates. For example, many children defined by the diagnostic criteria of Conduct Disorder also may carry a diagnosis of ADHD. The capacity for self-regulation, self-control, and the inhibition of impulses may be a common symptom shared among both conditions and stem from a shared neurodevelopmental process. It is important to recognize co-occurring conditions formulating both treatment plans and appropriate educational programs. Failure to do so may render a program or intervention plan marginally effective or, even worse, ineffective.

We have identified ADHD and autism spectrum disorders (ASD) as frequent co-occurring conditions in youngsters with emotional and behavioral struggles. The core cognitive component of ADHD is difficulties with aspects of executive functioning or self-regulatory skills. Weaknesses in executive functioning are apparent in many neurodevelopmental disorders. As you may recall from Chapter 4, executive functions refer to a set of brain-based processes that underlie regulation of behavior and cognition. These processes include response impulse control, expression of emotion, working memory, and planning skills. For example, the expression of anxiety or depression may, in part, depend upon a child's capacity for emotional control, frustration tolerance, and flexibility. Similarly, youngsters with autism often demonstrate weaknesses in both cognitive and behavioral control related to executive function deficits.

A child who is melting down at home after school, annoying others, misunderstanding social situations, and without friends can be a child with Asperger's syndrome or Pervasive Developmental Disorder, Not Otherwise Specified, both autism spectrum disorders. The frequency of autism spectrum disorders has risen dramatically over the past decade. Recent studies by the Centers for Disease Control and Prevention (CDC, 2009) suggested that one in 110 children may show symptoms of an ASD. This is a significant increase over the reported rate of 1 in 150 children reported just a few years ago. A dysregulation of emotion due to an ASD must be evaluated with a focus on intervention. The core features of ASD include weaknesses in social reciprocity and ritualized, routinized, or repetitive behaviors; therefore, a child with autism could meet the part of the definition of emotional disability of unusual thoughts or feelings under normal circumstances. Children described as on the autism spectrum typically have trouble forming and maintaining peer relationships, may be described as rigid or inflexible, and may have communication difficulties or sensory sensitivities. Such weaknesses may manifest through a tendency to shut down or avoid others when overwhelmed. These behaviors may be interpreted as defiant, oppositional, or noncompliant. Recognizing these underlying co-occurring conditions may allow a more reasoned and effective intervention plan.

How Frequently Do Behavioral Disorders and ADHD or Autism Spectrum Disorders Co-Occur?

Rates of co-occurring conditions vary among studies but most research indicates that nearly half of youngsters identified with a behavioral disorder meet the diagnostic criteria for ADHD. Both conditions share a basic difficulty in a student's ability to regulate his behavior in a manner consistent with the expectations of a given environment. Both conditions are typically addressed through the development of a behavior plan that regulates antecedent conditions and consequences. Physicians may use similar medications to treat these disorders.

Not all youngsters with ASD demonstrate significant behavioral problems. However, the nature of autism predicts difficulties in social relationships and inflexibility, which are catalysts for behavioral issues. Addressing the behavioral problems of a child with ASD through only contingency management—that is, rewarding desirable and punishing undesirable behavior—may yield little success. Evidenced-based programs for youngsters with ASD include social skills training, language services, and environmental modifications, which may need to be different than those used with students with EBD. Recognizing these co-occurrences is likely to result in a more comprehensive and effective intervention plan. Many youngsters with ASD will demonstrate co-occurring differences in their capacity for mood and behavioral regulation. It is important to determine the primary neurodevelopmental condition in order to prioritize treatment. For example, identifying anxiety as the primary disorder in a child with an ASD may result in an opportunity loss for important interventions designed for enhancing social reciprocity, social thinking, language skills, and nonverbal communication.

Conversely, failing to recognize a co-occurring anxiety disorder in a child identified with ASD or a learning disability may reduce the efficacy of interventions designed to treat the primary disorder. In all, differential diagnoses of neurodevelopmental disorders in preschoolers remains a challenging task and often is facilitated by the use of multiple professionals including physicians, neuropsychologists, psychologists, special educators, and related therapists.

Are There Brain-Based Functions or Dysfunctions That Are Consistent Among Co-Occurring Conditions?

One of the frequent findings in children with co-occurring conditions such as those discussed in this section involves weaknesses or deficits in executive functions. Executive functions are the neurologically mediated control processes of the brain impacting the expression of emotions, cognitive skills, and adaptive behavior. Recognition and assessment of executive functions may yield helpful information in effective intervention planning.

Giftedness and Behavior

The term *gifted* is used in schools to describe students whose cognitive ability or talents far exceed those of the average student. Sometimes schools use a relative definition, such as the top 5% of students needing a more challenging curriculum. Broader definitions may use gifted to describe children whose high potential must be nurtured or to describe a process of asynchronous development that recognizes not only intellect and talent, but also emotional traits such as heightened sensitivity.

The relationship between giftedness and challenging behaviors is worth consideration. Research has long studied the association of artistic talent and creativity with mood instability, depression, and substance abuse; although certainly not as extreme, gifted youngsters may have increased risk for emotional and behavioral challenges than their more typical peers. Three factors may underlie this risk (Webb, 2000).

1. First, gifted children are almost always described as extremely intense and highly sensitive. This intensity may be evident in their intellectual pursuits, interests, and in their emotional responses. Intensity may manifest as restlessness, intolerance, or power struggles. Heightened sensitivity may include sensory sensitivities, emotional sensitivity, and tendency to overempathize with the plight of others. Both intensity and sensitivity may increase the risk of behavioral issues in the classroom.

2. Second, situational factors common to gifted children may increase the risk of behavioral problems. Gifted youngsters may be more likely to challenge authority in an effort to explore or understand. They may experience impatience and boredom because of the pace of instruction. These situational factors may create conflict with peers or teachers in a structured classroom setting.

3. Third, gifted children may be at risk for misdiagnoses stemming from limitations in the knowledge and training of behavioral health specialists. Limited understanding of the common social, emotional, and behavioral characteristics of gifted children may result in overdiagnosis or misdiagnosis of disorders such as ADHD, ODD, or mood disorder.

Table 7 describes some of the potential behavior challenges that can be caused by characteristics of gifted children also considered to be strengths of their giftedness.

The next chapter will look at the variety of medications that may be prescribed to help children with their various diagnoses.

Table 7

Possible Behavior Problems Associated With Characteristic Strengths of Gifted Students

Strengths	Possible Problems
Acquires and retains information quickly.	Impatient with slowness of others; dislikes routine and drill; may resist mastering foundational skills; may make concepts unduly complex.
Inquisitive attitude, intellectual curiosity; intrinsic motivation; searching for significance.	Asks embarrassing questions; strong-willed; resists direction; seems excessive in interests; expects same of others.
Ability to conceptualize, abstract, synthesize; enjoys problem solving and intellectual activity.	Rejects or omits details; resists practice or drill; questions teaching procedures.
Can see cause-effect relations.	Difficulty accepting the illogical, such as feelings, traditions, or matters to be taken on faith.
Love of truth, equity, and fair play.	Difficulty in being practical; worry about humanitarian concerns.
Enjoys organizing things and people into structure and order; seeks to systematize.	Constructs complicated rules or systems; may be seen as bossy, rude, or domineering.
Large vocabulary and facile verbal proficiency; broad information in advanced areas.	May use words to escape or avoid situations; becomes bored with school and age peers; seen by others as a "know it all."
Thinks critically; has high expectancies; is self-critical and evaluates others.	Critical or intolerant toward others; may become discouraged or depressed; perfectionistic.
Keen observer; willing to consider the unusual; open to new experiences.	Overly intense focus; occasional gullibility.
Creative and inventive; likes new ways of doing things.	May disrupt plans or reject what is already known; seen by others as different and out of step.
Intense concentration; long attention span in areas of interest; goal-directed behavior; persistence.	Resists interruption; neglects duties or people during period of focused interests; stubbornness.

Table 7, continued

Strengths	Possible Problems
Sensitivity, empathy for others; desire to be accepted by others.	Sensitivity to criticism or peer rejection; expects others to have similar values; need for success and recognition; may feel different and alienated.
High energy, alertness, eagerness; periods of intense efforts.	Frustration with inactivity; eagerness may disrupt others' schedules; needs continual stimulation; may be seen as hyperactive.
Independent; prefers individualized work; reliant on self.	May reject parent or peer input; nonconformity; may be unconventional.
Diverse interests and abilities; versatility.	May appear scattered and disorganized; frustrations over lack of time; others may expect continual competence.
Strong sense of humor.	Sees absurdities of situations; humor may not be understood by peers; may become "class clown" to gain attention.

Note. Adapted from Clark (1992).

chapter 12

Medications*

YOU are not alone when the mention of medication for your child's challenging behavior brings forth a host of mixed emotions. A parent may have a positive view of medications from personal experience, feedback from others, or research. Another parent may have a negative view of medications and insist that there is no way he will put his child on medication. Yet another parent may want to learn more. This chapter is written for all parents, no matter what your thoughts and feelings are toward medications. Remember, only you can give consent for your child to receive medication.

An educator may have feelings about a parent's decision to medicate her child. You may know children who you think should be on medication, or know children who you believe take too much medication. Medication often is given at school, and educators are asked to give a prescribing doctor

---

*This chapter was contributed by Maria Hammill, M.D.

Myth	Truth
Once you start psychiatric medication, you have to take it for life.	How long one needs to be on psychiatric medications will depend on what conditions the medications are being used for, ranging from as needed use to maintenance treatment. Some people may need to take medications to stabilize mood and behavior for months to years. It is important to have the continued use of medications be evaluated regularly to determine risk and benefit. Most medications for depression and mood stability take 3–4 weeks to start working but how long one needs to take the medication will depend on the severity of symptoms and is determined on a case-by-case basis.
Medications should be used as the last resort.	In some conditions, nonmedication strategies (e.g., therapy, school accommodations, behavior modification) may not be effective or possible without medication. One example is that when the student is extremely inattentive, hyperactive, and impulsive, other interventions cannot be implemented. Medication must be considered throughout the diagnostic and treatment phases as part of a comprehensive treatment plan rather than as a last resort.
All psychiatric medications are addictive or habit forming.	The majority of psychiatric medications are not addictive. The medications that can be addictive are those used for anxiety (e.g., Ativan, Xanax, Klonopin, or Valium) and the stimulants for ADHD (e.g., Ritalin, Dexedrine, or Adderall). There are prospective studies that show that treatment children with ADHD who were treated with stimulants had lower incidence/prevalence of substance abuse in adulthood compared to children who had untreated ADHD.
Psychiatric medications will alter one's personality and make one act like a "zombie."	When psychiatric medications are given for the right indication and dosed correctly, it can enhance the person's personality, improve functioning, and increase one's ability to reach his full potential. Some antipsychotic medications used for aggressive and out-of-control behavior can be sedating when given at higher doses.

feedback as to whether a medication is working. It is important that you have information relevant to your student's performance and that families maintain some degree of privacy. Balancing these needs may be challenging but definitely worthwhile in the end.

The more knowledge a parent or educator has about medications, the more power he or she will have to work in partnership with the school staff for success. Medications may not work for everyone but it is a treatment option that you may need to consider. In many cases, when prescribed correctly and monitored closely, medications have made a world of difference in a child's quality of life and can help transform failure into success. Changes in your child may positively impact the quality of life for parents and siblings now and in the future.

The chapter will address the following questions:

- What factors are considered when making the decision to medicate?
- What symptoms can improve with medications?
- Who is in charge of medication management?
- What are the different types of medications?
- How can the effects of medication be effectively monitored?

This chapter will focus on the role of medications as part of a comprehensive treatment plan in helping students with EBD achieve school success. This chapter will help you through the process of considering medication use, monitoring medication response, and developing strategies to communicate with doctors and teachers.

Psychiatric medications often are in the news, resulting in confusing, sensational, or even inaccurate information. The use of medicines for mood and behavior symptoms in children is often viewed as controversial despite the availability of well-designed research supporting the safe and beneficial effects in some conditions. This chapter will provide parents and teachers with current information regarding the different medications that can be helpful for the child and access to the research examining the safety and effectiveness of such medicines.

Tool 12.1 provides tips for parents and teachers on understanding the issues related to medication.

To Medicate or Not: Factors

A decision to seek medication consultation often is driven by several factors, including:
- mounting school pressure due to behaviors suggesting threats to anyone's safety,
- increasing legal pressure to treat students who have exhibited symptoms and behaviors that are in violation of the law,
- risk of losing daycare and school placement,
- when the emotional or behavioral skills interfere with a child's learning, and
- when the parents and the child agree that other interventions are not enough.

Research

The push to seek medication consultation may come from home, school, daycare, the legal system, different treatment providers, or other sources where the student has regular interaction. Severe behavior and mood symptoms such as danger to self and others often trigger the most rapid response. Academic underachievement or failure to progress in school especially after different interventions have been tried is another common reason. Researchers studying national trends in the use of psychiatric medications in children published a 10-year prospective study of practice patterns in youth regarding the use of psychiatric medications (Olfson, Marcus, Weissman, & Jensen, 2002; Zito et al., 2003). It showed enough benefit to encourage consideration of medications as an important intervention.

In 1996, the National Institute of Mental Health established Research Units in Pediatric Psychopharmacology (RUPPs). These are

- Aggressive/dangerous behaviors

- Anxiety, phobias, and panic attacks

- Attention/concentration/memory issues

- Oppositional/defiant behavior

- Impulsive/hyperactive behavior

- Mood swings/Instability

- Psychosis/delusions/hallucinations/paranoia

- Sleep problems (insomnia/nightmares/sedation)

- Bowel/bladder problems

- Excessive absences/school refusal

- Physical complaints without an organic basis

Figure 20. Common symptoms of students with EBD that can benefit from medication consultation and treatment.

networks located in academic research settings throughout the country devoted to do multisite clinical trials to study the safety and efficacy of commonly used psychiatric medications that have no adequate data and are being used in children. Some of the sites are in highly regarded universities such as Yale, Columbia, and Johns Hopkins. The teams are led by experts in pediatrics, child psychiatry, psychopharmacology, and clinical research and design. These are not sponsored by drug companies. Several protocols have come out of the RUPPs such as the use of antidepressants for anxiety, depression, and bipolar disorders and the use of antipsychotics for children with autism and behavioral disturbances. They have ongoing clinical trials for all types of treatment such as childhood-onset schizophrenia, mood disorder, ADHD, anxiety, and bipolar disorders that include medications, cognitive-behavior therapy, and other interventions.

Figure 20 lists behaviors identified by schools and parents that may respond to medication.

Table 8

Symptoms Treated by Different Types of Physicians

Type of Physician	Symptoms Treated
General Pediatrician	ADHD, bowel/bladder disorders, symptoms due to medical conditions
Developmental Pediatrician	Genetic disorders, ADHD, autism, behavioral and learning difficulties
Family Physician	Mild depression, anxiety, ADHD
Pediatric Neurologist	ADHD, autism, seizures, migraines, brain injuries, sleep disorders
Child or Adult Psychiatrist	ADHD, depression, anxiety, bipolar disorder, Oppositional Defiant Disorder, schizophrenia, autism, sleep disorders, learning and speech/language disorders

Types of Prescribing Doctors

There are several physicians who can provide medication consultation and management. The different medical specialists are listed in Table 8 with the disorders that they frequently manage.

A child psychiatrist will have the most education and training in managing psychiatric disorders in children. It is better to choose a Board Certified physician because he or she has completed formal training in his or her specialty in a United States accredited program and passed a series of examinations to validate his or her knowledge. The physician who is recommending medication must be able to fully explain the reasons why a particular medication is recommended, what risks and benefits should be considered, and how she arrived at the diagnosis and recommendation.

A parent should feel that his questions are addressed by the physician and there is a clear understanding of what to expect. When the parent calls the doctor for any adverse reactions, the physician should be responsive and available. During the initial visit, it is important to ask if any tests are needed before starting medication to ensure safety.

It is important to know if the type of medication prescribed can be stopped abruptly if there is a side effect and how your physician handle after hours or emergency calls. To guide parents in selecting a physician to manage medical concerns, the following questions can be used:

- What is your initial diagnosis and how did you arrive at that conclusion?
- What diagnostic tests are needed to confirm the diagnosis?
- What are the different treatment options?
- What follow-up and monitoring is needed?

Treatment Settings

There are many settings where health providers can provide medication consultation and treatment. The setting often is determined by the urgency and complexity of the condition. The mildest symptoms typically are managed in an outpatient office setting while the most severe symptoms such as extreme aggression, psychosis, and suicidal and homicidal thoughts and behaviors are initially seen and managed in a hospital setting.

The following treatment settings provide medication management from the least restrictive and most common to the most intensive setting, which is less common:

- *Doctor's office/clinic:* The child is stable and cooperative and the frequency of follow up can be weekly to monthly depending on the symptoms and types of medications used.
- *Intensive outpatient program (IOP):* The frequency can vary from daily to several times a week for 2–3 hours a day. The child needs more frequent monitoring but is stable enough to go to school and sleep at home. Individual, family, and group therapy may be included in addition to psychiatric medication management.
- *Partial hospital or day program (PHP):* The child attends the program from Monday to Friday during school hours only. The child participates in individual, group, and family therapy and receives medication management. Time also is allotted for schoolwork.

- *Inpatient or hospital setting:* This is for emergency situations when the child is suicidal, homicidal, psychotic, or not safe to manage at home. The average stay is generally from 3–7 days for crisis stabilization. It can be in a medical center or a psychiatric hospital. In most hospital or inpatient settings, there is a children's unit for those younger than 13 years of age and an adolescent unit for those 13 to 18 years old. A parent cannot stay overnight with the child but can visit daily for family meetings. In addition to the medication management, the child participates in a hospital classroom for several hours a day. There is individual, group, family, and behavior therapy. Medication management in this setting often is aggressive in terms of dosing, combinations of drugs, and using injectables if needed to contain dangerous behaviors. This is possible because of the availability of 24-hour monitoring and access to laboratories and doctors with expertise in different areas (i.e., cardiologist, neurologist, and others if necessary).
- *Residential treatment setting (RTC):* This is a long-term setting where school and treatment are provided within a setting that is a combination of inpatient (hospital) environment and intensive academic placement. The child stays in this program anywhere from 30 days to a year and a periodic review is done to assess continued placement in this setting. Medication management; behavior modification; small class settings; individual, group, and family therapy; and other interventions are provided. The psychiatrist makes regular rounds from daily to several times a week to assess medications and all the interventions provided acting as the team leader. The use of medications in this setting also can be aggressive but not as much as in the hospital setting. If the child has a medical crisis, he may frequently utilize the emergency system unless the RTC is part of a hospital setting.

Symptoms That May Respond to Medication

As we discussed in Chapter 7, EBD is an educational disability, not a clinical diagnosis. As we discussed in the previous chapter on diagnoses, it is not listed in the *DSM-IV-TR* reference as a psychiatric diagnosis. Medications traditionally have been classified based on a clinical or psychiatric diagnosis when they are approved for indication; currently there are no medications approved or indicated for the educational condition labeled as *emotional disability* by the Food and Drug Administration (FDA). Recently newer psychiatric drugs have been approved for irritability, aggression, and agitation in children and adolescents due to developmental disorders such as autism. Challenging behaviors, emotional disturbances, and lack of behavioral control may be described by a number of diagnostic terms ranging from ADHD to mood disorders. EBD, however, encompasses a range of mood, thought, and behavioral symptoms of psychiatric disorders.

Attention, Concentration, and Memory

Attention, concentration, and memory difficulties are frequently found in school-age children. This can be due to conditions such as ADHD, learning disorders, hearing and vision problems, and neurological conditions such as seizures and head trauma. There are two main groups of ADHD medications: stimulants and nonstimulants. The main factors to consider when deciding which ADHD medication is best suited for your child include:
- overall health including weight, height, and sleep problems;
- presence of neurological, gastric, cardiac, and liver disease;
- treatment costs;
- risk of abuse;
- onset of action, duration of effect;
- ability to swallow pills;

- drug interactions; and
- other coexisting psychiatric disorders.

ADHD medications can improve attention span, reduce distractibility, improve memory, and reduce hyperactive, impulsive, and disruptive behavior. Stimulants work quickly, ranging from half an hour to 3 hours from intake and can last up to 12 hours. Some students take their stimulants on school days only and have drug holidays (off stimulants) on weekends or during vacations. The most common reason drug holidays are done is because of side effects such as appetite suppression or sleep problems. In older children, especially teenagers who drive or work, it is recommended that they stay on their stimulants 7 days a week. Nonstimulants build up from several days to weeks before the improvement of symptoms can be noticed and have to be taken daily.

Research. Medication effects on children with ADHD have been well researched. A 5-year naturalistic, longitudinal, observational study of 21,000 children followed from kindergarten to fifth grade who were given standardized tests for reading and mathematics in the United States was published in *Pediatrics* (Sheffler et al., 2009). The study had 600 children with ADHD and two-thirds were taking medications. Medication use was associated with gains in mathematics and reading. The gains were only 40% of the amount needed to bridge the gap between medicated and unmedicated students. The authors of the study still advocate for a combination of medication, behavioral, and school intervention. Keep in mind that medication works better for some children than for others.

Side effects and warnings. In the last few years, there have been news headlines warning about the risk of sudden cardiac deaths associated with stimulants, triggered initially with reports from Canada involving Adderall. A series of hearings were conducted within the Food and Drug Administration involving a team of experts including pediatricians, cardiologists, and child and adult psychiatrists. The recommendation is that all stimulants can have a small potential for cardiac risk in individuals with structural lesions of the heart. It is recommended that a careful history must be obtained for the individual and the family for abnormal heart rhythm, syncope, fainting spells, heart attacks, hypertension, and strokes. The need to obtain cardiac clearance, echocardiograms, or an electrocardiogram (ECG or EKG) prior to starting stimulant medication is to be made by the prescribing physician depending on his risk assessment of the individual patient. Atomoxetine (Strattera) also has three "black box" warnings that include risk of increased suicidal ideation, liver toxicity, and cardiac rhythm disturbance.

Depression and Anxiety

Depression in school-age children is a very serious and potentially life-threatening medical condition that if untreated may have devastating consequences to the child and others. Depression is the third leading cause of death in the 10–14-year-old age group in the United States (Anderson & Smith, 2005). In the 2005 U.S. Youth Surveillance Report, 19% of 15–19-year-olds had suicidal ideation and 9% attempted suicide (Eaton et al., 2010). Three to five percent of youths with depression accounts for 60% of suicide attempts for all ages. Some estimates predict that 35%–50% of youths with depression will attempt suicide and 2%–8% will complete it (Eaton et al., 2010).

Research. Selective Serotonin Reuptake Inhibitors (SSRIs), a type of antidepressant, has a protective effect on depression. There have been several studies in Europe and the United States that as the number of prescriptions for SSRIs decrease, the suicide rates increased during the period from 1980 to 1999. Examples of SSRIs include Prozac, Zoloft, Paxil, Celexa, Lexapro, and Luvox.

Recently, two major NIMH-sponsored studies called Treatment for Adolescent Depression Study (TADS) and Treatment of Resistant Depression in Adolescents (TORDIA) provided useful guidelines regarding the use of antidepressants and their efficacy. The TADS study compared use of Fluoxetine (Prozac) alone versus cognitive-behavioral therapy (CBT) alone and the two treatments in combination (TADS Team, 2004, 2007). The combination was the most effective in accelerating remission and also minimizing suicidality. The

TORDIA study showed that the combination of CBT with an SSRI or Venlafaxine (Effexor) was better than medication alone and either medication was equally effective (Brent et al., 2009).

The American Academy of Child and Adolescent Psychiatry recommended that a combination of medication and cognitive-behavioral therapy for moderate to severe anxiety in youths is more effective that either therapy or medication alone. Anxiety disorders in children and adolescents refer to separation anxiety disorder (SAD), generalized anxiety disorder (GAD), phobias, panic disorder, social phobia, selective mutism, Obsessive-Compulsive Disorder (OCD), and Posttraumatic Stress Disorder (PTSD). SSRIs are considered first-line medication treatment, as they are the only ones that have consistently shown efficacy in placebo-controlled studies in pediatric anxiety disorders excluding OCD and PTSD. These studies were focused on Prozac, Luvox, Paxil, and Zoloft. Medications other than SSRIs such as Effexor, tricyclic antidepressants (TCAs), Buspirone, and Benzodiazepines have not been shown to be safe and effective for pediatric anxiety disorders but have been used as alternatives in combination with SSRIs or alone.

Obsessive-Compulsive Disorder (OCD) is another condition that has been researched and found to respond to medication treatment. OCD is characterized by the presence of recurrent thoughts (obsessions) or behaviors (compulsions) that are intrusive and repetitive, causing marked distress. A common example is a fear of contamination causing excessive handwashing.

Research for anxiety. A major NIMH study called Pediatric Obsessive-Compulsive Disorder Treatment Study (POTS) looked at state-of-the art treatments for OCD alone or in combination. The study found that a combination of medication and cognitive-behavioral therapy was more effective than either therapy or medication alone.

Mood

Some medications require medical testing. Bipolar disorder or manic-depression characterized by major mood swings is treated with either a single medication or a combination of medications that are classified as mood stabilizers, antipsychotics, or antidepressants. Antidepressants such as SSRIs, tricyclics, and other classes are only used during the depressed state and discontinued during the manic phase of bipolar disorder. Mood stabilizers generally refer to lithium carbonate, antipsychotics, or anticonvulsants (also known as antiepileptic or antiseizure drugs). These drugs frequently require laboratory tests and other work-up before starting and during the course of treatment due to their potential side effects and to avoid toxicity.

Antipsychotics. Antipsychotics (also called neuroleptics) are used primarily for schizophrenia and as major tranquilizers but also are used for the treatment of mania and the agitated states of bipolar disorder. There are only a few antipsychotics that have been approved for those below 18 years old and they are mainly approved for irritability, aggression, and agitation. These include Haloperidol (Haldol), Pimozide (Orap), Thioridazine, Risperidone (Risperdal), Aripiprazole (Abilify), and Quetiapine (Seroquel). These medications are generally sedating, weight gaining, and can cause muscle spasms or stiffness or extrapyramidal side effects. They can cause rare side effects and should be discussed with your doctor.

There is a "black box" warning issued by the FDA regarding the risk of increased suicidal thinking with the use of antidepressants across all ages including children. This means that there must be a clear warning given to the person who is giving informed consent to the use of antidepressants. This warning is to alert clinicians and patients to monitor for worsening depression, suicidality, and agitation at the beginning, during a dose adjustment, and when stopping antidepressants.

Aggression, Impulsivity, Hyperactivity

Because EBD frequently manifests as lack of control of behavior, medications that are used for this group of symptoms also are used for other problems such as ADHD and bipolar disorder. There are a few medications that have FDA approval for irritability especially in autism for children. These medications are Risperidone (Risperdal) and

Aripiprazole (Abilify). Lithium also is used for aggression and poor impulse control. ADHD medications and anticonvulsant medications also are used for aggression, impulsivity, and hyperactivity. The doses and monitoring guidelines for these medications are the same when used to control behavior as for other conditions.

The use of medications in children with EBD should be viewed in the same way as one views medication use in other medical conditions such as asthma or heart disease. All medications have potential adverse effects. The risk and benefit ratio must be frequently reviewed. No one can truly predict with accuracy what the child's positive or negative response is going to be while on a particular medication. The only way to know the medication effect is to have the child take the medication and monitor him or her closely. When working with children and medications, the rule is "Start low and go slow."

You might also hear the term "off-label use" from doctors. It means that the medication is not approved by the FDA to be used for the age or diagnosis it is being prescribed. Doctors can prescribe "off-label" any medications that are currently available in the pharmacy as long as they are explained to the parents. Psychiatric medications for children take longer to be approved by the FDA due to stricter guidelines and research data and clinical experience from adults are frequently used to extrapolate its use in children.

Medication can be helpful in improving the symptoms of EBD and increasing the chances of school success. It should be considered earlier rather than later and must be viewed as part of a comprehensive treatment plan. The use of medication must be determined on a case-to-case basis between the patient, parents, and the physician as the results and potential benefits and adverse events can vary. There is more interest and ongoing research than ever in the use of psychiatric medications in children and adolescents. Medications, when carefully monitored and used appropriately, can be a very effective and safe intervention in ensuring school success.

Children have shown significant improvement of their EBD symptoms with medication, and many medications enable them to achieve their goals and a better quality of life. As parents, it is important to consider the potential benefits of medication as one of the tools that can help a child with challenging behaviors be able to compete on a level playing field. Medication, therapy, or other treatments may extend into adulthood, so teaching a child what tools she needs for success may be part of her development of self-awareness, self-advocacy, and self-determination skills.

Tool 12.1

Tips for Parents and Teachers on Medication for Children With ADHD

Ten Tips for Parents:

1. Seek the best help for medication consultation! Ask your pediatrician, therapist, family, and friends for names of physicians. Make sure to check their credentials.

2. Do not be afraid to ask questions. The physician must be able to explain what he or she is recommending to your satisfaction. If you are not sure whether to ask a question, ask anyway.

3. Learn as much as you can about the medication.

4. There is no magic cure. Medication can help but it must be used in combination with other nonmedication interventions.

5. If the medication is not working, reevaluate or get a second opinion. The diagnosis may be correct but there can be another coexisting condition that is not being addressed. Children are constantly developing and their diagnosis is always evolving or changing.

6. Always consider nonmedication options along with medications. Lifestyle and daily routines such as sleeping patterns, nutrition, and activities can improve or worsen EBD symptoms.

7. Review your family history for psychiatric disorders and medication response of relatives. Most psychiatric disorders such as ADHD, anxiety, and depression have a genetic or familial predisposition. This information will help your physician with considerations for diagnosis and treatment.

8. Do not change your child's medication without the physician's consent. Some medications can have dangerous effects if stopped abruptly or when doses are changed.

9. Use daily logs to monitor changes you observe in your child while on medication. Changes in mood, behavior, weight, appetite, sleep, energy, and school performance are hard to recall when you see the

physician. It is important to bring this information at every physician visit. This will help guide medication adjustment.

10. Are brand medications better than generic? There is no simple answer as it can vary from one medication to another. Generic drugs cost less but not all drugs are available in generic form. Newer drugs are not available as generics for several years. There are several companies that can make the generic drug, therefore the quality control can vary. The child might be sensitive to the inactive ingredient of the drug such as the coloring or dye and this can affect her reaction.

Ten Tips for Teachers:

1. Do not suggest medications to parents.

2. Be open and flexible to suggestions from parents and medical providers as their goal is the same as yours. We all want the child to behave and perform to the best of his or her ability.

3. Stimulant medications for ADHD work quickly, therefore there will be a major change in behavior and performance when the child has missed his or her daily dose.

4. Medications for mood take 2–6 weeks to start working; however, the side effects can occur early. Sedation, agitation, and appetite changes can be caused by medications.

5. Tell parents right away if you notice any significant change in mood, attention, alertness, orientation, and behavior, as these changes can be signs of medication toxicity or due to a serious medical condition such as seizures.

6. Anger and defiance can mask depression and anxiety in school-aged children. Active listening and patience generally will work better than negative reinforcement and can help reduce tension in a volatile situation. Adolescents are highly sensitive to shame and embarrassment, especially in a school setting. It is extremely important to talk to them privately instead of in the presence of their peers.

7. Never compromise your safety and that of your students.

8. Call parents to share positive and negative feedback about their

child. This will improve your credibility to both the child and the parents.

9. Refrain from making comments about the child's medication in class, as each child has a different sentiment about medication. The child could become the object of teasing or bullying once peers know he or she has a condition or takes medications.

10. Open communication is always best between the school and the family. Teachers have a very important role and influence in a child's life and, next to the parents, no one spends as much time with the child as teachers do.

chapter 13

Self-Determination and Self-Advocacy

SCHOOL success is ultimately measured by how well schools prepare students to meet the challenges of adult life. Successful adult life includes setting goals, having employment and a career, living independently, and having successful relationships. In order to achieve these outcomes students need to begin to learn and practice the skills of adult living and decision-making while they are in school. Educators and families are usually so centered on the *current* year and the *current* progress that long-term future goal setting does not get equal consideration. This chapter introduces parents to the world of advocating for students with emotional and behavioral challenges beyond K–12 and will answer the following questions:

- What is self-determination and why is it important to school success and success beyond school?

Myth	Truth
Once my child applies to college the college will give him accommodations and services.	College and universities are not allowed to ask about disability status when students apply. Also, in order to receive accommodations for a documented disability students must self-disclose to the Office of Disability Student Services and present any documentation to be given to students' course instructors.
Job experience is not helpful.	Structured internship programs or programs where there is a job coach who can help students navigate the challenges of working with others and completing tasks is very helpful and can ensure future employment.
There is little support for students once they leave school.	People with disabilities must take initiative to access adult services but services do exist at the state and federal level.

- What are the factors of a successful transition from school to work or postsecondary education?
- What supports are available for students with emotional and behavioral challenges after K–12 schooling?

Self-Determination

The theory of self-determination relates to the "can do attitude" necessary for all students to succeed. Promoting self-determination has become a best practice in special education. Self-determination is the ability to know one's personal needs and to take action to meet those needs.

Self-determination is "a combination of skills, knowledge and beliefs that enable a person to engage in goal directed, self-regulated, autonomous behavior" (Field, Martin, Miller, Ward, & Wehmeyer, 1998, p. 2). Basically, self-determination is the ability to know yourself and get what you want from life. Sometimes, in schools and at home, adults do not let students with emotional and behavioral challenges make choices, try new things, or do things independently. At school and at home we need to help students find their strengths and talents and then have them practice attaining goals and making choices.

With practice and guidance, students can learn to be self-determined and to advocate for their needs. Students with emotional and behavioral challenges need this more than other students; they need to believe in themselves and recognize their strengths. Additionally, they need plenty of opportunity to practice the skills of self-knowledge, self-advocacy, and goal setting. Self-determination can be taught in schools through developed curricula (Field & Hoffman, 1996; Fullerton, 1994; Halpern et al., 1997; Martin & Marshall, 1995).

The spirit of self-determination and empowering students to help make their own choices also can be modeled and highlighted at home and in the community. Adults surrounding students with emotional and behavioral disabilities must have high expectations for students, recognize strengths, and allow youths to practice real-life situations. Below is a list of ways self-determination can be built in to schools and classrooms:

- if students have a documented disability, have them participate in their IEP meeting;
- have students complete inventories that identify their strengths;
- practice short-term goal setting with a built-in planning time and then a built-in reflection time;
- offer choices in ways to complete assignments that give students ownership of the process as well as the content; or
- have mentors or older students come in and discuss goals and future planning.

Often when we hear about transition and think about postsecondary outcomes, parents and educators do not think about students from elementary schools and middle schools. This is a big mistake. Students at all levels of schooling must start learning about self-determination and planning for transition. Self-determination can be taught in elementary and middle school. Simple goal setting and exposure to the strengths of each individual will help bolster the positive attributes of each individual. Social skill exercises and practice in real-life situations can help students become better able to manage their connection with their community throughout their school career.

Transition can be thought of as a broad category rather than only as a plan for postsecondary outcomes. For example, the transition from elementary school, to middle school is often a stressor on all students. Students in elementary school often have one teacher. In traditional middle school, however, students transition to changing classes and having many teachers. This change increases the chances of a breakdown in communication between family and school and decreases the likelihood that teachers form strong relationships with each student. Dealing with the social stress of middle school where peer relationships and acceptance play a large role in the activities also can impede progress. Parents and teachers need to build a support team for a student with challenging behaviors. Before a change in school happens, students should tour the school, meet key teachers, be involved in creating a back-up plan if the students feels they need help or support, and be introduced to a few mentor students who can help ease the transition process. Parents and educators should recognize that change often is difficult for students with challenging behaviors. Each change in schooling, teachers, activities, and family situations should be discussed, defined, given rules, and practiced, if possible.

Factors of Successful Transitions to Post-K–12 Schooling

Students with emotional and behavioral challenges have a variety of postsecondary education options to consider. Some students will go on to higher education, vocational, or technical schools whereas other students will enter the workforce. Most living-wage jobs require at least some postsecondary education, training, or certification. Readiness for college and career requires increasingly similar sets of skills. College and career readiness requires proficiency in a set of reading, writing, mathematics, and social skills. Regardless of where students go next, there are factors in the transition planning process that need to be considered. The top five transition principles are: (1) know your strengths and disability or needs, (2) have a realistic plan, (3) use the resources available, (4) build in plenty of practice, and (5) create a back-up plan and seek help when needed.

Know Your Strengths and Disability or Needs

Before students can advocate for themselves they need to understand their strengths and weaknesses and be able to explain these to others. This process needs to be started in middle or high school. Students should know the name of their disability and things that they can do without aid or accommodation and tasks where they know they will have some difficulty and need supports. The better students can explain their needs the better they can help set up situations where their needs are recognized and a reasonable plan is created. Make sure that students understand their unique learning needs or triggers and develop a plan to communicate this to others.

Adult services are systems of eligibility, not systems of entitlement. Students in K–12 schools are entitled to a free appropriate public education. The public schools are charged with finding children with disabilities in order to serve them appropriately. Adult services and postsecondary education providers do not have similar mandates for students with disabilities. The Americans With Disabilities Act Amendments Act of 2008 provides certain "reasonable" accommodations and protections for Americans with disabilities. But adults with disabilities must self-advocate and qualify for accommodations and services. Parents of adult children with disabilities must realize that they will not be allowed access to their child's adult records without written permission. Preparation for this transition is necessary so that each student knows his or her rights and can begin to be the main person who is the advocate for these rights.

Have a Realistic Plan

Future plans for higher education or the workforce should start early. In order to go to community colleges or universities, students need to be sure that they are enrolled in the correct classes so that they will meet the requirements of the college or university. Often these classes must be taken early in the student's career. Families should be aware of courses and course credit beginning in ninth grade if not earlier. Part of a realistic plan is to test out options. If students are interested in a particular field or course, have them take an internship, get a part-time job, or take a supplemental course over the summer to begin to test their ideas about jobs and future directions. In addition, if a student has a documented disability, it is the student's responsibility to communicate with the university's disability services office. Students may choose not to disclose their disabilities; however, if there is a problem, it is difficult to go back and try to get accommodations later in the process. The question of whether or not a student should disclose a disability is a personal one.

Students should investigate programs that include a vocational assessment and skills component to help them begin to work on skills for a selected job. Completing a career and vocational assessment will help lead a student to a job that is aligned with his strengths. There are technical colleges and vocational training schools that may be good options for further skill development. The more a student can be exposed to his options early the more he can "try out" different options.

All states and the District of Columbia have federally supported vocational rehabilitation agencies established to support adults with disabilities. Students and their families should be sure that referrals are made to their local agency at least three semesters before graduation or high school completion. This agency will provide funding for postsecondary education and training. Students and their families may have to exhaust other sources of financial aid, such as grants and loans, before they will qualify for rehabilitative services funding.

Use the Resources Available

Students who want to attend higher education need to be aware of resources that are available to them as they apply to colleges and resources. Students with documented disabilities with current eligibility can petition the College Board, which administers the SAT, or ACT, which administers the ACT test, for an accommodation while taking the exam. This must be done before scheduling the exam. Before enrolling in college there are courses one can take to "get the feel" of college and also summer programs that introduce higher education to students. Once on campus it is up to each individual to contact the institution and find out about disability services that are available. Interviews about tutoring services, taking a reduced load, or the openness of faculty toward accommodating students with disabilities can take place while visiting colleges.

Students who enter the workforce can take advantage of internship programs and career and technical schools in their area. Some schools offer school-to-work options with job coaches to help a student transition to work while still in school. These programs give students the support and coaching they need to make a successful transition to the workforce. Students who enroll in an apprenticeship program or internship program or work in high school are more likely to attain and retain employment.

Some key personnel who can be helpful in the transition process include (Kochhar-Bryant, Bassett, & Webb, 2009):
- *Transition counselors*: If a student has a documented disability, secondary transition specialists can help begin to plan for transition. By law, transition planning needs to be incorporated into a student's IEP beginning at age 16.
- *School counselors*: School counselors can help students choose courses and apply for college and job-training programs.
- *Disability support specialists*: Disability support specialists can

support students at a college or university and can serve as the liaison between faculty, staff, administrators, and other social service agencies.

- *Vocational rehabilitation counselors*: Vocational rehabilitation counselors work for the state's vocational rehabilitation agency and help people with disabilities prepare for employment.
- *Social Security administration*: The federal social security administration operates programs for people with disabilities who work.

Build in Plenty of Practice

A key indicator of future adult life success and satisfaction is employment during high school. Students with and without disabilities who hold even a part-time paid or volunteer job have more positive records of postsecondary employment. Parents are strongly encouraged to support their child with emotional and behavioral disabilities to experience some employment success as early as feasible. Middle school is not too early to begin volunteer employment.

In order to transition from K–12 education, students need to know how to communicate, interview, get along with others, and manage finances. These skills need to be explicitly taught and practiced to help ensure smooth transitions from school. Students should be exposed to work and higher education environments, take advantage of support groups and coaching to discuss new environments, and know the expected rules and norms. Successful transition means that students are not just dropped at the door of their new experience but that students are aware of the new environment and have practiced the necessary skills to succeed in that environment.

Create a Back-Up Plan and Seek Help When Needed

All plans need a back-up due to unforeseen circumstances. Many times students who are starting fresh in higher education or work think that they want to "try" without any supports and see how they do. Although this is a wonderful show of independence and determination, it is advisable to have frequent check-ins and an established back-up plan in case of difficulty. For example, students may want to have an early meeting with their instructors to determine their progress in a course. It usually is advisable to have more supports in the beginning and then to gradually wean off of the supports as a person progresses. In addition, there needs to be a counselor, a parent, or someone connected to the student to be a sounding board for his ideas and thoughts. Students need to identify a coping plan in times of stress and have a written plan to ask for help if school or work becomes too difficult.

Conclusion

WE hope you come to the end of this book with a sense of hope and direction. Students with emotional and behavioral challenges, whether identified in the special education system or not, *do* have a chance to lead successful and happy lives. We hope you have seen the importance of attitude and its effects on progress and have gained a multitude of strategies and ideas to help facilitate behavioral change. We hope you will remember that the disabilities that these students face are invisible, yet real and often painful. Society has misunderstood the nature and needs of emotional and behavioral challenges for too long. It is time to advocate for these students and to use positive, therapeutic interventions to help them lead the lives they want. We hope your student with emotional and behavioral challenges seeks and finds school success.

References

Albrecht, S. (2009). The messages from the pioneers in EBD: Learning from the past and preparing for the future. *Teaching Exceptional Children Plus, 5*(4). Retrieved from http://escholarship.bc.edu/education/tecplus/vol5/iss4/art4

Algozzine, B. (1977). The emotionally disturbed child: Disturbed or disturbing? *Journal of Abnormal Psychology, 5,* 205–211.

American Occupational Therapy Association. (2008). *Occupational therapy in educational settings under the Individuals with Disabilities Education Act.* Retrieved from http://www.aota.org/Consumers/WhatisOT/CY/Fact-Sheets/38507.aspx

American Occupational Therapy Association. (2009). *Occupational therapy and school mental health.* Retrieved from http://www.aota.org/Practitioners/Resources/Docs/FactSheets/School/School-MH.aspx

American Psychiatric Association. (2000). *Diagnostic and statistical manual of mental disorders, Text revision* (4th ed.). Washington, DC: Author.

Americans with Disabilities Act, 42 U.S.C. §§ 12102 et seq. (1990).

Anderson, R. N., & Smith, B. L. (2005). Deaths: Leading causes for 2002. *National Vital Statistics Report, 53*(17), 1–92.

Anne Arundel County Public Schools. (2010). *Disproportionality resource guide: Addressing the disproportionate identification and representation of African American, Hispanic, and speakers of other languages in special education in Anne Arundel County Public Schools.* Annapolis, MD: Author.

Baer, D., Wolf, M., & Risley, T. (1987). Some still current dimensions of applied behavior analysis. *Journal of Applied Behavior Analysis, 20,* 313–327.

Bower, E. M. (1982). Defining emotional disturbance: Public policy and research. *Psychology in the Schools, 19,* 55–60.

Bradley, M. J. (2003). *Yes, your teen is crazy: Loving your kid without losing your mind.* Gig Harbor, WA: Harper Press.

Bradley, R., Henderson, K., & Monfore, D. (2004). A national perspective on children with emotional disorders. *Behavioral Disorders, 29,* 211–223.

Brent, D. A., Emslie, G. J., Clarke, G. N., Asarnow, J., Spirito, A., Ritz, L., . . . Keller, M. B. (2009). Predictors of spontaneous and systematically assessed suicidal adverse events in the Treatment of SSRI-Resistant Depression in Adolescents (TORDIA) study. *The American Journal of Psychiatry, 166,* 418–426.

Bullock, L., & Gable, R. (2006). Programs for children and adolescents with emotional and behavioral disorders in the United States. A historical overview, current perspectives, and future directions. *Preventing School Failure, 50*(2), 7–13.

Burns, M. K., & Dean, V. J. (2005). Effect of acquisition rates on off task behavior with children identified as having learning disabilities. *Learning Disability Quarterly, 28,* 273–282.

Callahan, K. (1994). Wherefore art thou, Juliet? Causes and implications of the male dominated sex ratio in programs for students with emotional behavioral disorders. *Education & Treatment of Children, 94,* 228–244.

Campbell, S. (2002). *Behavior problems in preschool children: Clinical and developmental issues.* New York, NY: Guilford.

Carrie, E., Dunlap, G., & Horner R. (2002). Positive behavioral support: Evolution of an applied science. *Journal of Positive Behavioral Interventions, 4,* 4–16.

Caseau, D. R., Luckasson, R., & Kroth, R. L. (1994). Special-education services for girls with serious emotional disturbance: A case of gender bias? *Behavioral Disorders, 20,* 51–60.

Centers for Disease Control and Prevention. (2009). *Prevalence of autism spectrum disorders—Autism and developmental disabilities monitoring network, United States, 2006.* Retrieved from http://www.cdc.gov/mmwr/preview/mmwrhtml/ss5810a1.htm

Chen, S. (2010). *Girl's arrest for doodling raises concerns about zero tolerance.* Retrieved from http://www.cnn.com/2010/CRIME/02/18/new.york.doodle.arrest/index.html?hpt=C1

Chugani, H., Behen, M., Muzik, O., Juhasz, C., Nagy, F., & Chugani, D. (2001). Local brain functional activity following early deprivation: A study of postinstitutionalized Romanian orphans. *NeuroImage, 14,* 1290–1301.

Clark, B. (1992). *Growing up gifted.* New York, NY: Macmillan.

Cohen, S. (1983). The mental hygiene movement, the development of personality and the school: The medicalization of American education. *History of Education Quarterly, 23,* 123–149.

Cooper-Kahn, J., & Dietzel, L. (2009). *Late, lost and unprepared: A parents' guide to helping children with executive functioning.* Bethesda, MD: Woodbine House.

Coutinho, M. J., & Oswald, D. (1996). Identification and placement of students with serious emotional disturbance. Part II: National and state trends in the implementation of LRE. *Journal of Emotional and Behavioral Disorders, 4,* 40–53.

Cruickshank, W. (1967). The development of education for exceptional children. In W. Cruickshank & G. Orville Johnson (Eds.), *Education of exceptional children and youth* (pp. 3–42). Englewood Cliffs, NJ: Prentice Hall.

Cullinan, D., Epstein, M., & Lloyd, J. (1983). *Behavior disorders of children and adolescents.* Englewood Cliffs, NJ: Prentice Hall.

Dahl, R. E., & Spear L. P. (2004). Adolescent brain development: Vulnerabilities and opportunities. *Annals of the New York Academy of Sciences, 1021,* 1–22.

Damasio, A. R. (1994). *Descartes' error: Emotion, rationality, and the human brain.* New York, NY: Putnam.

Davidson, R. J., Kabat-Zinn, J., Schumacher, J., Rosenkrantz, M., Muller, D., Santorelli, S., . . . Sheridan, M. (2003). Alterations in brain and immune function produced by mindfulness and medication. *Psychosomatic Medicine, 65,* 564–570.

Dickinson, M., & Miller. J. (2006). Issues regarding in-school suspensions and high school students with disabilities. *American Secondary Education*, *35*, 72–83.

Done, D. J., Crow, T. J., Johnstone, E. C., & Sacker A. (1994). Childhood antecedents of schizophrenia and affective illness: Social adjustment at ages seven and eleven. *British Medical Journal, 309,* 699–703.

Duhon, G. J., Noell, G. H., Witt, J. C., Freeland, J. T., Dufrene, B. A., & Gilbertson, D. N. (2005). *Identifying academic skill and performance deficits: The experimental analysis of brief assessments of academic skills.* Retrieved from http://www.joewitt.org/Downloads/Duhon%20Research%20on%20Skill%20vs.%20Performance%20Deficits%20(can't%20do%20vs%20won't%20do).pdf

Duchnowski, A., & Kutash, A. (2009). Integrating PBS, mental health services, and family driven care. In W. Sailor, G. Sugai, R. Horner, & G. Dunlap (Eds.), *Handbook of positive behavior support, Vol. X. Issues in clinical child psychology* (pp. 203–222). Washington, DC: American Psychological Association.

Eaton, D. K., Kann, L., Kinchen, S., Shanklin, S., Ross, J., Hawkins, J., . . . Weschler, H. (2010). Youth risk behavior surveillance—United States, 2009. *Morbidity and Mortality Weekly Report, 59*(SS05), 1–142.

Education for All Handicapped Children Act of 1975, Pub. Law 94–142 (November 29, 1975).

Epstein, M., Atkins, M., Cullinan, D., Kutash, K., & Weaver, R. (2008). *Reducing behavior problems in the elementary school classroom.* Retrieved from http://ies.ed.gov/ncee/wwc/pdf/practiceguides/behavior_pg_092308.pdf

Erickson, F. (1987). Transformation and school success: The politics and culture of educational achievement. *Anthropology & Education Quarterly, 18,* 335–356.

Field, S., & Hoffman, A. (1996). *Steps to self-determination: A curriculum to help adolescents learn to achieve their goals.* Austin, TX: PRO-ED.

Field, S., Martin, J., Miller, R., Ward, M., & Wehmeyer M. (1998). *A practical guide for teaching self-determination.* Reston, VA: Council for Exceptional Children.

Florida State Department of Education. (2002). *Determining a student's need for extended school year services.* Retrieved from http://www.eric.ed.gov/ERICDocs/data/ericdocs2sql/content_storage_01/00000196/80/1a/c2/a9.pdf

Forness, S., & Kavale, K. (2000). Emotional or behavioral disorders:

Background and current status of E/BD terminology and definition. *Behavioral Disorders, 25*, 264–269.

Fuchs, L. (2007). *NRCLD update on responsiveness to intervention: Research to practice.* Retrieved from http://www.nrcld.org/resource_kit/general/RTIResearchtoPractice2007.pdf

Fullerton, A. (1994). *Putting feet on my dreams: A program in self-determination for adolescents and young adults.* Portland, OR: Portland State University.

Genshaft, J. (2009). *Partnering with communities to promote children's mental health.* Retrieved from http://cfs.fmhi.usf.edu/news-detail.cfm?NewsID=565

Georgia Department of Education. (n.d.). *Emotional and behavior disorder (EBD).* Retrieved from http://public.doe.k12.ga.us/DMGetDocument.aspx/EMOTIONAL%20AND%20BEHAVIORAL%20DISORDER.pdf?p=6CC6799F8C1371F6B8F2A7669398C922E63F2BDC2C8B7BAE1D64B35B9DC25364&Type=D

Gettinger, M., & Seibert, J. K. (2002). Best practices in increasing academic learning time. In A. Thomas (Ed.), *Best practices in school psychology IV: Vol. 1* (4th ed., pp. 773–787). Bethesda, MD: National Association of School Psychologists.

Giedd J. N., Blumenthal J., Jeffries N. O., Castellanos, F. X., Liu, H., Zljdenbos, A., . . . Rapoport, J. L. (1999). Brain development during childhood and adolescence: A longitudinal MRI study. *Natural Neuroscience, 2*, 861–863.

Grobman, K. H. (2008). *Confirmation bias.* Retrieved from http://www.devpsy.org/teaching/method/confirmation_bias.html

Guralnick, M. J. (2000). *The effectiveness of early intervention.* Baltimore, MD: Brookes.

Hack, M., & Fanaroff, A. A. (1999). Outcomes of children of extremely low birth weight and gestational age. *Early Human Development, 53*, 193–218.

Halpern, A. S., Herr, C. M., Wolf, N. K., Lawson, J. D., Doren, B., & Johnson, M. D. (1997). *Next S.T.E.P.: Student transition and educational planning.* Austin, TX: PRO-ED.

Harmon, J. (1992). *Gender disparities in special education.* Madison, WI: Bureau for Exceptional Children.

Harry, B. (1992). Restructuring the participation of African American parents in special education. *Exceptional Children, 59*, 123–131.

Heim, C., Newport, J., Heit, S., Graham, Y. P., Wilcox, M., Bonsall, R., . . . Nemeroff, C. B. (2000). Pituitary-adrenal and autonomic responses to stress in women after sexual and physical abuse in childhood. *Journal of the American Medical Association, 284,* 592–597.

Honig v. Doe, et al. (86–728), 484 U.S. 305 (1988).

Hyter, Y. D., Rogers-Adkinson, D. L., Self, T. L., Simmons, B. F., & Jantz, J. (2001). Pragmatic language intervention for children with language and emotional/behavioral disorders. *Communication Disorders Quarterly, 23,* 4–16.

Individuals with Disabilities Education Improvement Act, Pub. Law 108-446 (December 3, 2004).

Ishikawa, S., & Raine, A. (2002). Psychophysiological correlates of antisocial behavior: A central control hypothesis. In J. Glicksohn (Ed.), *The neurobiology of criminal behavior* (pp. 187–230). Norwell, MA: Kluwer.

Ishikawa, S. S., & Raine, A. (2003). Prefrontal deficits and antisocial behavior: A causal model. In B. B. Lahey, T. E. Moffitt, & A. Caspi (Eds.), *Causes of Conduct Disorder and juvenile delinquency* (pp. 277–304). New York, NY: Guilford.

Johnson, S., Hennessey, E., Smith, R., Trikic, R., Wolke, D., & Marlow, N. (2009). Academic attainment and special education needs in extremely preterm children at 11 years of age: The EPICure Study. *Archives of Disease in Childhood, 94,* 283–289.

Joint Commission on the Accreditation of Healthcare Organizations. (2002). *Restraint and seclusion: Complying with Joint Commission standards.* Oakbrook Terrace, IL: Author.

Joseph, R. (1999). The neurology of traumatic dissociative amnesia: Commentary and literature review. *Child Abuse and Neglect, 23,* 715–727.

Kabat-Zinn, J. (2005). *Coming to our senses: Healing ourselves and the world through mindfulness.* New York, NY: Hyperion.

Kann, R. T., & Hanna, J. (2000). Disruptive behavior disorders in children and adolescents: How do girls differ from boys? *Journal of Counseling and Development, 78,* 267–274.

Kauffman, J., & Konold, T. (2007). Making sense in education: Pretense (including No Child Left Behind) and realities in rhetoric and policies about schools and society. *Exceptionality, 15,* 75–96.

Kauffman, J. M., & Landrum, T. J. (2009). *Characteristics of emotional and behavioral disorders of children and youth* (9th ed). New York, NY: Pearson.

Kearns, T., Ford, L., & Linney, T. (2005). African American students' representation in special education programs. *The Journal of Negro Education, 74,* 297–310.

Keeping Families Together Act, 108th Cong. (2003) (testimony of Tammy Seltzer).

Kendall-Tackett, K. A. (2000). Physiological correlates of childhood abuse: Chronic hyper-arousal in PTSD, depression and irritable bowel syndrome. *Child Abuse & Neglect, 24*, 799–810.

Kern, L., & Hilt, A. M. (2004). An evaluation of the functional behavioral assessment process used with students with or at risk for emotional and behavioral disorders. *Education and Treatment of Children, 27*, 440–452.

Klinberg, T., Forsberg, H., Westerberg, H., & Hirvilkoski, T. (2002). Training of working memory and children with ADHD. *Journal of Clinical and Experimental Neuropsychology, 24*, 781–791.

Knitzer, J., & Olsen, L. (1982). *Unclaimed children: The failure of public responsibility to children and adolescents in need of public mental health services.* Washington, DC: Children's Defense Fund.

Kochhar-Bryant, C., Bassett, D. S., & Webb, K. W. (2009). *Transition to postsecondary education for students with disabilities.* Thousand Oaks, CA: Corwin Press.

Kraft, R. (2000). Extended school year services (ESY)—What the courts have said. *Future reflections, 19*(1). Retrieved from http://www.nfb.org/images/nfb/publications/fr/fr19/Issue1/f190119.htm

Kutash, K., Duchnowski, A. J., & Lynn, N. (2006). *School-based mental health: An empirical guide for decision-makers.* Tampa: University of South Florida, The Research & Training Center for Children's Mental Health, Louis de la Parte Florida Mental Health Institute.

Loeber, R., Burke, J. D., Lahey, B. B., Winters, A., & Zera, M. (2000). Oppositional Defiant and Conduct Disorder: A review of the past 10 years, Part I. *Journal of the American Academy of Child and Adolescent Psychiatry, 29*, 1468–1484.

Long, J. E., Long, N. J., & Whitson, S. (2009). *The angry smile: The psychology of passive-aggressive behavior in families, schools and workplaces* (2nd ed.). Austin, TX: PRO-ED.

Luckasson, R., & Smith, D. (1995). *Introduction to special education. Teaching in an age of challenge.* Boston, MA: Allyn & Bacon.

Martin, J. E., & Marshall, L. (1995). Choicemaker: A comprehensive self-determination transition program. *Intervention and School Clinic, 30*, 147–156.

Martin, E., Martin, R., & Terman, D. (1996). The future of children. *Special Education for Students With Disabilities, 6*, 25–39.

Maryland State Department of Education. (2009). *Discipline and students with disabilities.* Retrieved from http://www.marylandpublicschools.org/nr/rdonlyres/5f4f5041-02ee-4f3a-b495-5e4b3c850d3e/22802/disciplineofstudentswithdisabilities_september2009.pdf

National Association of School Psychologists. (2005). *Position statement on students with emotional and behavioral disorders.* Retrieved from http://www.nasponline.org/about_nasp/pospaper_sebd.aspx

National Center for Education Statistics. (2008). *Number of 14 through 21 year old students served under the Individuals with Disabilities Education Act, Part B, who exited school by exit reason, age, and type of disability: United States and other jurisdictions, 2004-05 and 2005-06.* Retrieved from http://nces.ed.gov/programs/digest/d08/tables/dt08_111.asp

National Institute of Child Health and Human Development. (2000). *Report of the National Reading Panel. Teaching children to read: An evidence-based assessment of the scientific research literature on reading and its implications for reading instruction.* Retrieved from http://www.nichd.nih.gov/publications/nrp/smallbook.htm

National Institute of Mental Health. (2001). *Teenage brain: A work in progress.* Retrieved from http://www.nimh.nih.gov/health/publications/teenage-brain-a-work-in-progress-fact-sheet/index.shtml

National Institute of Mental Health. (2005). *Half of all lifetime cases of mental illness begin at age 14.* Retrieved from http://www.medicalnewstoday.com/articles/25768.php

Nelson, J. R., Benner, G. J., & Cheney, D. (2005). An investigation of the language skills of students with emotional disturbance served in public school settings. *Journal of Special Education, 39,* 97–105.

Newman, L., Wagner, M., Cameto, R., & Knokey, A.-M.(2009). *The post–high school outcomes of youth with disabilities up to 4 years after high school.* Retrieved from http://www.nlts2.org/reports/2009_04/nlts2_report_2009_04_complete.pdf

Nippold, M. A. (1993). Developmental markers in adolescent language: Syntax, semantics and pragmatics. *Language, Speech, and Hearing Services in Schools, 24,* 21–28.

Nippold, M. A., Mansfield, T. C., Billow, J. L., & Tomblin, J. B. (2009). Syntactic development in adolescents with a history of language impairments: A follow-up investigation. *American Journal of Speech-Language Pathology, 18,* 241–251.

No Child Left Behind Act, 20 U.S.C. §6301 (2001).

Nock, M. K., & Kurtz, S. M. S. (2005). *Direct observation in school settings:*

Bringing science to practice. Retrieved from http://www.wjh.harvard.edu/~nock/nocklab/Nock_Kurtz_2005.pdf

O'Connor, T., Rutter, M., Beckett, C., Keaveney, L., Kreppner, J., & the English and Romanian Adoptees Study Team. (2000). The effects of global severe privation on cognitive competence: Extension and longitudinal follow-up. *Child Development, 71,* 376–390.

Olfson, M., Marcus, S. C., Weissman, M. M., & Jensen, P. S. (2002). National trends in the use of psychotropic medications by children. *Journal of the American Academy of Child and Adolescent Psychiatry, 41,* 514–521.

Ontario Ministry of Education. (2005). *Social skills anchor charts.* Retrieved from http://www.edu.gov.on.ca/eng/studentsuccess/lms/files/SocialSkills.pdf

Oswald, D., Best, A., Coutinho, M., & Nagle, A. L. (2003). Trends in special education identification rates of boys and girls: A call for research and change. *Exceptionality, 11,* 223–237.

Passaro, P. D., Moon, M., Wiest, D. J., & Wong, E. H. (2004). A model for school psychology practice: Addressing the needs of students with emotional and behavioral challenges through the use of an in school support room and reality therapy. *Adolescence, 39,* 503–517.

Pediatric OCD Treatment Study Team. (2004). Cognitive-behavior therapy, setraline, and their combination for children and adolescents with obsessive-compulsive disorder. *Journal of the American Medical Association, 292,* 1969–1976.

Penno, D. A., Frank, A. R., & Wacker, D. P. (2000). Instructional accommodations for adolescent students with severe emotional or behavioral disorders. *Behavioral Disorders, 25,* 325–343.

Pliszka, S. R. (2003). Psychiatric comorbidities in children with Attention Deficit Hyperactivity Disorder: Implications for management. *Pediatric Drugs, 5,* 741–750.

Quake-Rapp, C., Miller, B., Ananthan, G., & Chiu, E. (2008). Direct observation as a means of assessing frequency of maladaptive behavior in youths with severe emotional and behavioral disorder. *American Journal of Occupational Therapy, 62,* 206–211.

Raine, A., Venables, P. H., & Mednick, S. A. (1997). Low resting heart rate at age 3 years predisposes to aggression at age 11 years: Findings from the Mauritius Joint Child Health Project. *Journal of the American Academy of Child and Adolescent Psychiatry, 36,* 1457–1464.

Ratey, J. J., & Hagerman, E. (2009). *Spark: The revolutionary new science of exercising the brain*. New York, NY: Little, Brown and Company.

Redl, F. (1959). Strategy and techniques of the life space interview. *American Journal of Orthopsychiatry, 29,* 1–18.

Reid, R., Gonzalez, J. E., Nordness, P. D., Trout, A., & Epstein, M. H. (2004). A meta-analysis of the academic status of students with emotional/behavioral disturbance. *The Journal of Special Education, 38,* 130–143.

Rescorla, L., Ross, G. S., & McClure, S. (2007). Language delay and behavioral/emotional problems in toddlers: Findings from two developmental clinics. *Journal of Speech-Language, and Hearing Research, 50,* 1063–1078.

Rice, E., Merves, E., & Srsic, A. (2009). Perceptions of gender differences in the expression of emotional and behavioral disabilities. *Education and Treatment of Children, 31,* 549–565.

Richardson, A. J. (2006). Omega-3 fatty acids in ADHD and related neurodevelopmental disorders. *International Review of Psychiatry, 18,* 155–172.

Rutter, M., & the ERA Research Team. (1998). Developmental catch-up and deficit following adoption after severe global early privation. *Journal of Child Psychology and Psychiatry and Allied Disciplines, 39,* 465–476.

Sage, D., & Burrello, L. (1994). *Leadership in educational reform: An administrator's guide to special education*. Baltimore, MD: Brookes.

Salk, J. L. (2004). *What ED teachers say about race, class, and gender in their work in special education* (Unpublished doctoral dissertation). University of Saint Thomas, Minnesota.

Sampson, P. D., Streissguth, A. P., Bookstein, F. L., Little, R. E., Clarren, S. K., Dehaene, P., . . . Graham, J. M., Jr. (1997). Incidence of fetal alcohol syndrome and prevalence of alcohol-related neurodevelopmental disorder. *Teratology, 56,* 317–326.

Scheffler, R. M., Brown, T. T., Fulton, B. D., Hinshaw, S. P., Levine, P., & Stone, S. (2009). Positive association between Attention-Deficit/Hyperactivity Disorder medication use and academic achievement during elementary school. *Pediatrics, 123,* 1273–1279.

Schwarz, J. (2004). *Childhood conduct problems may predict depression among young adults*. Retrieved from http://uwnews.org/article.asp?articleid=4311

Selden, S. (2000). Eugenics and the social construction of merit, race, and disability. *Journal of Curriculum Studies, 32,* 235–252.

Shanahan, T. (2006). *The National Reading Panel report: Practical advice for teachers*. Naperville, IL: Learning Point Associates.

Shaw, P., Eckstrand, K., Sharp, W., Blumenthal, J., Lerch, J. P., Greenstein,

D., . . . Rapoport, J. L. (2007). Attention-Deficit/Hyperactivity Disorder is characterized by a delay in cortical maturation. *Proceedings of the National Academy of Sciences, 104,* 19649–19654.

Shore, A. N. (2001). Effects of a secure attachment on right brain development, affect regulation, and infant mental health. *Infant Mental Health Journal, 22,* 7–66.

Smith, D. D. (2007). Emotional or behavioral disorders defined. Retrieved from http://www.education.com/reference/article/emotional-behavioral-disorders-defined/?page=4b

Snyder, S., & Mitchell, D. (2006). Eugenics and the racial genome: Politics at the molecular level. *Patterns of Prejudice, 40,* 399–412.

Spearing, M. K. (2002). *Overview of schizophrenia.* Retrieved from http://www.schizophrenia.com/family/sz.overview.htm

Spira, E. G., Bracken, S. S., & Fischel, J. E. (2005). Predicting improvement after first-grade reading difficulties: The effects of oral language, emergent literacy, and behavior skills. *Developmental Psychology, 41,* 225–234.

Stullken, E. (1931). Special education for behavior problems. *The Phi Delta Kappan, 14,* 5–8.

Sugai, G., & Horner, R. (2002). Evolution of discipline practices: School-wide positive behavior supports. *Child and Family Therapy, 24,* 23–50.

Sullivan, A. L., A'Vant, E., Baker, J., Chandler, D., Graves, S., McKinney, E., & Sayles, T. (2009). Confronting the inequity in special education, part I: Understanding the problem of disproportionality. *NASP Communique, 38*(1), 14.

Swap, S. (1978). The ecological model of emotional disturbance in children: A status report and proposed synthesis. *Behavioral Disorders, 3,* 186–196.

Szasz, T. (1974). *The myth of mental illness.* New York, NY: Harper.

TADS Team. (2004). Fluoxetine, cognitive-behavioral therapy, and their combination for adolescents with depression. *Journal of the American Medical Association, 292,* 807–820.

TADS Team. (2007). The treatment for adolescents with depression study: Long-term effectiveness and safety outcomes. *Archives of General Psychiatry, 64,* 1132–1143.

U.S. Department of Education. (2000). *Twenty-second annual report to Congress on the implementation of IDEA 1997.* Washington, DC: U.S. Government Printing Office.

U.S. Department of Education. (2006). Assistance to states for the education of children with disabilities and preschool grants for children with disabilities, final rule. *Federal Register, 71*(156), 46540–46845.

U.S. Department of Education, National Center for Education Evaluation and Regional Assistance, Institute of Education Sciences. (2008). *Digest of Education Statistics*. Retrieved from http://nces.ed.gov/programs/digest/d08/tables/dt08_111.asp

Von Ravensburg, H. (2006-2008). *IDEA 2004: The reauthorized FBA*. Retrieved from http://www.pbis.org/common/pbisresources/publications/SSRN_d1151394.pdf

Wagner, M., Kutash, K., Duchnowski, A. J., & Epstein, M. H. (2005). The Special Education Elementary Longitudinal Study and the National Longitudinal Transition Study: Study designs and implications for children and youth with emotional disturbance. *Journal of Emotional and Behavioral Disorders, 13*, 25–41.

Wagner, M., Newman, L., Cameto, R., & Levine, P. (2005). *Changes over time in the early postschool outcomes of youth with disabilities*. Retrieved from http://www.nlts2.org/reports/2005_06/nlts2_report_2005_06_complete.pdf

Walker, H., & Severson, H. H. (1990). *Systematic screening for behavior disorders (SSBD): A multiple gating procedure*. Longmont, CO: Sopris West.

Walter, U. M. (2006). *Best practices in children's mental health*. Retrieved from http://kuscholarworks.ku.edu/dspace/bitstream/1808/3886/1/bestpracticesreport18.pdf

Webb, J. T. (2000, August). *Misdiagnosis and dual diagnosis of gifted children: Gifted and LD, ADHD, OCD, Oppositional-Defiant Disorder*. Paper presented at the annual conference of the American Psychological Association, Washington, DC.

Wehby, J. H., Lane, K. L., & Falk, K. B. (2009). Academic instruction for students with emotional and behavioral disorders. *Journal of Emotional and Behavioral Disorders, 11*, 194–197.

Weinfeld, R., & Davis, M. (2008). *Special needs advocacy resource book: What you can do now to advocate for your exceptional child's education*. Waco, TX: Prufrock Press.

Wisconsin Department of Public Instruction. (2009). *Services for children with an emotional behavioral disability*. Retrieved from http://www.dpi.state.wi.us/sped/ed.html

Witt, J. (2006). *Core concepts of RTI*. Retrieved from http://rti4success.org/images/stores/coreprinciplesandessentialcomponentsofrti.pdf

World Health Organization. (2010). Depression. Retrieved from http://www.who.int/mental_health/management/depression/definition/en

Yurgelun-Todd, D. (2007). Emotional and cognitive changes during adolescence. *Current Opinion in Neurobiology, 17,* 251–257.

Zito, J. M., Safer, D. J., dosReis, S., Gardner, J. S., Magder, L., Soeken, K., . . . Riddle, M. A. (2003). Psychotropic practice patterns for youth: A 10-year perspective. *Archives of Pediatrics and Adolescent Medicine, 157,* 17–25.

About the Authors

Michelle R. Davis, M.Ed., is the director of ABCs for Life Success and Special Needs Advocacy, delivering education consulting services to educators, families, and schools for students with a wide variety of special and gifted education needs. An experienced, passionate advocate for children, she is skilled in child-centered evaluation, program analysis and development, navigating the special education process, and developing effective individual student plans that prepare students for success in school and in life. She is an adjunct professor at The George Washington University. Her *Special Needs Advocacy Resource Book* forms the curriculum for her Special Needs Advocacy Training Institute. She also cohosts an Internet radio show, "Teach Your Children Well." She can be found online at http://www.abc4lifesuccess.com and http://www.specialneedsadvocacyinstitute.com.

Vincent P. Culotta, Ph.D., ABN, is a Board Certified neuropsychologist and president of NeuroBehavioral Associates in Columbia, MD. NeuroBehavioral Associates serves children and adolescents with learning, attention, and neurodevelopmental differences through neuropsychological assessment and consultation. Dr. Culotta completed his undergraduate degree from Pennsylvania State University, doctoral work in clinical psychology from the University of Memphis, and specialty training in the neurosciences at the University of Maryland Medical School. Dr. Culotta has served as the director of neuropsychology in the neurosurgery division of the University of Maryland's R. Adam's Cowley Shock Trauma Center. His research and clinical interests include disorders of executive functioning, dyslexia, autism spectrum disorders, and traumatic brain injury. Dr. Culotta serves on the boards of several academic institutions and supervises the clinical and research training of graduate students. Dr. Culotta is a frequent speaker and invited lecturer at regional and national conferences, provides professional training and consultation, and has published numerous articles regarding neurodevelopment and brain-based disorders of children and adolescents.

Eric A. Levine, Ed.D., is an educational consultant who specializes in providing services to children, families, and private and public schools. Dr. Levine has worked in public and private day and residential treatment centers and has provided program development and evaluation services to children and program staff in myriad educational settings. In addition to supporting families in the IEP process, Dr. Levine is working on collaborative projects in the areas of over-representation of African American students in special education and employability skills for incarcerated youth.

Elisabeth Hess Rice, Ed.D., is an associate professor of special education at The George Washington University. A former classroom teacher of students with a variety of learning and emotional challenges, Dr. Rice is dedicated to meeting the needs of troubled students through effective teacher training, research, and education. Her current research interests include girls with emotional behavior disorders, professional development, school and university partner-ships, and effective, scientifically sound interventions for students with social, emotional, and behavioral difficulties that highlight children's strengths and capabilities.

About the Contributor

Maria Hammill, M.D., has been a Board Certified Child Psychiatrist in private practice in Maryland for 15 years. She is highly respected for her expertise in the diagnosis and treatment of children and adolescents with attention deficit disorders, mood disorders, autism, and other developmental and learning disabilities. She is a popular consultant and speaker to other physicians in the diagnosis and treatment of anxiety, depression, and attention deficit disorder across the age spectrum. She works in collaboration with schools, therapists, psychologists, advocates, and different agencies to provide comprehensive treatment for her patients. She has trained in child psychiatry at Johns Hopkins Medicine in Baltimore, MD, and adult psychiatry at the Medical College of Virginia at Virginia Commonwealth University.